Colleges and Universities for Change: America's Comprehensive Public State Colleges and Universities

Fred F. Harcleroad
Allan W. Ostar

AASCU Press
Washington, D.C.

Library of Congress Cataloging-in-Publication Data

Harcleroad, Fred F.
Colleges and universities for change.

Bibliography: p.
Includes index.
1. State universities and colleges—United States—
History.   I. Ostar, Allan W.   II. Title.
LB2329.5.H327   1987   378'.053   87-19277
ISBN 0-88044-085-6 (alk. paper)
ISBN 0-88044-086-4 (pbk. : alk. paper)

All AASCU Press books are produced on acid-free paper
which exceeds the minimum standards set by the
National Historical Publications and Records Commission.

Table of Contents

About the Authors

FRED F. HARCLEROAD earned his B.A. and M.A. degrees from a comprehensive state university, served over two decades in the California State Universities, and was founding president of the California State University at Hayward in 1959. One of three honorary members of the American Association of State Colleges and Universities, he was a member of the Board of Directors for several years. His varied writings include a baseline historical study of the "Developing State Colleges and Universities" in 1966–67 and five other related studies of these diverse institutions.

ALLAN W. OSTAR did his undergraduate work at the Pennsylvania State University and graduate study at the University of Wisconsin, and has worked toward the advancement of public higher education for the past 35 years. In 1965 he became the first full-time head of the American Association of State Colleges and Universities (AASCU) in Washington, D.C. Since 1968 he has been awarded honorary doctoral degrees from 22 universities in recognition of his contributions to higher education.

Acknowledgment

We are grateful to many persons over many years for shaping the ideas which appear in this venture. Previous baseline studies of the "Developing State Colleges and Universities" (1960s), and the "Regional State Colleges and Universities" (1970s) served as background for this complete history of the "Comprehensive State Colleges and Universities" of the 1980s. Special thanks are due to C. Theodore Molen, Jr. for his contributions to 3 of these studies, and to Bradley Sagen, Jack Rayman and Suzanne Van Ort for their contributions to these original historical materials. We are grateful also to several persons who provided important ideas and assistance in the preparation of this historical study, including: Larry Dennis for valuable help with chapter 5, Scott Miller for his report on which chapter 6 is based, and Karen Heger and Meredith Ludwig for extensive assistance with the appendices. Several persons have made significant contributions to the final effort necessary to complete and publish the book, including: Juanita Bugg, Larry Eiser, Joanne Erickson, Joan Hurley, Jane Otten and Allan Watson.

Nevertheless, the authors assume all of the responsibility for the ideas and opinions contained in this historical analysis of this important segment of American higher education, and for the identficication of key public policy issues that will affect its future.

Preface

In slightly over two centuries, the people of the United States of America have built one of the strongest, most open and democratic republics on our globe. Waves of immigrants, by the millions, have flowed in constantly and continue in huge numbers to this day. Education, always a basic need of both new and continuing groups, has provided the major avenue for these millions to achieve some degree of financial independence and to make their personal contribution to overall improvement of the total society. The states, with basic responsibility for education, have had to adapt constantly to maintain the flow along this broad avenue.

In their wisdom, the people have required and supported constant change in both the financing and form of their education. Tax-supported elementary education was implemented in the 1820s and 1830s, along with tax-supported state normal schools (copied from France and Germany), to provide needed teachers. In the late 1800s, state tax-support was ruled legal for high schools, and the resulting expansion of basically free secondary education provided a better educated populace for a developing industrial nation. Another half-century later, in the 1940s and 1950s, a grateful country made the G.I. Bill available to finance postsecondary education for millions of veterans of World War II. The new principle of direct federal support of needy students who wished a college education became an integral part of the current overall financing pattern of higher education in the U.S.

Similarly, the form, organization, and content of postsecondary education have been subject to social invention in the U.S. The need to broaden collegiate education from the limited, classical English curriculum reached a climax in the 1850s. The Land-Grant College Act of 1862 opened the way for "agriculture and mechanic arts" to be made available to the "industrial classes in new public colleges." By the end of the nineteenth century, a second educational invention was needed, and the junior/community college developed. Of course, hundreds of classically oriented liberal arts colleges continued to be opened at this same time, many by religious groups concerned about the increasingly secular society. In the late 1800s, doctoral education developed on the German model with its research emphasis. A century later, many of the formerly open land-grant universities have been adapted to the research model emphasizing graduate education and are critically important, leading international research centers.

This process of adaptation and change has been constant and continued into the 20th century. In the 1920s, Alfred North White-head, in his great essay on technical (professional) education, pro-vided a philosophic basis for a change in recognition of "work" as a critical part of education at all levels of American society. He wrote that "work should be transfused with intellectual and moral vision and thereby turned into a joy." Further, he emphasized the "neglect of technical education as an ingredient in the complete development of ideal human beings. This neglect has arisen from two disastrous antitheses, namely, that between mind and body, and that between thought and action." The need for emphasis on "profession" and "work" is further amplified by Whitehead in his statement: "There can be no adequate technical education which is not liberal, and no liberal education which is not technical: That is, no education which does not impart both technique and intellectual vision. In simpler language, education should turn out the pupil with something he (she) knows well and something he (she) can do well. This intimate union of practice and theory aids both."

A half century later, Richard Millard, philosopher and student of Whitehead, extended this thesis and pointed out that vocational education, broadly conceived, is the "central aim of education" and is at the "cutting and most relevant edge of the educational process in the 20th century." Thus, the development of a type of higher educa-tion institution designed to recognize this philosophic thrust became an essential need in the United States as the century progressed.

This volume presents the thesis that the U.S. surely has invented a third new type of higher education institution during the last thirty years: the publicly controlled, professionally oriented, comprehensive state universities and colleges. Multi-purpose institutions, primarily concerned with teaching and public service, they emphasize pro-grams of professional education designed to meet our complex socie-ty's needs for well-educated persons in the Whitehead mold. In order to meet his requirements, concurrently, these institutions provide and require a general/liberal, basic education component taken in tan-dem/parallel with the professional specialization. This modern muta-tion differs drastically from the classical English college with a fixed curriculum, from a liberal arts college with some pre-professional majors and a few professional fields, from specialized technical institutions, and from the doctoral institutions emphasizing research and newly discovered knowledge. Comprehensive, public state colleges and universities are, indeed, far different and represent a new type. Our book documents their development and their contributions to society—yesterday, today, and tomorrow.

—FRED F. HARCLEROAD
—ALLAN W. OSTAR

CHAPTER 1

A New Collegiate Institution For A New Society

It was 1691. Colonial Virginia had tried twice unsuccessfully to found a college. James Blair, the Virginia representative of the Episcopal Church through the Bishop of London, was sent to England to obtain permission of King William III and Queen Mary II to found a college and find some financial support. In 1693, a charter was granted to the College of William and Mary in order to provide pious education for the youth of good letters and manners and to propagate the Christian faith among the Indians. A Crown grant of two thousand pounds accompanied the charter. Two hundred seventy years later in 1963, many of the now fifty states of the U.S.A. also started new institutions, publicly controlled comprehensive colleges and universities. Examples from that one year include Alabama (University of South Alabama), Colorado (Metropolitan State College), Florida (University of West Florida), Maryland (University of Maryland, Baltimore County), Michigan ((Saginaw Valley State College), Minnesota (Southwest State University), Missouri (University of Missouri at St. Louis), and North Carolina (North Carolina School of the Arts). This group of eight public institutions started in one year signifies the great effort of the states during the 1960s decade when sixty-five similar new public institutions were started.

How are these far distant events related? In one major way: both are part of a major current development in higher education. In the past three decades (1950s–1980s), the people of the United States have completed the creation of a new, unique type of higher education institution, the comprehensive public state college and university. Developed by the conversion of 270 existing institutions, many of them special-purpose, and the building of over 130 new comprehensive institutions (see Table 1), this group of 406 institutions shares the following characteristics:

- Publicly established and/or controlled by state governance systems,
- Primarily comprehensive institutions emphasizing professional programs,
- Predominantly awarding baccalaureate and master's degrees,
- Meeting diverse needs of different states primarily at the baccalaureate and master's levels but including less than baccalaureate programs and doctoral programs in selected professional fields,
- Requiring faculty primarily to teach and remain at the cutting edge of knowledge in their fields,
- Predominantly open-access institutions that emphasize equal opportunity, and
- Receiving primary funding from state taxes, with a tradition of low or moderate tuition charges.

TABLE 1
Dates of Establishment of Current Comprehensive State Colleges and Universities

Dates	AASCU Members	Eligible for AASCU	Total	% of Total
1600–1699	1	0	1	1
1700–1799	2	1	3	
1800–1809	–	–	0	
1810–1819	1	–	1	1
1820–1829	3	2	5	
1830–1839	8	–	8	2
1840–1849	4	1	5	1
1850–1859	16	1	17	4
1860–1869	24	1	25	6
1870–1879	28	2	30	7
1880–1889	27	2	29	7
1890–1899	45	2	47	12
1900–1909	39	1	40	10
1910–1919	29	4	33	8
1920–1929	28	2	30	7
1930–1939	11	1	12	3
1940–1949	14	4	18	4
1950–1959	13	6	19	5
1960–1969	57	8	65	16
1970–1979	16	2	18	4
1980s	0	0	0	–
TOTALS	366	40	406	100

Comprehensive public colleges and universities are clearly distinct from the types of institutions adopted from European backgrounds. In addition, they differ greatly from the first two institutional types established in America: the land-grant universities, which developed in the middle 1800s and were formalized by the Morrill Act of 1862, and the junior/community colleges, which started around the turn of the century. The contributions of the land-grant universities and the junior/community colleges have long been recognized. Only recently has it become clear that the comprehensive universities and colleges have a distinctive mission that makes them unique. As a result, these new institutions have been studied extensively during the past decade and emulated in dozens of countries throughout the world. What growth and characteristics led to this attention?

Almost three million students were reported as attending these institutions in 1983, one in every four in all of higher education.* They enrolled almost 40 percent of all students attending institutions offering baccalaureate degrees or beyond. They granted over 35 percent of the total bachelor's degrees completed in 1982, almost 31 percent of the master's degrees, over 30 percent of first professional degrees, and over five percent of the doctorates. Many of these degrees, particularly at the bachelor's level, were earned in badly needed, often newly planned and organized educational degree programs. A major reason for their uniqueness is the breadth and strength of their offerings of professional programs.

This same report of the institutions belonging to the American Association of State Colleges and Universities provided very interesting data on several aspects of their condition and operation. With regard to students, 66 percent were full-time, with 34 percent part-time. Fifteen percent of the students were first-time attendees.

The distribution of institutional sizes indicated great differences among the colleges and universities. Twenty-seven percent were under 3,000, and 29 percent between 3,000 and 6,000, over half of the institutions thus being under 6,000 and able to offer quite personalized education. The remaining numbers varied between 6,000 and 37,000 with percentages as follows: between 6,000 and 9,000 there were 15 percent; from 12,000 to 15,000 seven percent; from 15,000 to 18,000, four percent; from 18,000 to 21,000, two institutions; from 21,000 to 24,000, one institution; and from 24,000 to 37,000, two percent. With regard to location and urban/rural

---

*In August 1984 data were secured for 358 institutions which were members of AASCU at that time, 88 percent of the total eligible (see Appendices 1 and 2). These data were augmented statistically, where appropriate, to apply to the entire group.

characteristics, 27 percent of the institutions were from a standard metropolitan statistical area with a population over 500,000, 28 percent were from standard metropolitan statistical areas with less than 500,000, and 45 percent were actually rural institutions located outside of a standard metropolitan statistical area.

These institutions were scattered all over the United States with significant numbers in each of the various regions. New England, the first area to be reported, had eight percent of the institutions; the Mid-East, 15 percent; the Great Lakes area, 12 percent; the Plains areas, ten percent; the Southeast, 30 percent; the Southwest, ten percent; the Rocky Mountains, five percent; and the Far West, nine percent, with outlying institutions composing only one percent.

Financing the institutions and their costs for attendance were reported in the same study. State and local appropriations provided 48 percent of each year's current fund revenue. Tuition charges to students supported, on the average, 36 percent of instructional expenditures. Educational and general expenditures were 77 percent of current fund expenditures, indicating the emphasis on the educational program within this type of institution. Faculty-student ratios based on both headcount and full-time equivalent faculty were at a 20:1 ratio—higher than many private colleges but actually rather close to the faculty-student ratio maintained in many of the institutions of the United States.

Fee charges for students were relatively reasonable when compared with costs of many professional schools and certainly those of the private liberal arts colleges and universities of the United States. The average state resident cost for tuition and fees was $1,024 for undergraduate students and $1,115 for graduate students, certainly relatively inexpensive compared with many other institutions. The costs for nonresidents were appreciably higher, however, with the rate for nonresident undergraduates averaging $2,452 for the academic year and the graduate nonresident tuition and fees at an average of $2,376 per year. The overall cost for resident students averaged around $3,000 per year for tuition, fees, and room and board, with the comparable costs for graduate students running under $4,500 a year. Although these are significant costs and mark a considerable increase over the past two decades. In 1983–84, they were much more reasonable than those of any but the two-year colleges.

The comprehensive public colleges and universities owe their remarkable growth to their flexibility and diversity. Their ability to adapt and change has made them a crucial segment of the higher education community. However, their main emphasis on professional programs supported by especial, sometimes noteworthy, general education programs makes them unique and provides their distinctive mission.

Why and how has American society changed so drastically that another new type of higher education unit has been required? Several partial reasons can be itemized, such as (1) the post-war movement toward an egalitarian, classless society; (2) the population explosion and increased demand for spaces to attend higher education; and (3) the G.I. Bill and federal assistance to the states for funding higher education (both students and buildings.) New and existing types of institutions have contributed mightily to meeting these needs. Most existing ones have grown, adapted admission standards, and provided, again, preparatory/remedial/developmental program units for poorly prepared students. Many new institutions have been set up, particularly new liberal arts colleges and new junior/community colleges.

However, the main factors demanding a new type of higher education institution are part of the restructuring of our total industrial society. Four different historical eras can be defined leading to this current era, and higher education has changed with each. First, the agricultural era extending to around 1850 was based mainly on land as a key resource, horse and foot transportation, and a very dispersed settlement pattern throughout the United States. The second period, from 1850 through 1920, centered around manufacturing. The key resource for this era was raw material, mainly metals, transported by water and by rail. Much larger cities developed during this period with major beginnings of population concentration. The third major era was from around 1920 through approximately 1950–60, with an emphasis on services. The key resource during that time could be considered the people of the country, with transportation by auto and by air. During this era, the huge concentrations of populations and the big "metropolis" developed. People began to talk about the entire geographic area from Boston to Washington, D.C., as BosWash, with beginnings of San San from Los Angeles down through San Diego.

Since the 1960s, during the developing fourth era, there has been a change to a communications/international focus, with information as the key resource. Major new ways have been developed for the production of wealth, and activities for handling information are expanding rapidly. Patterns of work have changed greatly. Numerous people now work at home on a part-time or extended basis without going regularly to work places. Obviously we have crossed a new threshold, made a sharp break with the past. A term sometimes used for this period is "the post-industrial society", one which is more and more based on knowledge.

The need for knowledge has led the land-grant institutions to emphasize their research institute responsibilities for the development of new theoretical knowledge, and the patterns of organization and development of these institutions reflect this major requirement. Advanced education is the major means by which people can work their way into professional jobs in a post-industrial, knowledge-based, communications/international telecommunications society. Vast new professional areas of knowledge for which people need to be educated and trained have become very important to the successful operation of the society. The new comprehensive public university and college group has changed drastically as a direct result of this change in our society. The massive need for a huge infrastructure of persons highly educated at the baccalaureate and master's degree level has not been met by the more limited or different changes in other four-year and doctoral institutions. The need for a total institution providing for millions of graduates in new and changing professional fields has been the great impetus to the establishment of this new type of collegiate institution for the society of the current decades.

An illustration of the importance of this change in occupational-vocational-professional work is shown in the 1984 fall report of the Maryland State Board for Higher Education. This compared the percentage of 1982 graduates who were unemployed one year after graduation with their undergraduate major. A high proportion of these students came from the state's comprehensive public four-year and master's degree institutions. In the area of computer and information sciences, less than one percent were unemployed. In the agricultural and natural resources areas, less than four percent were unemployed. Comparable figures were true for the new health professions, 4.3 percent, for engineering 4.7 percent, for architecture and environmental design 5.6 percent, education 6.2 percent, and mathematics and business management 6.3 and 6.6 percent, respectively. In the social sciences, physical sciences, fine and applied arts, and foreign languages—the major fields of the liberal arts colleges of the past century—the unemployment rate ranged above ten percent to over 14 percent. This study indicated that the Maryland unemployment rate at the time the survey was conducted was seven percent, and the national unemployment rate was ten percent. Maryland's rate was better by almost three percent than the national rate. If these figures are applied to the national rate, the striking differences between the new professional areas and the old liberal arts and science areas becomes even more apparent.

Another study published simultaneously by the Maryland State Board for Higher Education indicated that almost 12 percent of 1982 graduates were employed in the business area as accountants, financial analysts, bankers, or brokers. An additional 9.7 percent were employed as managers, executives, or proprietors. With the personnel and purchasing, almost one-fourth of all 1982 graduates were employed in the business field. In the education field, as administrators, teachers, counselors, or librarians, there was a continuing high proportion, 9.3 percent. The greatest change was in the computer programmer/computer analyst, area where 7.7 percent were employed in this single relatively new field. In the sales agent/representative area, an additional 6.9 percent were employed. At the same time, 5.8 percent were employed as engineers and architects, four percent as health professionals, 2.2 as health technicians and 2.1 in engineering or science technician work. All told, over 80 percent of the 1982 graduates were employed in professiona/technical work. Sixteen percent were employed in nonprofessional, operative, skilled-craft, or secretarial work, and 3.2 percent were in the armed forces.

A third factor reported in this same Maryland study showed the close relation of some academic majors and appointment to professional positions. In the computer and information science area, 88 percent reported that they were in a job directly related to their major. This was true of 74 percent in the health professions, 73 percent in engineering, 63 percent in education, and 52 percent in business and management. In mathematics, graduates were in directly related jobs in 48 percent of the cases, in public affairs and services 47 percent, in agriculture and natural resources 45 percent, biological sciences 44 percent, communications 41 percent, and home economics 41 percent. In the areas of interdisciplinary studies, fine and applied arts, psychology, letters, and social sciences, the incidence of employment related to undergraduate major ranged from 37 percent in interdisciplinary studies and, dropping drastically, to 18 percent in the social sciences. Once again, these very interesting and useful findings indicate not only the growing need for professional service in these newer fields required by our information society, but the high potential for direct employment of persons who have graduated in these areas (Report, Insert, pp. 2–4).

An important characteristic of our new, professional institutions is their concern and provision for a strong general education for these highly educated professionals. As these state institutions developed during the post-World War II period, most have experimented with and developed updated modern, general/liberal education programs.

Montclair State College in New Jersey provides a good example of this concern. Its mission statement reads:

The mission of Montclair State College as a *multi-purpose public institution** is to develop *educated persons** of inquiring, creative and disciplined intelligence to be *competent in careers** that are fulfilling and to be socially responsible contributors to society.

In the area of general education, the statement goes on: The College aims to provide all of its baccalaureate graduates with a *fine general education.** Its graduates must be competent in the basic intellectual disciplines, aware of human experience in the arts and in society, and understand the development of scientific theories through objective observation of the way nature works. Its aim is education, not merely training. Its graduates must have developed their affective and intellectual faculties through encounters with the great works of literature, philosophy and history. Its graduates must also understand foreign cultures and languages to educate them beyond the provincialism of time, place, religion, or race to become world citizens.

To implement these goals, the college faculty, following an extensive study of many years, established a new, revised general education program in the early 1980s, requiring the following work for the baccalaureate degree as a part of the general education requirements:

1. Communication (9 semester hours), requiring competence in writing, reading, speaking, and listening.
2. An interdisciplinary course in contemporary issues (3 semester hours) dealing with moral and ethical problems and their possible realistic solutions.
3. Arts appreciation (through free elective).
4. A foreign language, including a two-course sequence emphasizing reading, writing, and speaking (6 semester hours) with placement exams and a competency examination at the end.
5. Humanities (6 semester hours), requiring a course in world literature from both Western and non-Western literary traditions, or a general humanities interdisciplinary course which provides for study of the values of different civilizations. It also requires a course in philosophy or religion emphasizing critical and creative response to philosophical and religious ideas, arguments, and perspectives.

---

*emphasis added

6. Mathematics, including a basic course in problem solving and analysis in mathematics (3 semester hours), plus a computer science course (2 semester hours) stressing the development of computer literacy.

7. The Natural/Physical Sciences requirements are, one laboratory science course (4 semester hours) and one non-lab course (3 semester hours) designed particularly to provide the ability to appreciate and utilize the scientific method.

8. The Social Sciences (12 semester hours) require a course in American or European history designed to provide perspective on long-range historical developments and the influence of the past in shaping the contemporary world. A second course is required in non-Western cultural perspectives, along with two other non-history courses. These should include the assumptions, principles, and methodologies of one particular social science discipline, and a topical course focusing on analytical techniques and methods of inquiry in a particular theme, problem, or issue in the social sciences.

9. Physical education (1 semester hour) requires one physical activity which is designed to improve skills and give better understanding of how regular exercise improves the quality of life.

10. A minority cultures requirement is designed to ensure that all graduates of the College are acquainted with the life, history, and cultural contribution of a group recognized by the larger society as constituting a disadvantaged subculture in the U.S. A large group of courses is available for selection to meet this requirement: Minorities in Business, Afro-American Art, The Development of Black Thought, and Women in Politics.

11. In addition, general electives are designed for selection of courses providing creative expression in a particular art form, and individual and professional issues in professional coursework or fields of study. General education electives must be taken outside the student's major so the study of individual and professional issues cannot be totally subsumed in the professional program.

This relatively extensive and creative, general/liberal education program provides a specific case example to illustrate the general point made above: although these institutions emphasize professional education in the developing professions of the late years of the twentieth century, they demand a program designed to provide a much broader general education. Taken parallel and simultaneously with professional education coursework, the program differs dramatically from the previous pattern of higher education used in many institutions, i.e., two years of general/liberal education (breadth or distribution) in the freshman and sophomore years followed by concentration or specialization in the upper division, often in liberal arts fields.

The historical background of this group of institutions provides a basis for understanding in more depth the reasons for their change into a unique group with a clear mission. This background logically breaks down into three main periods: (1) Origins of Change (1693–early 1900s); (2) Changing Missions (1920–1960); and (3) Emergence of New Components of Higher Education (1960–1985). Consideration of these periods follows and will explicate further the thesis of this book.

A few very significant themes recur through these various time periods. For the entire three centuries, at least three stand out. First, the need for higher education institutions to offer preparatory programs has been constant. As new additional groups of students have been accommodated, for whatever reason, special programs for makeup or preparatory work have been absolutely necessary and offered continuously. Whether they are called remedial work, developmental programs, or preparatory divisions, they have been established, often with considerable faculty complaint and sometimes concern by the college's constituents. Second, once an institution has been established and built, even though funds may run out and the institution closes, facilities continue to be used. Most often another college opens—sponsored by a church, a public group, or a governmental unit. Third, the expanding knowledge base has forced institutions, often reluctantly, to add to or materially change collegiate-level programs or to be left behind to close their doors. Students continually assess institutions with their feet, deciding where they will attend, in what programs they will enroll, and which they will complete. Also, funding sources dry up when priorities of a society or a state change and the institutions fail to react rapidly enough to be funded.

In the two centuries since the American Revolution and the development of our current form of government, at least three additional themes recur often and are important to note here also. First, voluntary nonprofit organizations and associations have played a critical role in the establishment and continuing support of both private and public institutions. American governmental structure provides three basic types of enterprise to produce necessary goods, services, and amenities for the entire society: (a) private, profit-seeking enterprises; (b) governmental enterprises funded basically from taxing either the profits of the private group or the salaries paid from the income it generates; and (c) nonprofit voluntary organizations which operate in the public interest. These are tax-free in the main and supported by tax-deductible contributions. Second, voluntary nonprofit accreditation associations for the past century have affected the ebb and flow on institutions through their appraisal and reporting activities. Third, state-federal relationships regarding education at all levels due to (1) constitutional limitations on the central government and (2) federal funding powers, have been a constant influence and have affected the development of higher education institutions in countless ways.

These six themes crop up continually, along with other issues of importance to particular periods. With these in mind, we go back to the beginnings of today's new type of collegiate institutions and their gradual evolution toward their present unique mission.

CHAPTER 2

Origins of Change (1693–1920s)

Some of the institutions in the comprehensive public college and university group evolved over a period of almost three centuries, while others have developed only within the last two decades. Only two existing AASCU institutions were started in the first subperiod preceding the Revolutionary War in the United States: the College of William and Mary (1693) and the College of Charleston (1770). Basically, the period from 1693–1800 is separate, even though only two institutions from that period are today part of AASCU. The long remaining time period from 1800 until the 1920s breaks down into two additional subperiods, from 1800–1890s and from the 1890s through the 1920s. Accordingly, these three subperiods will be considered separately.

Early Beginnings (1693–1785)

James Blair returned to Virginia from his long trip to England with a royal charter which established the College of William and Mary on February 8, 1693. A royal grant of 2,000 pounds was provided also, for the College was charged to provide the colonists with an opportunity for a "religious and learned education" in a "place of universal study, or perpetual College of Divinity, Philosophy, Language, and other good Arts and Sciences." The charter stated categorically that the College was set up so that "the Church of Virginia may be furnished with a Seminary of Ministers of the Gospel . . . and that the Christian Faith may be propagated." The Virginia colony was a part of the Bishopric of London of the Anglican Church, and James Blair was the commissary (representative) of the Bishop of London. Virginia needed ministers, and the new College had a primary responsi-

13

bility for the primary professional education need of the day, training ministers. The colonial government for its part helped finance the College by levying taxes, first on skins and hides, and second on tobacco, with the funds used to support the new College. It was indeed well-supported, and in 1775–76, at the time of the Revolution, it was the wealthiest college in the 13 British colonies.

Virginia had tried to start its first college in 1619, when the Crown set aside 9,000 acres for a university at Henrico, but three years later an Indian massacre caused the death of those responsible and the loss of almost all records. In 1660, the Virginia Assembly tried again, but unsuccessfully. The 1693 founding was well-received and strongly supported by the people and the colonial government.

The College of William and Mary developed very well, living up to its charge. Though small in numbers, it trained many ministers and civil leaders of the colony, and respected its origins and professional purpose, following this stipulation in the early statutes of the College: "For avoiding the danger of heresy, schism, and disloyalty, let the president and masters, before they enter upon these offices, give their assent to the articles of the Christian faith, in the same manner, and in the same words, as the ministers in England, by act of Parliament are obliged to sign the Articles of the Church of England. And in the same manner too they shall take the oath of allegiance to the King or Queen of England." Most of the early professors at the College of William and Mary were ministers educated at Oxford, and the College president was an Anglican or Episcopal minister, head of the Anglican Church in Virginia, and the deputy or commissary of the Bishop of London.

Although operating a restricted classical curriculum, William and Mary began fairly early to modify and change it. Jefferson pushed, and the Board of Visitors abolished the Grammar School and the chair of Divinity. In their place on December 4, 1779, the Board established a chair for Modern Languages, and the nation's first professorship of law and police, filled initially by George Wythe, the eminent lawyer in whose offices Thomas Jefferson apprenticed to learn the law (Brown, 1982; Swindler, 1978). Both of these significant changes in curricular offerings were necessary and occurred in very difficult times. Another exceptional example of change came in 1776 when students were allowed to set up the first Greek letter organization, and Phi Beta Kappa was established (Rudolph, 1962).

In spite of its fine fiscal condition and willingness to adapt both curriculum and student organization, the College of William and Mary fell on hard times after the Revolution and endured a century of grave difficulties. They will be discussed later in the two following subperiods of this section.

The second prerevolutionary college, the College of Charleston, traces its beginnings to 1770, when a bill to establish it had been prepared and presented to the South Carolina General Assembly along with a detailed plan for governance, faculty, curriculum, location, and financing. Contributions to its endowment were received, and the bill passed a third reading—but an unrelated deadlock split the House, and it was "prorogued" (terminated) forthwith. Funds and books were collected and preserved for use at the College. However, the fight over a connection with the Church of England, and postponing establishment until after the Revolution, delayed the actual founding until 1785. In that year, the Assembly chartered three colleges but funded only one—at Charleston—requiring that the trustees be Protestant Christians. Six years later, a new act provided for complete religious freedom. In 1789, the College combined with an academy which had begun in 1785 and opened for students.

Thus, in reality, only the College of William and Mary was the first currently existing public higher education institution to operate before the Revolution. All other prerevolutionary institutions except Queens College (established in 1766) now Rutgers, the State University of New Jersey, continue to this day as privately controlled institutions—even though colonial and, later, state funds supported them to some degree up to the present time.

The Beginnings of Change (1785–1900)

During the period from the end of the Revolutionary War to the Civil War, a number of critical issues greatly affected the establishment and further development of publicly controlled colleges. Although sometimes closely related, five key issues will be presented separately. They are:

1. States' rights versus federal responsibility for higher education.
2. Secretarian, orthodox, and religious versus secular, "revolutionary" state control of colleges.
3. Tax-supported versus fee-supported educational institutions.
4. Education for a privileged elite versus open, egalitarian institutions.
5. Classical versus professional education for the developing industrial society.

The decisions regarding these basic issues vitally affected this period in American history and all of its institutions, including higher education.

State Versus Federal Control of Colleges

This issue centered around states' rights was a heated one in the decades from 1785 until 1860. Proposals for a national university, for example, were highly unpopular and always defeated. Plans for the new nation led to the continuation of state rather than federal control of higher education. As part of the development of the Constitution and of the new country, education played a very limited role. In fact, the Federalist Papers contained no reference to schools, colleges, education, or universities.

One of the very fundamental debates about the development of the Bill of Rights, however, ultimately had a very controlling influence in the development of postsecondary education in the United States. In 1789, as a part of the debates in the Congress about the establishment of the new nation, James Madison proposed what has now become the Tenth Amendment of the United States Constitution: "The powers not delegated by this Constitution nor prohibited by it to the states, are reserved to the states respectively." By the time the Tenth Amendment was approved and made a part of the Constitution, it included, at the end, the following phrase: "or to the people."

In making his proposal for including this amendment, Madison said that "the great object in view is to limit and qualify the powers of the [federal] government, by excepting out of the grant of powers those cases in which the government ought not to act, or to act only in a particular mode." The word *education* does not appear in the Constitution of the United States and is therefore not a power delegated by the states to the federal government. A few collegiate-level institutions which are designed to meet delegated powers of the Constitution, including the "common defense," have been developed by the federal government. Their number is quite small, and they are mainly institutions for training members of the various armed services. For example, the first, the U.S. Military Academy, opened in 1802 primarily to prepare engineers, and its graduates served all aspects of the society. However, during the past two centuries, the states of the United States have been the basic source of controlling laws and of charters granted to postsecondary institutions.

Religious Versus Sectarian Control

The religious, denominational college prevailed totally in the colonies from 1636 until the Revolution, and set a strong pattern for organizing and controlling the vast majority of colleges until the Civil War. Nine of the thirteen colonies were basically church-states, and in six of them the Anglican Church was the "established" church. These states were Virginia, New York, North Carolina, South Carolina, Georgia, and Maryland. Massachusetts, New Hampshire, and Connecticut also had an "established" religion, the Congregational (Puritan) Church. Pennsylvania, Rhode Island, Delaware, and New Jersey had no "established" church and had separated church and state early in their history—but their three colonial colleges (Delaware had none until 1833) were still highly religious, and even in Pennsylvania the training of ministers was a main function. In Rhode Island, Brown University was "New Light" Baptist. In New Jersey, the College of New Jersey (now Princeton) was Presbyterian, and Queens College (now Rutgers) was of the Dutch Reformed Church (Tewksbury, 1932).

The full separation of church and state was a major goal of the Revolution at both state and federal levels. Much of the population, however, still was concerned about "godless" secularism. While this significant group of the population preferred religious freedom without an established church, many still preferred a varied group of private religious colleges over those established and controlled by the secular state.

Actual disestablishment of religion was slow coming in to some states. In Virginia, Thomas Jefferson proposed in 1779 that the College of William and Mary become a state university. He lost this political battle largely due to Presbyterian opposition and Episcopal unwillingness, and it did not come to pass. In 1788, his bill for religious freedom did pass, and separation of both church and state became a fact. Simultaneously, William and Mary lost its former prestige and its state tax resources. Three decades later, in 1819, Virginia finally established a new, so-called "revolutionary" university (i.e., state established, funded, and controlled) when the Legislature established Jefferson's University of Virginia. The College of William and Mary again became a state-controlled and funded university a century later—but that is another story for discussion at another period in history.

New York's disestablishment took a totally different path. The

University of the State of New York, in actuality a supervisory board over all education, was created in 1784, a partial victory for those favoring "revolutionary," state-controlled higher education since Columbia University was also included. The Board of Regents was charged with visiting every school and college yearly and reporting to the legislature on the quality of the institutions—the first beginning of accreditation. In 1787, Columbia received its own Board, still subject to yearly review by the Board of Regents of the new state university system. This arrangement did allow other churches or nonprofit organizations to establish competing institutions, such as Union College (1795) and Hamilton College (1812). Also, it left the way open for the new academies (such as St. Lawrence Academy in Potsdam in 1816) and eventually for state-controlled normal schools. In contrast, Massachusetts did not disestablish the church/state relationship for fifty years, in 1833, just in time to set up its own normal schools.

In Connecticut, still another type of action was finally taken with regard to the position of Yale University and the state. Although Yale University was close to the state traditionally, it was not legally a part of the colonial government. Following the Revolution and during the Revolutionary period, in 1784, petitions were presented to the legislature regarding the alteration of the Yale charter in order that other institutions could be established under state control or that state representation would be included on the Yale Board. These were not passed at that time. In 1792, however, the legislature reorganized the Yale Corporation with official representation on the Board by the governor, lieutenant governor, and six state officials as ex-officio members. In this way, Yale maintained its high position in the state as a private institution and at the time was able to prevent the establishment of other institutions. The establishment of an official state university was delayed for decades.

In Rhode Island, a relatively comparable situation resulted for Brown University, with long-term effects. For example, the original land-grants to Rhode Island, in the period following the establishment of the land-grant colleges in 1862, were awarded to Brown University. Although not really used to establish agricultural and mechanical arts education, they were used for student scholarships, and minimal attention was given to the land-grant cause. In New Jersey, an attempt was made in 1793 to merge Rutgers and Princeton into one state-controlled institution. This proposed merger was never carried through, and the institutions remained separate colleges. The much later establishment of a state university of New Jersey at

Rutgers was delayed for decades as a result of this post-revolutionary decision.

In Pennsylvania, the University of Pennsylvania was basically a private institution established where a diversity of religious interests were already recognized. In 1779, the charter of the University of Pennsylvania was revoked, and a new institution, to be known as the University of the State of Pennsylvania, was established with a controlling representation from the state on the Board. The University of the State of Pennsylvania and the old College of Philadelphia existed as two rival institutions for ten years, with the College of Philadelphia quite concerned and protesting its charter revocation. Ten years later, in 1789, the original charter of the College of Philadelphia was reinstated, but the new university was retained for two more years. Finally, in 1791, the push throughout the state for a "revolutionary" state-controlled institution became less pressing. The College of Philadelphia and the University of the State of Pennsylvania were merged under a single board with minimal state representation. Only the governor served on the board, in an ex-officio capacity. Clearly, each of the various colonies, with their own sectarian versus church concerns, took very different actions in the immediate post-revolutionary period. As a consequence, the diversity of American higher education received a great impetus (Tewksbury, 1932, pp. 142–166).

Another push toward diversity came from the Dartmouth College court action in 1819, a major decision affecting the church/state issue. New Hampshire's legislature had established in 1816 a new, "revolutionary" state-controlled institution, Dartmouth University, to take over the assets of Dartmouth College and replace it. Three years later, in 1819, the John Marshall-written decision of the U.S. Supreme Court declared this action unconstitutional and an improper abrogation of contract law. Thus, it limited state action in this area both for educational institutions and all other private corporations as well. Suddenly, the air was cleared. Two different ways existed for states to charter or establish competitive colleges: first, independent, private, or church-related, denominational colleges; second, state-established colleges and universities. As a result, the denominational institutions grew by the hundreds, as did public, state-controlled institutions later.

A sidelight on the Dartmouth College decision was the struggle over this issue, between Jefferson and his old enemy, John Marshall. The struggle was basically a fight between conservative New Hampshire Federalists and Congregationalists on one side and the state's Jefferśonian Republicans (liberal revolutionaries) on the other. At the time, it appeared that Jefferson lost an important battle. In the long run, however, each won, for both ways of establishing colleges became acceptable and correct within the overall province of the state. The diversity of current American higher education under state chartering grew from this basic decision. At the same time, private colleges and business corporations, once chartered, are free from legislative supervision and control.

Tax-Supported Versus Fee-Supported Institutions

Colonies whose "established" churches had their own colleges often provided financial support. Taxes on such diverse items as skins, tobacco, surveyors, or ferries were designated for use by various colleges. Of course, a colony's funds often were insufficient to pay total costs, so endowments were sought from donors, and modest fees, often paid in kind, were required of students. After the Revolution, the separation of church institutions from state control led to the loss of many of these tax resources. Further, after the Dartmouth College decision, many states felt no obligation to support denominational colleges. The churches and the college's self-perpetuating boards of trustees had to pay their own way from whatever sources they could tap. Public colleges, however, were clearly the state's obligation. Regular political decisions had to be made regarding the value to the society of an educated populace, the amount of resulting taxes to be appropriated, and remaining costs to be assessed against individual students. The proportion varied greatly from state to state and time to time, but the principle of some tax support for public collegiate institutions was established very early.

Costs of elementary and secondary education however, were not so regarded. For two centuries, until the early 1800s, elementary education was something for families to provide, not the state. Tax money for secondary schools was finally ruled legal in the late 1800s and led to a great upsurge in numbers of publicly supported secondary schools. Until that time, most colleges maintained preparatory departments which often were funded in the same way as the college.

After the complete separation of states from established religions, low tuition or—in some cases—no tuition was charged to students in the publicly supported institutions, and state tax funds became their largest base for support. Private, independent institutions in most states, must secure funds from their constituents, having lost their prior right to direct forms of taxes and, in all but a few states, the right to request direct state appropriations. The Dartmouth College case had removed independent or denominational colleges from state control and left the states free from the requirement to consider financing for them. In spite of this quid pro quo, different states and, in recent decades, the federal government have considered the public interest served to some degree by independent institutions. As a result, some public tax funds are channeled to these institutions directly, or indirectly through their students. This competitive situation has existed for almost two centuries and often affected the establishment of new public institutions. For example, Queens College became Rutgers College in 1825, but it was 1917 before it became the State University of New Jersey. New York's public system, the State University of New York, was not established until 1958.

Elitism Versus Egalitarianism

The movement toward open state-controlled, funded, and operated institutions of higher education drew much of its support from the republican concern about elitism in colonial colleges—particularly in Anglican and Congregational colonies. Each of the early colleges came to be considered privileged, and essentially a "rich man's college" for a selected few students. As Rudolph has written further, "the [Dartmouth College] decision put the American college beyond the control of popular prejudice and passion; it assured the further alienation of the people from the colleges" (1962, pp. 201–217).

The real beginnings of an egalitarian approach to higher education took place with the push to elect Andrew Jackson as President in 1828. Colleges which considered the classical curriculum preeminent and the only way to educate leaders for government and commerce (with a few "charity" students admitted) had difficulty adjusting to Jacksonianism. Actual hostility to denominational, religious colleges for being open basically to the privileged class seemed an unfair accusation to college leaders. In the 1830s, many took steps to react to the times. One planned to set up a college designed for "children of the poor to rise by their wisdom and merit into stations hitherto occupied by the rich", as proposed for Kenyon College in 1830. Other existing institutions even went so far as to set up programs to prepare teachers for the newly developing "common" schools and public school systems. The move toward egalitarianism of the post-revolutionary period, particularly during and after the Jacksonian era, started a movement toward "education for all" through state-controlled and financed higher education—a movement that has constantly gathered a momentum which continues to this day.

Classical Versus Professional/Liberal Education

Classical education maintained a preeminent position long after its direct usefulness had ended. When all significant writings were in Latin and Greek, these great classical Western languages were essential to acquire an education. However, when eminent writings were translated and available in the customary English language and new, great ideas became available only in English, the justification of Latin and Greek—for so called "mental discipline" and improving the mind—became artificial. They were no longer relevant to the changing needs of a new, dynamic, expanding democratic republic. A more urban country with improvements in transportation, agriculture, and commerce, and with an exploding industrialization required new approaches to curriculum offerings. Many of these developed through new forms of specialized educational institutions—dozens of them in existence today in often revised forms.

The demise of the classical college curriculum took many decades, and in some locations today versions still exist which are quite close to the early American colonial curriculum. During the period after the Dartmouth College decision, literally hundreds of new denominational colleges were started throughout the entire United States. By the time of the Civil War, over 900 institutions had been established in the thirty-four states of the Union. Tewksbury's famous dissertation on the founding of American colleges and universities before the Civil War included a complete study of sixteen of the thirty-four states. Those sixteen had already founded 516 institutions; 412 had closed and 104 were still operating, for a mortality rate of 81 percent. Tewksbury used a broad spectrum of the various states, large and small in all sections of the country; it is probably justifiable to expand his findings from the sixteen states he covered to the thirty-four states that existed. He also found that 182 permanent college and universities were founded before the Civil War. Accordingly, at the same rate of mortality, there were over 900 institutions founded.

Rudolph's analysis of colleges which died in the United States before the Civil War came to over 700 (1962 p. 219). He also found, for example, that 55 new Catholic colleges were started between 1850–1866, with 25 abandoned by 1866. The sizes of the remaining institutions were also quite small. Lafayette College, for instance, established in 1828, had a Board of Trustees larger than the student body in 1848. Denison College in Ohio had 65 students in 1853, 20 years after its establishment. Of the nine permanent colleges established in the colonies prior to the Revolution, all except Harvard became smaller and lost enrollments between 1825 and 1860. At Harvard, after the violent student revolutions of the 1820s, modest changes had taken place in the curriculum offerings, and slight beginnings had been made in the elective system. In addition, the Lawrence Scientific School had been established in the late 1840s, with a lesser degree known as the Bachelor of Science degree; the students in the Lawrence School helped to maintain the size of the Harvard enrollment. Yale also had established the Sheffield Scientific School, and its beginning enrollments tended to help the overall total enrollment of the university.

Most of the 182 institutions which survived during this period were small, however; some had taken small steps toward the curriculum revision required in order to meet the developing needs of the society. The new curricular response to demands for professionally trained people, with a liberal education background took place in many different types of institutions, including many new public institutions which developed from 1830 to the Civil War.

TABLE 2

Mortality of Colleges Founded Before the Civil War in Sixteen States of the Union

S.N.	State	Total Colleges	Living Colleges	Dead Colleges	Mortality Rate
1	Pennsylvania	31	16	15	48%
2	New York	36	15	21	58%
3	Ohio	43	17	26	60%
4	Virginia	32	10	22	69%
5	North Carolina	26	7	19	73%
6	Maryland	23	5	18	78%
7	Alabama	23	4	19	83%
8	Tennessee	46	7	39	84%
9	Georgia	51	7	44	86%
10	Louisiana	26	3	23	88%
11	Missouri	85	8	77	90%
12	Mississippi	29	2	27	93%
13	Texas	40	2	38	95%
14	Kansas	20	1	19	95%
15	Florida	2	0	2	100%
16	Arkansas	3	0	3	100%
TOTAL FOR 16 STATES		516 =	104 +	412	81%*

*Average mortality rate for 16 states

Source: Tewksbury, Donald G. *The Founding of American Colleges and Universities Before the Civil War*. New York: Teachers College, Columbia University, 1932. Reprint. Ann Arbor, Michigan: University Microfilms.

*Initial Development of State Institutions (1800–1890s)

In the seventy-five years following the actual founding of the College of Charleston in 1785, 62 existing public institutions were founded which are members or eligible for membership in the American Association of State Colleges and Universities. Many started as private academies or classical schools, others as normal schools, agricultural schools, technical institutes, colleges open to women and minorities, mechanics institutes, and YMCA or physical culture schools. At the time of their establishment, none of the institutions offered what was considered college-level work. Some perspective on the definition of "college-level work" during this period is provided by considering the 1847 establishment of Lawrence Scientific School at Harvard. The new degree allowed, the B.S. degree, and the "Scientific" program itself was regarded as of lower quality than the classical B.A. program. Nevertheless, most of these new public institutions developed degree programs at a later date.

The academies in particular were not collegiate, but preparatory for college, providing education for students continuing on to college. They taught a variety of practical subjects but functioned as teacher education institutions as well. It was primarily these academies that offered any preparation for service as teachers prior to the establishment of the normal schools. In many states, the academies remained as an important source of new teachers long after normal schools had been founded. The majority of the academies were located in New England; a few in the middle states, and still fewer in the South. They tended to be in the larger towns of the state rather than in the relatively secluded rural areas in which many private liberal arts colleges or normal schools were established.

A Case Example: Potsdam, New York

An interesting case example of an academy that became a normal school, then a teachers college, and finally a state university college of arts and sciences is the St. Lawrence Academy, founded originally in Potsdam, New York in September 1816. It was a product of the establishment of the University of the State of New York in 1787, which allowed local groups to set up academies and authorized the

*Significant portions of this section have been copied or paraphrased and corrected from a previous baseline study first conducted by Harcleroad in 1967. It is included in the bibliography as follows: Harcleroad, Fred F.; Sagen, H. Bradley; and Molen, C. Theodore, Jr. *The Developing State Colleges and Universities: Historical Background, Current Status and Future Plans.* Iowa City, Iowa: American Testing Program, 1969.

Board of Regents of the University of the State of New York to control them and be sure that they were functioning appropriately. The law did not prescribe the curriculum or designate required subjects; local trustees determined these. The regents, however, were required to visit and inspect the academies yearly.

The St. Lawrence Academy's career, long and distinguished, provided both an English Department and a Classical Program, the latter designed for college preparation. In 1826, the Academy reported 80 students in the English curriculum and 36 in the Classical, with state aid based only on the Classical students. The English Department was not supported since it was designed to provide an elementary and practical education for persons not intending to go on to college. In the Classical Program, Latin and Greek courses were the core subjects, in the "patrician tradition" and "good for mental discipline." A new addition to the Classical Curriculum came in 1832: biblical antiquities.

In 1835, the Academy established another department—mathematics and natural philosophy—creating within it a teacher department. Under the leadership of the Reverend Asa Brainerd during this early period, the Academy was very experimental and tried many ideas for courses which were somewhat unusual and out of the ordinary. The education of teachers had started in the early 1830s in accordance with plans established by the Regents. With a very early, special interest in the field of music, the Academy added that subject to the curriculum, establishing a leadership role in this field continuing to the present era.

A great debate took place in the State of New York in the 1840s and 50s regarding the way in which teacher education should be developed and cared for. Eventually, in 1844, a normal school was established in Albany for a five-year experimental period. Five years later, the state legislature determined that it had been successful and made provision for four academies, located strategically throughout the state, to provide for the education of teachers. St. Lawrence Academy was one of the four, and it served as a teacher education institution until 1868–69. At that time, the legislature determined to stop the education of teachers through academies at state expense, and invited communities to file applications for setting up new normal schools in their areas. Potsdam made a successful bid for one of the schools and, just after the Civil War, in 1869, began building Potsdam Normal School on the site of St. Lawrence Academy.

The story of this institution, a state-supported and controlled normal school, was very common during the nineteenth century. It well illustrates the process by which the states moved through a variety of avenues into the operation of a significant, specialized, and eventually collegiate higher education program. Although private academies flourished for a relatively brief time, the experience of St. Lawrence Academy was quite common. The normal school movement spread rapidly throughout all of the states, following the expansion of public schools. This expansion was, in fact, a logical extension of the fundamental principles of the young democracy, which promised equal freedoms and opportunities for all its citizens. Since education had been left to the several states by the new federal constitution, it was not surprising that pressure developed for rapid expansion of public education. Expansion came with surprising force and gained swift momentum; its principal outcome was the common school, whose purpose was to provide every child with a basic elementary education.

Development of Public Normal Schools

One of the first problems confronting advocates of common schools was preparation of adequately trained teachers. Horace Mann, Albert Carter, Henry Barnard, and a number of other educational reformers had studied the Prussian system of education. They attributed much of the Prussian success to the teacher training provided in the normal schools. Furthermore, they became convinced that if class distinctions were to be eliminated, all teacher preparation ought to be conducted under similar conditions. Therefore, they concluded, normal schools ought to be public and under state control.

The proposals' principal opponents represented two points of view. One group opposed the basic concept of common schools at public expense. The other group supported the idea of these schools but argued that existing academies should train the teachers. The arguments of the latter group resulted in state support of teacher education programs in academies in New York, Maine, and Wisconsin. Such schools proved unable either to prepare enough teachers or to prepare them sufficiently well, and other forms of teacher preparation became necessary.

Opposition from these groups prevented the establishment of public normal schools until 1839, 12 years after the establishment of the first private normal schools, but by the end of the nineteenth century there had been rapid development. Of the 406 institutions now defined as state colleges and universities, 103 were founded as normal schools between 1839 and 1900. The dates of the first establishment of state normal schools are:

State	Establishment	State	Establishment
Massachusetts	1839	Texas	1879
New York	1844	North Dakota	1881
Connecticut	1849	South Dakota	1881
Michigan	1849	Oregon	1883
Rhode Island	1852	Virginia	1884
Iowa	1855	Louisiana	1884
New Jersey	1855	Arizona	1885
Illinois	1857	Wyoming	1886
Minnesota	1858	Florida	1887
Pennsylvania	1862	Nevada	1887
California	1862	Colorado	1889
Kansas	1863	Georgia	1889
Maine	1863	Washington	1890
Indiana	1865	Oklahoma	1891
Wisconsin	1865	Idaho	1893
Vermont	1866	Montana	1893
Delaware	1866	New Mexico	1893
Nebraska	1867	South Carolina	1895
West Virginia	1867	Maryland	1896
Utah	1869	Ohio	1900
Missouri	1870	Kentucky	1906
New Hampshire	1870	Alabama	1907
Arkansas	1872	Tennessee	1909
North Carolina	1876	Mississippi	1910

The first public normal schools were founded at Lexington and Barre, Massachusetts in 1839, established under the direction of Horace Mann, lawyer and former president of the Massachusetts Senate; (Mangun, 1928, p. 72), then serving as secretary of the Massachusetts Board of Education. The normal school at Lexington moved eventually to West Newton and then in 1853 to Framingham. The school at Barre moved to Westfield in 1844 and later became the first coeducational normal school (Pilecki, 1984). For many years, while at Lexington and West Newton, the Framingham Normal School remained quite small. Fewer than 100 students were enrolled as late as 1880 (Mangun, 1928, p. 304). During this period, most public normal schools were quite small, and financing was quite limited.

The Western normal schools (so-called because they were west of the Alleghenies) were much broader in scope than those in the East and South. Between the 1840s and 1900, the states of the Midwest,

Rocky Mountain, and Pacific Coast areas were opening up, being settled, and establishing territorial and then state governments. Normal schools were a prominent feature of governmental planning for statewide education. Since no entrenched system of secondary education and higher education existed, the normal schools started in some cases as collegiate-level institutions responsible for the preparation of some teachers for the developing secondary schools. In some Western states, normal schools participated in the distribution of income from state lands and thus had stronger financial status.

An outstanding and somewhat unusual example occurred in Illinois where there was no state university at the time (1857): the establishment of the Illinois State Normal University placed it at the apex of the state education system. Truly a "college" for the education of teachers and administrators for all types of schools, it was planned for 600 to 1,000 students, with a fine arts gallery, a natural history museum , and "other such adjuncts as might serve the general purpose of a university" (Harper, 1939, pp. 80–84). Dramatically different from the Massachusetts normal schools, it served as an example for some states west of the Mississippi. Although individual circumstances in different states led to many separate forms of development, the Western normal schools had more responsibility for educating secondary school teachers and developed other educational areas of responsibility faster than most of those east of the Alleghenies.

The birth of the normal schools was marked usually by controversy with other institutions over duplication of educational missions. This has been present in all subsequent development of the present state colleges and universities. In each instance, state colleges and universities or their predecessor institutions were rebuffed in their first attempts to fulfill a particular mission. They were permitted to develop or to expand their functions only when the competitor institution proved unable to prepare enough graduates to meet the demand.

The earliest conflict came with the academies over the preparation of teachers for the common schools. In time, however, and particularly in the Midwest and West, the controversy extended to include the preparation of teachers for secondary schools. More recently, disagreement has arisen over offering master's degrees in fields other than teacher education. At issue currently is the question of which institutions ought to be permitted to award the doctorate. In each of these past controversies, the records indicate that state colleges and universities and their predecessors estimated correctly that competitor institutions would be unable to fulfill the demands made upon them. As to the present situation, while some may doubt the necessity of doctoral programs in state colleges and universities, history provides evidence that institutions of higher education have consistently underestimated the demands of society for graduates at every level.

Characteristics of the Normal Schools

The three original schools founded in Massachusetts showed some the characteristics which have persisted in normal schools well into the twentieth century.

First, many of the early normal schools were noncollegiate. School teaching was considered a transient occupation. While many college graduates taught school, few did so for an extended length of time. The normal schools hoped to attract graduates of academies and high schools who would then pursue a course of study designed to train teachers. In fact, however, many of the early students were recent graduates of the common schools. As a result, the level of training in many of the normal schools was quite low, and some students regarded as unfair the requirement that they must study (K. White, 1967, p. 16).

From the outset, normal schools and teacher education in some states were somewhat outside the sequential pattern of elementary and secondary education followed by attendance at a four-year collegiate institution. Many other colleges and universities provided preparatory divisions for students needing additional secondary education. However, fairly clear distinctions existed between this preparatory work and the course leading to a baccalaureate degree. In the normal schools for many decades the teaching certificate programs were, in reality, equated with secondary education. Even though high school diplomas were generally required for admission by 1910, it was not until the 1920s and 1930s that significant numbers of normal schools or teachers colleges were considered collegiate-level institutions. As late as 1908, the U.S. Commissioner of Education, examining relations between various institutions, noted that "the chief difficulty of adjustment from the side of the normal school arises from the fact that the normal school seems to be out of the main current of our scholastic life, which flows from the elementary school through the high school directly into the university" (Pangburn, 1932, p. 53).

A second general characteristic of the normal schools was state control. There were exceptions, of course. Several large cities established normal schools as part of their city high schools, but only a few of these, e.g., Chicago State University and Northeastern Illinois University, survived to become teachers colleges and eventually state universities. The basic relationship between state colleges and universities and the state was determined at the time of their founding as normal schools. For the most part these institutions operated either directly under the State Board of Education or under a Normal School Board. In either case, control was exercised by the state government and later, often, by a statewide board for higher education institutions.

The location of new schools often reflected the political realities of the state and the pressure which a given community could exert. Where political influence was an insufficient guarantee of a normal school for an area, enterprising local officials frequently raised the sums of money necessary to capture the prize. The founding of the present University of Wisconsin at Whitewater in 1865 presents an interesting combination of the effect of money and political influence. It appears that a state senator used his influence to secure the appointment to the Board of Regents of a friend who was similarly inclined. "Together they helped convince the Regents that Whitewater's $29,000, though less than the amount offered by Racine and some others, was a better deal for the state than the other contenders in the district could claim" (Wyman, 1968, p. 57). Many other similar instances have been recorded.

Thus, despite state control, normal schools often were essentially local in constituency, aspiration and operation. From the beginning, the community of Platteville, Wisconsin, for example, assumed the responsibility for the maintenance and repair of the Platteville Normal School's building and property. This school, established in 1866, began in 1839 as Platteville Academy. (Wyman, 1968, p. 23). The same conditions prevailed at New Britain, Connecticut (1849) and in many other places (Fowler, 1949, p. 25). The local orientation is also evident in the decision of most states to establish several small normal schools rather than to expand existing institutions.

Third, by intention, the normal schools are specialized institutions. They were designed to prepare teachers for the common schools or, in a few cases, the secondary schools of the state. It is important to note that the normal schools were planned solely to serve the larger society collectively and not students individually, except as they were prepared for a useful profession. The goal was to develop human resources for the service of society, not primarily to assist individuals to fulfill themselves. In 1880, for example, it was the stated aim of Kirksville Normal School "to give culture and learning, not for the benefit of the student, but that it may be used in the education of the masses" (Borrowman, 1865, p. 187).

Fourth, despite their singleness of purpose, few normal schools were purist enough to devote the entire curriculum to professional work in teacher training. One of the continuing debates in teacher education has been whether prospective teachers should *first* secure a proper education in the subject matter they are to teach and then follow this by training in *how* to teach, or whether courses in teacher training should be accomplished by study in specific subject fields. Although many favored the purist approach, the majority of normal school students who came with only a common school education were poorly prepared in the subjects to be taught. Thus, the normal schools were forced to devote a substantial part of the program to further subject matter education. Subjects such as arithmetic, algebra, natural science, chemistry, botany, art, agriculture, music, grammar, and geography formed the basis for the introduction of secondary school subject matter courses. Later, they provided the foundation for movement to the teachers college and eventually to the development of multi-purpose institutions.

The common schools developed far more rapidly than had been anticipated. According to U.S. Office of Education statistics, the number of students enrolled in public schools nearly doubled from 7,561,000 in 1870 (the first year in which records were kept) to 14,379,000 in 1895. Although most of the growth was in the common schools, significant growth had occurred by 1895 at the higher level in the secondary schools. The number of teachers increased from 220,000 to 400,000.

Enrollment data are available for 69 of the institutions which were later to become state colleges and universities. The total enrollment in these institutions in 1890 was 29,866 or approximately 425 per institution. Despite the tremendous increases in the number of students attending public schools, normal school enrollment had increased by less than 12,000 (from 17,927 to 29,8560 between 1880 and 1890). The average increase in size was from 315 students per institution in 1880 (for 57 institutions) to 425 in 1890 (for 69 institutions) (USOE, Commissioner of Education, *Annual Report,* 1880, 1890). These figures illustrate the local or regional orientation mentioned earlier. Rather than expand existing institutions, more institutions were opened contributing to the rather slight increase in the average enrollment per institution. Of the 69 institutions reporting enrollments in 1890, only three enrolled more than 1,000 students; none enrolled more than 2,000. On the other hand, six normal schools still enrolled less than 100 students (see Table 3).

The typical normal school was controlled by the State Board of Education or the state Normal School Board. The Board or department was treated as a code department by state government, received a line appropriation from the legislature, and often was subject to scrutiny and intense political pressure. In many states the normal school board was elected to ensure representation from immediate areas served by the school. Such representation often reinforced state control of the institution at the local level and reflected the desire of the state government and the Board to subject the school to continuing supervision. Some states, such as Wisconsin, designated a person to be the resident regent, and in other states local committees were set up to supervise the institution between Board meetings.

The schools were financed essentially from state appropriations with some funds from student fees, although these were generally quite low. Some scattered data on financing are available prior to 1900 indicating the generally limited support provided. The U.S. Office of Education figures for 1900 show average institutional receipts of $27,500 and an average total expenditure of approximately $56 per student at the turn of the century. In 1900, 75 percent of the total receipts came from state appropriations. Facilities in the late nineteenth century consisted usually of one building which housed all classrooms, offices, and the model training school. (The building is typically still in use today.) Average library holdings in 1890 were 2,000 volumes per institution.

In spite of controversy, low financing, poor facilities, and frequent outside attacks, the normal schools had made significant contributions to American life by 1900. A variety of curricula were available in many of the institutions, preparing for both elementary and secondary teaching and principalships. Fairly extensive electives in a number of normal schools made it possible for students to obtain some depth in a good range of subject matter fields. The normal school at Albany, New York required high school graduation for admission in 1890, and the Massachusetts normal schools did likewise in 1894. By 1900, at least one-fourth of the matriculants in 38 percent of the largest schools were high school graduates. Although the quality of the normal schools was very uneven throughout the country as a whole, a significant number were well recognized for their work as specialized institutions.

TABLE 3

The Size of AASCU Institutions: 1870–1940

Size	1870	1880	1890	1900	1910	1920	1930	1940
More than 15,000								
10,000–14,999								
6,000–9,999								1
4,000–5,999						2	3	
2,000–3,999				2	5	7	27	20
1,000–1,999			3	9	26	35	62	57
500–999	1	10	20	31	38	52	75	72
100–499	28	42	41	54	88	69	49	88
Less than 100	4	5	6	7	4	14	3	5
Number of Institutions	33	57	70	103	161	179	219	243

Sources: USOE, Commissioner of Education. *Annual Report.* (1870). *The Biennial Survey of Education in the United States.* (1916/18).

Note: Since the 1950 data on teachers colleges were summary data rather than by specific institutions, a frequency distribution was impossible.

Specialized Types of Institutions

In addition to the academies and the normal schools, the states, in the nineteenth century, either created or in the main took over partial or full funding and partial or full control of a number of other diversified types of institutions. Several maritime schools and military institutions were created; some ultimately became members of the AASCU. The Citadel, for example, established in 1842, has become one of the leading military colleges of the United States. A large number of technical and trade schools, started at various times, have become significant members of the state-controlled institutional group.

Some appropriate examples are the Newark Technical School (established 1881), now the New Jersey Institute of Technology; the Ferris Industrial School (established 1884), now Ferris State College; the Dakota School of Mines (established 1894), now the South Dakota School of Mines and Technology; the Industrial Institute and College of Louisiana (established 1885), now Louisiana Tech University; the Southwestern Louisiana Industrial Institute (established 1898), now the University of Southwestern Louisiana. The Lowell Technical Institute, established in 1895, as a proprietary textile institute is now the University of Lowell, formed by a merger of Lowell Technological University and Lowell State College. The West Virginia Trade School, started in 1895, has become the West Virginia Institute of Technology; the Bradford-Durfee College of Technology, established in 1895, and the New Bedford Institute of Technology were later combined to form Southeastern Massachusetts University; and the Montana School of Mines, established in 1893, is now the Montana College of Mineral Science and Technology. This significant group of technological institutions indicates the states' major effort during the end of the nineteenth century either to take over and support or to develop technical institutions.

The municipal college or university was another type of institution. Buchtel College, established in 1870 in Akron, Ohio, by the Universalist Church, became the Municipal University of Akron. Eventually it was made a state institution and is now the University of Akron. In 1865, the Congregational Church established Lincoln College in Topeka, Kansas, on the site of the current State Historical Museum. Three years later, because of financial support from a New England philanthropist, Deacon Ichabod Washburn, Lincoln became Washburn College. The city of Topeka chartered Washburn as a municipal university in 1941 and supported it through tax funds. In return, the Board of Trustees turned the College's physical assets over to the new urban university supported in part by the city and a local Board of Regents. Uniquely, the old Washburn College Board of Trustees continued to exist and still administers the endowment funds of the former college, strictly for the benefit of Washburn University.

Kansas provides a second example of the municipal university in Fairmount College, a private institution. Fairmount opened its doors to a small group of students in 1895 and continued as a private college until 1926. At that time, it became the Municipal University of Wichita and was financed as a public, municipal institution for many years. Its tuition was approximately twice that of the state-supported institutions, however, and after a long campaign the municipal university became a state university in 1963. The Toledo University of Arts and Trades was established in Toledo, Ohio, in 1872 as a municipal institution and is now the state-supported and state-controlled University of Toledo.

Another group of institutions opened during the latter part of the nineteenth century were specifically designed for the higher education of black people, and many were eventually taken over by the states as part of their state system. The Ashmun Institute in Pennsylvania, for example, established in 1854, is now Lincoln University. The Biblical Institute established in 1867 in Maryland is now Morgan State University. The Slater Industrial Academy in North Carolina, established in 1892, is now Winston-Salem State University. These numerous examples of specialized institutions, illustrate this step toward the new institutional group with which we are concerned.

Development of Teachers Colleges to the 1920s

The transition from the normal school to the teachers college took place over a period exceeding half a century. The wide variety of normal schools and their great diversity of programs make it hard to pinpoint the actual move to true collegiate-level instruction. Certainly, the forces for change were at work as early as the 1860s and culminated in the 1920s. Two main factors contributed to the changes during this period: (1) the rapid expansion of public secondary education from 1880 to 1920, and (2) the development of accreditation systems for secondary and higher education.

In the late nineteenth century, the United States turned to public secondary schools to provide necessary human resources in much the same way it had turned to the common schools earlier in the century. Although the first public secondary school was founded in 1821 in Boston, the significant development of public secondary education occurred after 1880. Between 1880 and 1930, enrollment in the public secondary schools increased form 110,000 to 4,399,000 students, doubling approximately every decade and requiring enormous numbers of teachers prepared to teach in these schools.

The aim of the common school was to to develop the basic skills of reading, writing, and arithmetic and to transmit subjects such as history and geography, presumed necessary for all educated citizens. It was assumed that those who had mastered these subjects in the common school could, with a limited amount of training in pedagogy, teach the same material to incoming students. Secondary education, in contrast, involved instruction in the same subject matters taught at the collegiate level and was presumed to demand a baccalaureate level of education for prospective teachers. Further, secondary education was forced to a higher level of teacher competence because the colleges could impose sanctions against those schools which failed to employ teachers with the required credentials.

As with the common schools, perhaps the most significant problem faced by secondary schools in the late nineteenth century was that of securing teachers with even minimal preparation. Faced with a shortage of teachers, many of the smaller rural high schools began to recruit teachers from among those students preparing to teach in the common schools. Thus, the normal schools found themselves preparing secondary teachers even in states which had not adopted plans providing for such functions on a legal basis.

The normal schools willingly accepted the opportunities presented by the rapid development of secondary education. As early as 1875, the Department of Normal Schools of the National Education Association had recommended the establishment of higher normal schools to prepare teachers for the secondary schools. As noted previously, the normal schools possessed the foundation upon which to develop secondary teacher programs when the opportunity arose. Because of academic deficiencies in their students, both Eastern and Western normal schools had offered remedial instruction in subject fields for decades. Also, because of the emphasis upon mental discipline as the basic approach to education, secondary-level subjects had often been taught to teachers for the common schools because they were said to strengthen their mental faculties.

The normal schools were able to take advantage of the demand for teachers of secondary-level occupational programs—manual training and secretarial studies—because of the lack of these programs in most existing colleges and universities. Some states, for example, Wisconsin, established special-purpose normal schools in fields such as industrial arts and physical education, and other states, like New York, permitted normal schools to develop in one or more subject areas. Potsdam educated secondary school teachers of music and Oswego educated those in industrial arts. Just as with the introduction of subject matter studies into the normal schools, the introduction of teacher education programs in areas such as industrial arts and business education provided the base for later state college programs in various technological and business fields.

Initial expansion of the functions of normal schools into the preparation of secondary teachers was, as stated earlier, essentially a Midwestern and later a Western phenomenon. The Eastern states were dominated by the older established universities and colleges which had the necessary power to prevent normal schools from developing secondary teaching programs. Midwestern normal schools, developing at approximately the same time as the public universities and private colleges, were able to appropriate a larger share of the political power in the state.

Eastern private liberal arts colleges also graduated larger numbers of potential teachers (often a high percentage of their graduates), and the demand for new institutions to prepare secondary teachers was somewhat less intense than in the Midwest. Some states took over

existing private colleges, funding them if they added the preparation
of teachers as an important curricular offering.

An excellent illustration of this type of situation occurred in Virginia in the 1880s at the College of William and Mary. For almost a
century after the Revolutionary War, the College had serious financial
problems. Essentially a private college and closely related to the
Episcopal Church, it made some very interesting curricular adjustments in an attempt to increase its enrollment. In 1812, for example,
the Professorship of Humanities was eliminated and replaced with
instruction in gunnery, fortification, and architecture. The professorships of law and police, moral philosophy, and chemistry, remained
vacant because there were insufficient funds to provide programs in
these fields. Often in grave trouble, the College was able to struggle
through very serious times for decades but finally closed during the
Civil War, from 1861 through 1865. Following another very difficult
period from 1865 to 1880, it closed again in 1881. It reopened finally
in 1888, after the Commonwealth of Virginia agreed to provide the
financial support necessary if the College would establish a program
of teacher education. Thus, the College of William and Mary became
a major, state-controlled, teacher preparation institution for Virginia.

A combination of factors prevented normal schools in several states
from developing into public liberal arts colleges similar to those
established in the private sector. The normal schools were forced to
remain as specialized institutions somewhat outside the mainstream
of higher education and, in so doing, adopted an ideology of teacher
education which influenced their programs well into the twentieth
century.

The political fact was that in many states a combination of organized opposition from existing colleges and universities plus economy-minded legislators was able, often for decades, to prevent normal schools from becoming four-year, multi-purpose public colleges.
Denied access to this status and, in some states threatened by their
opponents with the loss of secondary teacher programs, normal
school presidents often contended that preparation for secondary
teaching demanded separate programs and, indeed, separate institutions. The argument was that those who were going to teach subject
matter should be taught separately or differently from those who
were pursuing a liberal education as an end in itself or acquiring
knowledge for entry into developing professional fields.

The strength of the opposition to the development of normal
schools as collegiate institutions was so great that although public
secondary education experienced significant growth in the late nine-

teenth century, it was not until 1903 that the first normal school made the transition to a baccalaureate degree-granting institution. (The institution is now Eastern Michigan University at Ypsilanti.) It was only after World War I that significant numbers of normal schools were changed to teachers colleges. Almost two-thirds of these institutions made the transition in the 1920s.

Early Efforts in Accreditation

Accreditation of secondary schools and colleges by nongovernmental, voluntary organizations first developed in the 1880s, with a major effect on the development of normal schools. As early as the 1870s, institutions such as the Universities of Michigan and Indiana had admitted the graduates of certain high schools without qualifying examinations. The need for some standards was aptly illustrated by John Eaton, Commissioner of Education, when he reported in 1873 that "at least 75 percent of the students in the West and in the South (college students) must have been prepared for college by the colleges themselves in their own preparatory departments" (quoted in Selden, 1960, p. 98).

The development of the regional accrediting associations, beginning with the New England Association of Colleges and Secondary Schools in 1885, brought the real force to accreditation. The large public universities, in particular, realized that they could not advance if they continued to enroll students directly from the common schools or from high schools in which the level of work was not much better. Hence, it was in the best interests of the universities to develop higher standards for secondary and normal schools. Pressure for improvement of the high schools came also from business and organized labor, which saw the necessity for a well-trained population. The accreditation movement was facilitated considerably by the fact that development of secondary schools resulted in a significant increase in college enrollments. This, in turn, increased the need for a supply of potential teachers making it somewhat easier to enforce increased professional standards.

Additional regional voluntary accrediting associations grew up throughout the nation. The Middle States Association of Colleges and Schools was organized in 1887, and the North Central Association of Colleges and Secondary Schools and the Association of Colleges and Secondary Schools of the Southern States in 1895. They developed college accrediting standards in 1910 and in 1919, respectively.

The story of the Association of Colleges and Secondary Schools of the Southern States aptly illustrates the need for these associations. It was organized in the autumn of 1895 in Atlanta, Georgia, at a meeting of voluntary delegates from a number of southern colleges and universities. The faculty of Vanderbilt University, seeing the need, had issued invitations to this spontaneously called meeting and stated three purposes:

1. Organize southern schools and colleges for cooperation in mutual assistance.
2. Elevate the standard of scholarship and effect uniformity of entrance requirements.
3. Develop preparatory schools and cut off this work from the colleges.

Agnew, in his official history of the Association, has emphasized that "throughout the South there were private academies and 'colleges,' most with inadequate faculties and ill-defined curricula. Many students were at the 'preparatory level.' From this educational anarchy, the Southern Association sought to bring about order by defining the difference between preparatory schools and colleges. The major thrust of the Association for the first 15 years was to establish requirements for graduation from secondary schools and to establish admission and graduation requirements for colleges and universities."

The Northwest Association of Schools and Colleges, formed for similar purposes in 1914, established its formal institutional accrediting standards in 1921. Only the West was left without a regional accrediting association by that decade, and it remained without one until the period shortly after World War II. Until that time, the Northwest Association provided accreditation services in all of the Western states, including California.

By 1917, the North Central Association was accrediting teacher education institutions separately. Five normal schools and teachers colleges were on the first list, a separate unclassified list which also included two junior colleges. As one key requirement, high school graduation was a prerequisite for admission to each accredited institution. Such a requirement not only affected the secondary teacher preparation programs but helped also to advance elementary teacher preparation to the collegiate level. Accreditation pressures led eventually to specialization in not more than two or three fields, such as English and social studies. This enhanced the collegiate standing of normal schools by forcing the institution to develop faculties of greater specialization. By 1917, as an example, the North Central

Association required teacher education faculties to instruct only in their teaching speciality.

The changes that took place in state control and funding of higher education during the nineteenth century were truly awesome. From a few institutions established by 1800—only two of which are currently AASCU institutions—hundreds of diverse institutions were meeting the expanding needs of the nation by 1920. Even greater changes were in store, but the bases had been developed—274 AASCU-type institutions were in place and ready for take-off during the next expanding decades.

CHAPTER 3

Changing Missions: 1920s–1960

The decades from the end of World War I to 1960 included two postwar expansions, the most severe depression of the past century in the 1930s, and the massive, disrupting World War II. The era of manufacturing based on raw materials and developing urbanization gradually gave way to a service-dominated era based on people as a resource, rapidly improving transportation by highway and air, and heavily populated metropolitan areas. Expanding governmental services and service industries greatly increased needs for trained personnel. The changes ensuing resulted in major expansions of publicly financed and state-controlled higher education. The rate of change accelerated rapidly—in institutional missions, in the numbers and sizes of institutions, and in overall diversity of programs.

As single-purpose institutions, most with a teacher education or technology emphasis, the developing teachers colleges and state colleges had been relatively overlooked in national studies; little consideration had been given to their possibilities of service to meet expanding needs. By the end of this 40–year period, however, comprehensive public colleges and universities had experienced astonishing growth and expansion of programs. By 1960, they were recognized as constituting a significant portion of American higher education.

Undergraduate enrollments increased significantly during this 40–year period. Surveys of the U.S. Office of Education from 1919–20 through 1959–60 show the following undergraduate enrollments: 582,000 in 1920, 1,053,000 in 1930, 1,396,00 in 1940, 2,436,000 in

*In this chapter also, significant portions have been adapted or reproduced without quotes or used in corrected or updated form from Harcleroad, Sagen, and Molen, 1966.

41

1949–50 and finally, in 1960, 2,894,000. In the first decade, the 1920s, enrollments almost doubled, and over the 40–year period undergraduate enrollments in institutions of higher education increased by almost 400 percent.

The pressure for additional opportunities for higher education during the early 1900s and particularly after World War I led many students to attend nearby normal schools and teachers colleges and to press for broadening of the curriculum in additional fields. This also caused continual pressure for collegiate status for all previously specialized institutions, especially institutes of technology, normal schools, and teachers colleges.

By the 1920s, two million students were enrolled in public high schools (Stabler, 1962, p. 49). These vast numbers of high school graduates clamoring for places did not, however, create the initial pressure for additional higher education opportunities, although, college age population (18 to 21) grew from 5,930,765 in 1900 to 9,753,537 in 1940, a gain of only 64 percent (McQuery, 1952, p. 171). The real pressure arose for existing institutions to accommodate local high school graduates who lacked transportation facilities and funds and were hampered from attending distant institutions. This phenomenon was particularly strong in the Midwest, where the population was more dispersed and where public universities and private colleges did not dominate the education scene as they did in the East. As a result, the "collegiate" movement remained basically regional in the early years of this period. The Eastern normal schools remained two-year institutions with primary emphasis on elementary education, and some of the Western and Southern normal schools were just in the initial stages of development. Midwestern institutions took the lead, along with a few other scattered institutions from South Carolina, New Mexico, Utah, New York, and Colorado.

Development of the Teachers Colleges

The early beginnings of the degree-granting teachers colleges came in the 1890s, answering the need for secondary teachers with majors in their teaching fields, coupled with professional course sequences in the art and science of teaching. In 1890, the normal school established in 1844, in Albany, New York, in 1844 became the first baccalaureate degree granting teachers college. The second, Michigan State Normal School at Ypsilanti, became Michigan State Normal College in 1899 (Isbell, 1971, p. 142).

By 1918, 27 degree-granting teachers colleges existed in 14 states as follows:

Name of Institution	*Location*
Colorado State Teachers College	Greeley, Colorado
Southern Illinois Normal School	Carbondale, Illinois
Illinois State Normal School	Normal, Illinois*
Western Illinois State Normal School	Macomb, Illinois
Indiana State Normal School	Terre Haute, Indiana
Iowa State Teachers College	Cedar Falls, Iowa*
State Normal School	Emporia, Kansas
Fort Hays State Normal School	Fort Hays, Kansas
State Manual Training Normal School	Pittsburgh, Kansas
Michigan State Normal School	Ypsilanti, Michigan*
State Normal School	Cape Girardeau, Missouri
State Normal School	Kirksville, Missouri*
State Normal School	Maryville, Missouri
State Normal School	Springfield, Missouri
State Normal School	Warrensburg, Missouri
State Normal School	Chadron, Nebraska
State Normal School	Kearney, Nebraska
State Normal School	Peru, Nebraska
State Normal School	Wayne, Nebraska
New Mexico Normal University	Las Vegas, New Mexico
New York State College of Teachers	Albany, New York
State Normal School	Bowling Green, Ohio
State Normal School of Miami University	Oxford, Ohio*
State Normal School of Ohio University	Athens, Ohio
Winthrop Normal and Industrial College	Rock Hill, South Carolina
State Normal School of Univ. of Utah	Salt Lake City, Utah

Source: American Association of Teachers Colleges (AATC), 1922, p. 12.

In 1917, presidents of five of these institutions (marked by *) met informally (another example of the "voluntary" system in the United States) and established the American Association of Teachers Colleges (AATC, 1922, p. 14) with annual meetings held thereafter for over 40–years. By 1920, the Association had 46 members in three classifications: Class A, 35 member institutions already conferring bachelors degrees; Class B, eight members with authority to confer degrees but none yet conferred; and Class C, three institutions currently offering four-year programs but not yet accorded degree-granting authority.

Four were added in 1921, one in Class A and three in Class B, with one in Class B moved to Class A. In 1922, the membership rose dramatically to 71 with seven new Class A members, eight in Class B and two in Class C and four to be admitted after classification was completed. Sixty-four of these 71 institutions are members of the American Association of State Colleges and Universities. A few were private institutions, and four are now members of the National Association of State Universities and Land-Grant Colleges.

The AATC took action through a formal resolution adopted unanimously in 1922 to encourage the various states to require a bachelor's degree for certifying teachers:

> Be it resolved by the American Association of Teachers Colleges that the recognized necessity of more adequate preparation of teachers of all grades of school work demands that all state teacher training institutions should raise their standards to that of the standard Teachers College, and confer to a Bachelor's degree (AATC, 1922, p. 22).

It should be noted that in 1922 most institutions were still using the term *normal* in their title; some used this term until they were designated "college" or "university." An example is Michigan State Normal College, so named until 1955 when it became one of four designated as a Michigan state "college." The other three normal schools in Michigan (Mt. Pleasant in 1895, Marquette in 1899 and Kalamazoo in 1903) were changed to teachers colleges in 1927, became colleges of education in 1941, and colleges in 1955 (Isbell, 1971, pp. 362–63). However, most of the degree-granting "normals" followed the three or four step pattern of change from normal school to teachers college in the 1920s to 1940s, then colleges of education (for example, Colorado State College of Education in 1935–36), or state colleges from the 1930s through the 1950s.

A few other examples illustrate how the names of institutions changed to match their changing function. California normal schools followed this pattern of change through legislative action. The six normal schools became teachers colleges in 1921 and were authorized to grant baccalaureate degrees in 1923. In 1935, the institutions were authorized to drop the word *teachers* from their titles and to become "state colleges." Along with this designation, they acquired a very important liberalization of their function: they were allowed to admit students who were not expecting to teach. The primary function of the California state colleges was still the training of teachers, but they were allowed to offer extremely wide programs after 1935. For example, at that time San Jose State College began to offer programs in "police," eventually police administration. A wide variety of curricula developed, and in 1947 a further definition of the functions of the state colleges read:

> The primary function of the state colleges is the training of teachers. State colleges also may offer courses appropriate for general or liberal education and for responsible citizenship; offer vocational training in such fields as business, industry, public services, homemaking, and social services; and offer the pre-professional courses needed by students who plan to transfer to universities for advanced professional study. Courses in military science and tactics may be given in conformance with the laws of the United States made and provided with reference to ROTC units in educational institutions.

An extensive survey of California's higher education needs in 1948 indicated that the California state colleges were providing degree programs in many developing professional fields, including business, nursing, social service, engineering, agriculture, aeronautics, medical laboratory technology, sanitation (public health), physical therapy, occupational therapy, psychiatric technology (the first in the country at San Jose' State in 1956–57), recreation, music therapy, and journalism. In addition, two of the California state colleges were still operating junior colleges on their campuses by contract with local districts, and two other colleges, Chico State College and Humboldt State College, were operating what were essentially two-year college programs at state expense (Strayer, 1948, pp.20–22). A few additional examples will illustrate this type of institutional name change and timing throughout the United States.

- Ball State University in Indiana provides a good illustration. In 1894, a voluntary group of people formed the Eastern Indiana Normal University Association and purchased some land. Five years later, they completed an administration building and a residence hall for women, all part of a land development program planned for that section of Muncie, Indiana. The Eastern Indiana Normal University closed in 1902 and reopened as Palmer University. Two years later, it closed once more and reopened in 1905 as Indiana Normal School and College of Applied Science—closing again in 1907. It reopened as Muncie Normal Institute in 1912, was renamed Muncie National Institute in 1913, and closed again in 1917. Finally, in 1918, the buildings and 64 acres were given to the State of Indiana to be the basis for the Eastern Division of Indiana State Normal School. Four years later, a separate institution was established called The Ball State Teachers College and in 1929 the name changed to Ball State Teachers College. After seven different names in 35 years and many openings and closing, Ball State Teachers College remained so until its final name change to Ball State University in 1965.

- Western Oregon State College was chartered in 1856 as Monmouth University, which changed to Christian College in 1865 with support by the Disciples of Christ Church. A normal school was added in 1881, and its name was changed to the Oregon State Normal School. State support came in 1891 but stopped in 1909. The school closed, reopening in 1911 as the Oregon Normal School. In 1939, it became the Oregon College of Education, and much later, in 1981, was renamed Western Oregon State College.

- Central Connecticut State University began in 1849 as New Britain Normal School, changed in 1933 to the Teachers College of Connecticut, and in 1959 to Central Connecticut State College. Its present designation came in 1983.

- Winston-Salem State University in North Carolina started in 1892 as Slater Industrial Academy. It was renamed Slater Industrial and State Normal School in 1897, Winston-Salem Teachers College in 1925, Winston-Salem State College in 1963, and Winston-Salem State University in 1969.

- Johnson State College in Vermont, originally established as an academy in 1828 and changed to a county grammar school in 1836, became Johnson Normal School in 1866. It remained a normal school for 81 years, changing to Johnson Teachers College late in 1947. In 1962, it was renamed Johnson State College, one of the last to achieve this status.

- Livingston University in Alabama started as a female academy in 1839, became a normal school, and was renamed Livingston Academy in 1883. In 1907, the State of Alabama assumed control of the normal school and in 1929 changed the name to State Teachers College at Livingston. This became Livingston State College in 1957 and was renamed Livingston University in 1967.

- Longwood College in Virginia, originally established in 1839 as Farmville Female Seminary, became Farmville Female College in 1860. Virginia purchased the Farmville Female College in 1884, and it became Farmville Normal School. It was renamed the State Normal School for Women in 1914, and ten years later became the State Teachers College at Farmville. A quarter of century later, in 1949, it became Longwood College and in 1976 was made into a coeducational collegiate institution.

• Harris-Stowe College was formed by the merger of Harris Teachers College and the Stowe Teachers College in 1954 and renamed Harris-Stowe College in 1979. These two institutions came with a long history. Harris Normal School, begun in St. Louis in 1887, was the first teacher education institution established west of the Mississippi River. Stowe Teachers College began in 1890 as a normal school designed to prepare black elementary school teachers and was originally called the Sumner Training School. In 1910 Harris Normal School became Harris Teachers College. In 1929, the Sumner Training School became the Harriet Beecher Stowe Teachers College. The two institutions were finally merged in 1954 and became Harris-Stowe College in 1979.

• Mankato State University in Minnesota followed a pattern common to many of the Midwestern and Western normal schools. It started as a normal school in 1878, became Mankato State Teachers College in 1921, and Mankato State College in 1957. In 1975, as part of the renaming of hundreds of these institutions, it became Mankato State University.

• The Missouri normal schools followed relatively similar patterns. In 1871, the State Normal School for the Second District of Missouri was established, changed to Central Missouri State Teachers College in 1919 and to Central Missouri State Colleges in 1946. Southeast Missouri Normal School was established in 1873 and 1946 changed to SoutheastMissouri State Teachers College in 1919, and to Southeast Missouri State College in 1946. In 1972, these institutions became Central Missouri State University and Southeast Missouri State University.

• Sam Houston State University in Texas opened in 1879 as Sam Houston Normal Institute, was changed to Sam Houston State Teachers College in 1923 and four decades later became Sam Houston State College. After only four additional years, in 1969, it was renamed Sam Houston State University.

• The University of Northern Colorado opened as the State Normal School in 1888. In 1911, it was renamed Colorado State Teachers College, one ofthe early designations of this type, and in 1935 became Colorado StateCollege of Education. In 1957, it became Colorado State College, followed in 1973 by a change to its current university designation.

- Black Hills State College in South Dakota was established in 1883 as a normal school offering coursework at the level of the ninth grade. Forty years later, in 1924, it became a four-year, post-high school institution, Spearfish Normal School. In 1941, it was renamed Black Hills Teachers College, a degree-granting institution, and finally, in 1964, became Black Hills State College.

- The University of North Carolina at Greensboro originated in 1891 as the State Normal and Industrial School for women. In 1892, it was renamed the State Normal Industrial College, still for women. In 1929, the name was changed to North Carolina College for Women and in 1932 to The Woman's College of the University of North Carolina. Finally, in 1963, it became coeducational and was renamed the University of North Carolina at Greensboro.

These representative examples from various regions of the United States demonstrate the consistency of the development pattern of these specialized, single-purpose institutions during this period. In 1939, the midpoint of this period and the centennial of the first publicly established normal school, Harper summarized seven major developments in the state teachers colleges as they had evolved from the normal schools and played a major role in transforming teaching into a profession (Harper, 1939, pp. 114–120).

1. The concept of professionalized subject matter was developed during this century. This concept in the normal schools changed materially as they developed into teachers colleges and has been completely abandoned in present state colleges and universities.

2. There was a notable emphasis on laboratory learning and the scientific approach to the education of teachers. Programs of teacher education adapted the methods of science to analyses of students andthe teaching act. The laboratory approach, in contrast with the more sterile, theoretical approach, was strongly supported by the concerned public.

3. The state teachers colleges exhibited an essentially pragmatic attitude; their organization made adaptation and change the normal way to operate. Thus, it was very possible to adopt, from any source,methods and material which had a direct bearing on college problems.

4. Many parts of the extracurriculum were included in the orga-

nized program of preparation for teaching, particularly speech, music, art, and drama activities. Their inclusion in the regular program of studies enhanced the cultural development of the youth of the country.

5. The need for in-service education and follow-up work became clearly established. The filed service responsibilities to the surrounding region were a major factor in the development of these institutions.
6. They clearly demonstrated that teacher preparation institutions needed to remain close to the needs of the public schools and the public.
7. The institutions helped develop a personal interest in students and a spirit of professionalism in teaching staffs.

The stated purpose of most of these institutions remained teacher education, but programs changed considerably. Between two-thirds and three-fourths of the institutions still maintained two-year elementary programs, but the emphasis was decidedly upon baccalaureate-level instruction.

The professional education and subject-matter components of the program were separated, and specialization in areas such as social sciences, science, and language arts was developing. Academic divisions and, in some cases, departments were emerging; because of the shift in emphasis, professional "education" was often a single department within the institution. Substantial control over critical aspects of the teacher education program, such as methods courses and student teaching, often rested with the subject-matter divisions or departments.

Even before most of the normal schools completed the transition to teachers colleges in the 1930s, forces were set in motion which diminished the emphasis on teacher education and contributed to the multi-purpose state institution. The move away from the professional treatment of subject matter and towards a distinction between professional and subject-matter components was accelerated by accrediting agencies. They required that no secondary school instructors should teach more than two or three fields (more will be said about this later. As divisions of social and natural sciences and eventually departments emerged—such as history and chemistry—their emphasis was upon the preparation of teachers. Discipline-oriented faculty soon began to be attracted to those institutions, however, and degrees in many other majors developed. The changes described earlier in the California state colleges in the 1930's are good examples.

Another important change was the relaxation of requirements that every student be committed to a career in teaching. In many states, state law had required normal school students to sign a pledge that they would become teachers. Teacher education emphasis shifted gradually to graduation requirements: a student could not receive a degree from the institution unless he or she had a teaching certificate. Later it was stipulated that each student must complete the teacher education requirements but could graduate without being certified. By 1940, some institutions had dropped entirely the teacher education requirements for graduation. The pattern for transition at other institutions was readily predictable by the 1960's.

Graduate programs in the field of education started in the teachers college early in this period. Three of the 35 Class A members of the American Association of Teachers Colleges offered graduate programs leading to master's degrees in 1922: Colorado State Teachers College in Greeley, the New York Teachers Training School in Albany, and Winthrop Normal and Industrial College in Rock Hill, South Carolina. At least one nonmember offered the A.B. in 1920 and the M.A. degree in education in 1921, the Colorado State Normal School in Gunnison, whose pattern of growth is illustrative of other later efforts.

Previously, in 1916, this institution offered the Bachelor of Pedagogy (a four-year course) and the Master of Pedagogy based on the B.Ped. plus 60 additional hours, however. This was an active time in the building of this institution, and in 1923 the name was changed to the Western State College of Colorado. The same legislative bill made the institution "a liberal arts college with a professional school of education", the only public liberal arts college in Colorado. Its name remained the same in 1985, 62 years later. Western State College awarded its first M.A. in 1922 to an English major, for a thesis on "The History of English Prosody from Earliest Extant until Shakespeare." The next two M.A.s, in 1923, were in the fields of zoology and education. In the zoology thesis, a new zoological species was found and detailed, while the education thesis was a history of education in Colorado. Twenty years later, in 1941, 21 M.A. degrees were awarded. Western State provides a good illustration of growth in this area, with a total of 440 M.A. degrees earned between 1947 and 1960. Although 380 were in education, 60 (14 percent) were in other fields: social sciences (27), music (12), English (11), history/political science (5), English/speech (2), biology (1), French (1), and economics (1) (Faye, 1967, pp. 53–54, 62, 64, 106–107, 132–33).

Development of Specialized Technological Colleges

A new wave of technology oriented state colleges and universities also appeared in the four decades from 1920 to 1960. Many states, previously with only a land-grant college to draw on, felt the need to start another technologically directed institution. In some cases, the need developed as the land-grant college and/or state university grew more theoretical and research-centered and less open to new practice-oriented professional areas of study. In other states, the demands for highly trained personnel at the four-year and beginning graduate level were overwhelming, and additional programs had to be started.

Since doctoral universities are quite expensive and extremely jealous of their prerogatives, political tradeoffs made it wiser (1) to put some programs in existing colleges (such as engineering at San Jose' State or architecture at Ball State), (2) to create special satellite, independent branches of existing institutions, (3) to establish totally new institutions for more emphasis on the developing technologies, or, in a few cases (4) to merge two institutions with different previous missions. A preeminent example of the last-named case is the 1959 merger, of the Platteville State College and the Wisconsin Institute of Technology (started in 1908 as the Wisconsin Mining Trade School, in 1915 named the Wisconsin Mining School, and in 1935 expanded to a four-year degree program as the Institute of Technology) into the Wisconsin State College and Institute of Technology. (Wyman, 1968, pp. 41–42).

Creation of new and adoption of old existing institutions are common practices in American academic politics, and a number of instances give evidence of these methods of providing for the country's changing needs. The following examples are illustrative:

- Southern Technical Institute was established in 1948 as a separate satellite campus of Georgia Institute of Technology. Its location-,Marietta, is an important industrial city, critical to the country-'saircraft and defense production. Currently, it offers four- and five-year professional baccalaureate degrees and in addition to being regionally accredited it is accredited in the specialized field of engineering technology.

- Oregon Institute of Technology, established in 1946, occupies a specialized professional role in the Oregon System of Higher Education. It offers degrees at four- and five-year baccalaureate levels plus some below the B.A. or B.S. level, primarily in professional fields. Accreditation had been earned in several areas by 1982 including (1) radiographer education by the American Medical Association, (2) engineering technology, (3) dental hygiene, and (4) nursing-associate degree.

- Massachusetts Maritime Academy began in 1891 as the state's nautical training school. As this field constantly increased its technological base, however, the program was lengthened. The current name was given in 1942, and it became an accredited four-year bachelor's degree-grantinginstitution in 1946.

- California Polytechnic State University-San Luis Obispo, established in 1901 as a trade high school, became a four-year and master's degreeawarding professional institution in the late 1940s and 1950s. Itcontinues still to offer less than baccalaureate degrees in somesemi-professional fields. A fairly large institution, approaching 20,000 students in size, it has regional accreditation, plus specializedaccreditation in architecture, engineering, technology, landscapearchitecture, and social work.

- California State Polytechnic University-Pomona was originally a component part of California Polytechnic State University as a whole. It wasopened originally in 1938 and grew steadily in this developing industrial and research oriented area until it was made a separate institution after World War II. A professional institution, it offers baccalaureate andmaster's degrees coupled with a strong liberal arts and general education program. In addition to its institutional accreditation it has specialized accreditation in a variety of fields including art, business, engineering, music, nursing, social work, and teacher education. Again, this is a fairly large institution—around 15,000 students.

- The University of Alabama in Huntsville, established in 1950, is a separate campus of the University of Alabama System. The opening ofthis particular campus in the immediate post-World War II era has veryimportant strategic connotations. Following World War II, many of thepreeminent German rocket engineers came to the United States, and an important rocket research and development center was set up at Redstone Arsenal in Huntsville Alabama. This campus, established shortly thereafter, has contributed to this important national program. It, in Huntsville offers programs through the doctorate and is fully accredited institutionally by the Southern Association of Colleges and

Schools through it's commission on colleges. In addition its programs is nursing and engineering are fully accredited.

- Maine Maritime Academy was established early in World War II, during 1941, in order to assist with the developing need for ships' officers in the United States fleet. It is currently a professional institution offering a four-year baccalaureate degree program, and is institutionally accredited by the New England Association.

- West Virginia Institute of Technology had a long history of development as a less-than-baccalaureate institution prior to its current status. In 1895 it started as a preparatory school branch of West Virginia University, with a program characteristic of many institutions during the end of the nineteenth and beginning of the twentieth century. By 1917 it had been changed to West Virginia Trade School and in 1921 became a junior college called the New River State School. Ten years later it became New River State College and in 1941 was reoriented and made into a fully collegiate institution, the West Virginia Institute of Technology. It has developed broadly since this change and now offers both baccalaureate and master's degree programs. Fully accredited as an institution by the North Central Association, it offers fully accredited professional programs in dental hygiene, engineering technology, and teacher education.

- Louisiana Tech University, originally established in 1894 as the Industrial Institute and College of Louisiana, was changed to Louisiana Polytechnic Institute in 1921. After almost 50 years of operation as a polytechnic institute, its name was changed to Louisiana Tech University in 1970. The University now offers all degree programs from sub-baccalaureate through the doctorate in professional as well as liberal arts fields. Accreditation, including institutional accreditation is extensive—including specialized accreditation in architecture, art, business, dietetics, engineering, engineering technology, medical records administration by the American Medical Association, music, and teacher education.

- The University of Southwestern Louisiana started in 1898 as the Southwestern Louisiana Industrial Institute, offering its first classes in 1901. In 1921 it became a four-year institution, renamed the Southwestern Louisiana Institute of Liberal and Technical Training. After almost 40 years in this category, it was renamed and reoriented as the University of Southwestern Louisiana. Currently, a relatively large institution with close to 15,000 students, its extensive programs at the undergraduate and graduate levels lead to programs offering the doctorate level of instruction. Fully accredited institutionally, it also has specialized accreditation in the fields of architecture, engineering, medical records administration, music, and teacher education.

• Southeastern Massachusetts University traces its beginning back to 1895 and the development of the Bradford-Durfee College of Technology and the New Bedford Institute of Technology, which were combined in 1960 to form the Southeastern Massachusetts Technological Institute. Less than adecade later, in 1969, this new technological institute was converted to Southeastern Massachusetts University. In this capacity the institution is regionally accredited and has specialized accreditation in the fields of art, engineering, engineering technology, and nursing.

This representative listing of degree-granting institutions created during the latter part of the period under review clearly indicates the breadth of the movement throughout the United States. In addition to these newly established or newly created institutions, many of the technological schools in this group begun in the late 1890s were adapted, expanded, and accredited in the same type of degree programs in the wide variety of fields as those described above. Altogether, these institutions created during the past century provide a state-controlled and state-funded educational program at the collegiate level of great importance. Strategically located throughout the United States in key areas of industrial and research development, they are well placed to make a continuing major contribution to the welfare of the country through their particular specialties and technology oriented programs.

Accreditation, 1920–1960

By 1920, five of the six regional associations had been established, set up accrediting standards, and started to put them into operation. The Northwest Association performed this function in California for many institutions, even though there was no established regional accrediting association available until after World War II. The Western College Association was a membership discussion group which started in 1924 and eventually became an accrediting organization in 1948. A number of special programmatic associations began during this period: podiatry (1918), business (1919), law (1923), library science and music (1924), and dietetics (1927). These associations were in reality only precursors for the flood of specialized accrediting associations which have engulfed postsecondary education in the decades since that time.

We have noted previously that the North Central Association of Schools and Colleges had set up a special category for teachers colleges by the 1920s and had accredited five such institutions. As the American Association of Teachers Colleges developed and published its classification lists, it also began to establish standards for the teachers colleges. In a sense, these two movements coalesced in the middle 1920s, especially regarding the quality of the faculty of teachers colleges at that time. The American Association of Teachers Colleges adopted a resolution strongly encouraging all teachers colleges to require at least a baccalaureate degree and preferably the master's degree for all members of its regular faculty. In addition, they recommended baccalaureate training for members of the faculty and special laboratory training schools for student teaching supervision.

These strong recommendations had important effects on the appointment of future faculty members and even on the continuation of existing faculty members.

At Stout Institute (now Stout State University) in Wisconsin, for example, in 1923, 12 of the teachers were employed without a degree, 27 had bachelor's degrees and only six of the instructors had master's degrees. By 1930, President Nelson indicated in his report for the year that only three faculty members had less than the baccalaureate degree, only 15 had a baccalaureate degree alone and 25 members had completed the master's degree. Although Stout Institute had been a member of the American Association of Teachers Colleges, it had been subject to reinspection, and its membership was finally renewed in 1928. The North Central Association accredited it also in 1928, due its faculty upgrading and, the American Council on Education accepted it for membership at the same time. This was clearly a case of rapid faculty upgrading as a result of the accreditation movement (Wyman, 1968, p. 256).

A major study of the faculty preparation in all of the New York State normal schools, conducted in 1905 by Dennis L. Meriam, found that the problem of faculty preparation was serious. He reported that too few members of the faculty in the normal schools of the State of New York had collegiate standing, that many of the "higher" degrees were actually bachelor's of pedagogy without collegiate standing, and that many of the degrees were not taken from what Meriam considered institutions of "high standing". Some of the degrees listed were often honorary degrees, involving no academic study at all. A summary of faculty preparation in all of the New York State normal schools as of that date showed 151 of the 261 faculty members with no degrees of any type and 40 whose pedagogical or higher degrees were without collegiate standing. Seventy-four of the faculty had completed collegiate degrees with college standing, approximately one-fourth of the overall total. Four degrees were above the baccalaureate degree—one master of arts and three Ph.D.s. Meriam carefully points out, though, that some of these degrees and others listed were suspect. Five degrees, called Doctors of Philosophy, were received from Rochester University. Rochester University, however, did not offer the Ph.D. at that time except as an honorary degree, and thus some of the claimed advanced degrees were in fact not of this caliber. Four of the degrees were from Illinois Wesleyan University, one a master's degree and three Ph.D.s. As Meriam states:

> the standard of the degrees may be estimated when one reads in a recent catalog: "the graduate degrees of M.A. and Ph.D. are conferred only for work the nature and extent of which will be stated on inquiry. It is well-known that this work may be done wholly in absentia. The University does not give instruction in these courses, nor does it lay down a prescribed order of yearly or semi-yearly study . . . The latest editions of the text will be used in the preparation of examination papers . . . Ph.D. matriculants are required to present themselves at the University for the last examination" (Meriam, 1905, pp. 124–132).

In his study, Meriam also prepared a specific summary of the faculty at Potsdam Normal School over a period of 25 years prior to the turn of the century. Of the total number of 78 instructors, 20 were listed as holding collegiate degrees (Meriam, 1905, pp. 133–135).

Another vivid illustration of the problem occurred at Oswego in New York State. A new president, Ralph Swetman, arrived at Oswego in 1933 to find that 55 percent of the faculty had not completed degrees of any type. His board informed him that the state officials in Albany had mandated a rise in the level of the institution. In 1934, following his recommendation, the board of the institution announced that "faculty members were encouraged through leaves of absence to secure master's degrees by September 1, 1936." President Swetman issued an even stronger ultimatum which stated that no one on the faculty who failed to earn a master's degree would stay after

1935. By 1936, major changes had been made in both the composition and the degree accomplishment of the faculty, and by 1941 it was ranked in the highest 19 percent of the teachers colleges belonging to the Association. By 1944, of the 106 faculty members, 44 had bachelor's degrees, 39 had master's degrees, 18 had completed doctorates, and five others had doctoral degrees nearing completion. The rebuilding of the faculty to this enormous level in a period of one decade represented a huge upheaval on the campus and considerable personal suffering and college-wide tension (Rogers, 1961, pp. 176–179).

As the nation and its educational institutions entered the 1930s and a serious depression, budgets for educational institutions as well as every other publicly financed agency were seriously reduced. Selden pointed out that this led to a:

> consequent increase in accrediting by professional groups, which are always concerned with the effect of reduced appropriations on their schools. As enrollment in the graduate schools [had] doubled almost every decade, professionalism developed in the intellectual life of the campuses. Along with the increase in professionalism came the departmentalization of college and university faculties—and grave concerns for the securing and maintenance of accreditation for the various disciplines, particularly those in professional fields (Selden, 1960, p. 61).

While this professionalization was taking place and departmentalization was encouraging accreditation, the North Central Association adopted a new and much less objective basic principle for accreditation:

> an institution will be judged in terms of the purposes it seeks to serve and on the basis of the total pattern it presents as an institution in higher education, [and] the North Central not only abolished the old outdated standards but it evolved a radical approach by initiating a new additional purpose of accrediting, that of providing external stimulation to institutions for their continual growth and improvement . . . With the increasing use of the pattern which included both an institutional self-survey and a team of qualified institutional inspectors, the stimulation for college and university improvement was practiced more widely as a major purpose of regional accreditation (Selden, 1960, p. 41).

With these conflicting developments taking place, the presidents of many institutions made distinct efforts to move toward institutional accreditation and away from the increasing amount of professional accreditation. Although both the American Council on Education and the National Association of State Universities had tried in 1924 to place limits on the development of professional accrediting, the practice continued to expand. New professional associations with accrediting responsibilities were established in the 1930s for the following fields: chemistry (1936), dentistry (1938), occupational therapy (1935), physical therapy (1936), medical technology (1936 with AMA), journalism (1946), medical records (1943), architecture (1940), art (1944), and practical nursing (1945). Following World War II, as the trend seemed to be continuous, a number of presidents of major institutions came together and established a new National Commission on Accrediting (1948) to try again to stop the proliferation of new specialized associations and actually to cut back on the effects of those already in existence.

This new development had an important effect on existing teachers colleges and those which had already started in the 1930s to become state colleges. The key problem was how to arrange for the national accreditation of programs of teacher education. The National Commission on Accrediting in October, 1952 had informed seven of the professional accrediting bodies, including the American Association of Colleges for Teacher Education, that they should stop accrediting and begin work with the regional associations as a part of total institutional accreditation. Originally, teachers colleges had not been represented on the National Commission on Accrediting. As Herbert Welte pointed out, there were many discussions to try to obtain representation of this group on that Commission. He cites one of the three chairmen of the National Commission on Accrediting, Chancellor Gustavson of the University of Nebraska, who declared that he "refused to recognize teaching as a profession" (Welte, 1984, p. 1).

Another facet of the problem related directly to determining the best way to handle accreditation of teacher education, either as a special professional program or as an institutional type of accreditation. In 1950, a large group of teachers college presidents had banded together in a new voluntary organization called the Association of Teacher Education Institutions. They reasoned that the new organization would be comparable to the American Association of Universities, the American Association of Land-Grant Colleges, and other similar associations (Emens, correspondence, March 10, 1951, PP.2). Thirty of the presidents finally gathered in Chicago on March 31, 1951, established a constitution for this new organization, the Association of Teacher Education Institutions, and pushed for its recognition as a part of the entire operation of the National Commission on Accrediting.

John R. Emens, President of Ball State, was a member of the executive committee of the National Commission on Accrediting in 1952, representing this group and their association. He reported that:

> it was the objective of the National Commission on Accrediting to have all accrediting done on institution-wide bases rather than by units or divisions. It is the desire of the Commission that all accrediting will be done by the six regional accrediting associations with the advice and cooperation of the professional organizations interested in the accreditation of units or divisions of an institution. No institution is to be accredited unless it meets acceptable standards for all objectives named in its statement of purposes (Emens, correspondence including minutes of the ATEI Executive Committee Meeting, January 6, 1952).

The Association of Teacher Education Institutions represented a major change from the approach of the past, and included a number of institutions which had already broadened their mission or functions considerably beyond specialized programs in teacher education. The Association of Teacher Education Institutions, although it still used that name, turned out to be broader in type than originally expected. As a consequence, it lasted for only ten years, serving as the precursor for the association which was to take its place, the Association of State Colleges and Universities, created in 1961.

The expansion of the colleges after World War II, much of it based on the development of the G.I. Bill, led to one other facet of accreditationwhich had materially affected both ATEI institutions and their follow-up organization, the Association of State Colleges and Universities. Congress held extensive hearings in 1952 on flagrant abuses in the uses of the G.I. Bill since World War II. As a consequence, Public Law 82–250 was passed and its Section 253 stated:

> For the purposes of this Act the Commissioner shall publish a list of nationally recognized accrediting agencies and associations which he determines to be reliable authorities to the quality of training offered by an education institution (Harcleroad, 1980, p. 21).

Matthew Finkin, in a careful analysis of the effects of this legislative act, summarized its assumptions as follows:

First, the statute assumed that "nationally recognized accrediting agencies" existed and were of sufficient reliability that state government could permissibly piggyback its own approval of courses upon private agencies' decision-making processes. Second, reliance upon private determinations of educational quality would obviate the threat of federal control of education. Third, the role of the Commissioner of Education in determining that such nationally recognized agencies were of sufficient reliability would be essentially ministerial (Finkin, 1978, p. 2).

As a consequence, of course, this action of the federal government—with future funding of all types contingent upon an institution's approval by a "nationally recognized accrediting agency"—made it extremely important that all these developing institutions be included in whatever final settlement was made regarding the accreditation issues raised right after the end of World War II. The Association of Teacher Education Institutions, as a consequence, and its successor association, the Association of State Colleges and Universities, were extremely important in the postwar period as a result of this change in federal policy and the enormous increases in federal funding for institutions or for collegiate students occurring since 1960.

Teachers Colleges or State Colleges: The End of an Era

From 1920–1960, 79 institutions of the AASCU type were established in the 1920s, only 12 in the 1930s, 18 in the 1940s, and 19 in the 1950s (see Appendices 1 and 2). All were specialized, basically professionally oriented during the earlier years, but by the end of the 1950s the states were opening multi-purpose institutions with varied professional or arts and sciences curricula. In California, from 1947–59, five multi-purpose state colleges were started as upper-division and master's-level institutions. Several other states during this period changed junior colleges to four-year state colleges offering baccalaureate degrees. In addition, as previously described, a number of specialized degree-granting technologically based colleges were created.

During the war years, from 1940–45, some existing institutions had time for planning, a luxury difficult to duplicate since that time. As a result, some limited planning had been done for the returning flood of veterans and for the new and expanded functions which higher education was called upon to assume in the postwar years. How well higher education planned is open to discussion, but the situation would have been much worse had the time for planning not been available. State colleges, because they lacked the authorization to carry out new and expanded functions, were in many cases unable to translate into operational form the plans which contained realistic projections about the future. Consequently, many state colleges and universities (SCUs) were ill-prepared for the immediate postwar years.

In the early postwar years, higher education's most fundamental concern was providing access to higher education. Aside from a few states where state colleges had developed prior to the war, state colleges in their new role as multi-purpose institutions were still viewed as teacher training institutions and were given relatively little attention as major vehicles for the expansion and upgrading of educational opportunity.

The general status of SCUs in 1946–47 was described by the President's Commission on Higher Education:

> The great majority are called teachers colleges but increasing numbers are becoming state colleges or state colleges of education. Practically all grant the bachelor's degree, many grant the master's degree, and several grant the doctor's degree. Increasingly the teachers colleges, particularly those which have become state colleges, are offering other curricula in addition to those for prospective teachers (President's Commission on Higher Education, Vol. 3, 1948, p. 18).

Later in the report the Commission stated its conception of what teachers colleges should become:

> Teachers colleges, while striving constantly to improve their primary and all important function of educating teachers, should also utilize their facilities wherever feasible to help carry on the other aspects of the higher education program (President's Commission on Higher Education, Vol. 3, 1948, p. 70).

These passages constitute the most substantive references to SCUs in the Commission report. Possible additional functions of developing state colleges were recognized, but community colleges, state and land-grant universities, and private institutions were viewed as the major components of the higher educational system. However, during the 1950s and 1960s the state colleges grew so rapidly and expanded into so many new fields that the Commission Report was soon outdated.

The intensity of the cold war, and particularly "Sputnik" in 1957, focused the attention of the nation upon higher education and especially upon teacher education. Scathing articles in national publications denounced the "scandal" in teacher education, and major efforts were promoted to "take teacher education out of the hands of the teachers colleges." This of course did not happen and, in fact, SCUs today prepare almost as large a proportion of the nation's teachers as they have at any time in the past. However, the "crisis in teacher education" did focus the concern of the nation on state colleges and resulted in significant strengthening of programs, especially in the subject-matter fields. In particular, the increased emphasis upon content accelerated the trend away from the "professionalization of subject matter" in which courses in the academic disciplines had included instruction on how to teach those disciplines. Substantial preparation in one academic discipline was considered necessary for secondary school teachers, and many institutions considered a degree of specialization in one area desirable for elementary teachers as well.

SCUs were affected significantly, however, by some of the forces which created the enrollment surge following World War II and which affected higher education generally. The immediate increase in enrollments in SCUs, while not as great as in most other institutions, was composed chiefly of males rather than females. Veterans, while receiving the benefits of the G.I. Bill, were in many cases not able to travel great distances to seek higher education. Consequently there was an immediate demand for regional opportunities in curricula other than teacher education. And this demand, coupled with significant educational planning in a number of states, resulted in a large number of teachers colleges becoming state colleges during the immediate postwar years.

SCUs were also affected by the increased attention given to education as a whole. The end of World War II brought with it an assessment of the future of the country. What was it that the war had been fought to preserve? The answer, in part, was an opportunity for a more full and richer life for all in a free and open society. This answer brought with it an increased commitment to education as the path to this better life and to the preservation of a democratic society.

The postwar commitment to education thus affected SCUs not only as institutions of higher education but as institutions devoted primarily to the education of teachers. Indeed, the upgrading of programs for the preparation of teachers may well have done more to improve SCUs in the early postwar years than the addition of other professional or liberal arts programs. Major programs for students planning to teach in secondary schools shifted from such divisional programs

as the social sciences, language arts, and natural sciences to depart-
mental programs in English, history, and biology. Elementary education shifted to a four-year program, in some cases with a strong
"diversified" academic major, although many elementary teachers
continued to be trained in two-year programs until the late 1950s.

The numbers of teachers colleges existing in the late 1940s have
been well documented. An extensive study of the nature and needs of
higher education, conducted by John Millett for the Commission on
the Financing of Higher Education, and sponsored by the Association
of American Universities, found that the United States had 1,532
institutions in 1948–49. They enrolled a total of 2,236,571 students
by that time, a big increase from the end of World War II. Of this
number, 484 were considered professional schools with a total enrollment of 323,307. Of this 484 total, 200 were public, separate professional schools and 162 were teachers colleges. By 1950, eight additional teachers colleges had been accredited and added to the list,
making a total of 170 teachers colleges which were publicly supported, state-controlled professional schools. The Millett report focused heavily on the economic situation and sources of support for
the various types of institutions. The study found that between 1940
and 1950 there had been a 54 percent increase in average in-state
tuition at public universities and that charges for out-of-state students
had increased 81 percent. In spite of this rise, the average in-state
tuition charge at public universities in 1950 was still only $158 and the
average out-of-state charge $350. Many of the states provided all or
most of the budget for their colleges, or set a very low tuition fee
which students should pay. The teachers colleges and state colleges
actually had even lower overall average charges than public universities as a whole. This is an important factor in the development of state
college programs and their rapid enlargement in the years after
1950–1960.

In a study conducted almost ten years later, for the U.S. Department of Health, Education, and Welfare, Walter C. Eells and Harold
A. Haswell reported that there were still 168 publicly controlled
teachers colleges plus 28 independent technological institutions and
eight other professional schools which were funded and controlled by
the various states, a total of 194 institutions. A further study of the
teachers colleges showed, however, that they were rapidly moving
into baccalaureate and master's degree programs. More than three-
quarters of the institutions were giving master's degrees: 35 offered
the Master of Arts degree, 34 the Master of Science degree, and
others offered varied master's degrees in the field of education.

Three of the teachers colleges reported doctor's degrees, one a Doctor of Philosophy degree and all three offering the Doctor of Education degree. One of these, of course, is the current University of Northern Colorado which has been offering doctoral programs since 1930 (Eells and Haswell, 1960, pp. 32–34).

The changes in function and curricular offerings of all institutions, and particularly former teachers colleges, are well illustrated by Stabler's findings reported in 1958 at the conclusion of this period. He found that high school teachers, graduating from five different kinds of colleges and universities, were produced as follows: teachers colleges, only 17.6 percent; private general colleges, 22.3 percent; private universities, 10.3 percent; public universities, 27.0 percent; and public general colleges, 22.8 percent. Obviously, some of the institutions which he was classifying as public general colleges were state colleges which had been changed prior to 1958 from the normal school/teachers college group. This group still produces today from 35 to 40 percent of the high school teachers of the country—but only as one function rather than as a specialized primary function of the institution. As Stabler goes on to state:

> In more recent years as they have become state colleges [these institutions] have changed markedly. State legislatures have given more adequate appropriations and admission standards have risen. With its greater emphasis on liberal education and a more scholarly faculty the present state college is far different from the teachers colleges of the 30s and a totally different institution from the old normal school (Stabler, 1962, pp. 5, 54).
>
> The initial increases in enrollments in this group of institutions to almost 300,000 in the early 1950s, heralded the postwar "tidal wave" that was expected. Enrollments increased markedly in a decade, and by 1960 these colleges and universities had close to 1,000,000 students. Since then, the growth rate has accelerated, and they have prepared an even larger number of the total baccalaureate and graduate program graduates in the United States.
>
> This expansion led to increasing complexity in these now comprehensive institutions, evidenced primarily by a rapid development of new types of programs and an increase of between 400 and 500 percent in graduate enrollments. If these institutions had become larger but stayed basically undergraduate in scope, their structure and mission could have remained relatively simple. The growth not only in size but also in complexity of programs and degrees, however, resulted in major changes in the characteristics and goals of these institutions during the early postwar period. By 1960, their mission had changed abruptly— America had produced a third, wholly new type of higher education institution.

CHAPTER 4

Emergence of a New Major Component of Higher Education, 1960–1985

The enormous postwar changes in American society pushed it rapidly from a manufacturing and service orientation into a knowledge-based information and technology-oriented country. By 1960, publicly supported comprehensive institutions in the Association of Teacher Education Institutions realized that another type of association was needed. Accordingly, a group gathered voluntarily and created a new, different association, the Association of State Colleges and Universities.

This organization, established on February 23, 1961, grew out of the Association of Teacher Education Institutions (ATEI) which had been organized ten years before. The ATEI in itself was a major change for the public state colleges and universities. They had been members of the umbrella organization, the American Association of Colleges for Teacher Education, which encompassed all colleges and universities preparing teachers.

Teacher education, of course, has been a large part of the operation of all types of higher education institutions during the preceding century. As reported previously, the teacher education preparation program has been and still is a primary program at many private liberal arts colleges. It has also been a major program at many land-grant and state universities. For example, Indiana University, Michigan State University, Ohio State University, and Wayne State University are major suppliers of teachers and four of the largest ten contributors in the United States. This has also been true of graduate degrees in education; Columbia University's Teachers College, Indiana University, New York University, Michigan State University, the University of California at Berkeley, Wayne State University, and Temple University have been seven of the ten largest institutions in terms of graduates in the field of education.

Thus, development of the ATEI into a separate organization of colleges and universities in 1951 was a first significant change recognizing the breadth of program development away from specialization in the field of teacher education. After ten years of operation it became clear to much of the membership that the name of the organization was not really appropriate and that they should establish a new organization of public state colleges and universities. The new Association of State Colleges and Universities would recognize the unique characteristics of this newly developing and expanding form of postsecondary education in the United States. The group forming the association felt that the growing impact of the federal government on higher education, particularly as it related to research grants and other grants-in-aid, made it absolutely necessary that a strong national association should represent the interests of state colleges and universities.

A letter from William Selden in 1961 stated that the National Commission on Accrediting immediately thereafter, in early March 1961, had officially listed the new association "as one of the constituent members of the National Commission on Accrediting as a replacement for the Association of Teacher Education Institutions" (Selden, March 8, 1961). In May 1961, the American Association of Colleges for Teacher Education, as a courtesy for the new association in which many of its members had participated and still would participate, distributed a brief statement of the history and functions of the new Association of State Colleges and Universities. After delineating some of its history, its responsibilities, and in particular the accreditation function it had carried as the ATEI, the announcement noted that:

> ASCU will devote the greater portion of its time and efforts to the needs of its member institutions in three other [leaving out accreditation] major aspects of over-all institutional administration, namely; financial and business affairs, student affairs, and public affairs (letter and announcement sent to John Emens from Elizabeth James, Secretary to Dr. Pomeroy, Executive Secretary of the American Association of Colleges for Teacher Education).

Similarly, Lloyd B. Young, the first president of the Association of State Colleges and Universities, stated in a letter to John Caldwell, President of the American Association of Land-Grant Colleges and

$28 billion by 1971. Funding for the National Institutes of Health, the National Science Foundation, the National Aeronautics and Space Administration, and the Department of Defense have increased phenomenally since 1970, thus increasing the emphasis on research in interested universities wanting to participate.

Although relatively few universities were active participants during World War II, the number of universities with research as a main function and with federal research dollars as a major source of income has increased enormously and spread into every state of the United States. As a consequence, many of the land-grant institutions, the state universities, and the private institutions have become major research centers, and this has become their major emphasis. Although they do provide education in many professional areas, including new professions, their emphasis is at a different level from that of the AASCU institutions—namely, at the advanced theoretical level which is exceedingly important for the country. This major postwar change in the emphasis and efforts of the public land-grant institutions and the public state universities has been an important factor in the need to develop the comprehensive, publicly supported state colleges and universities emphasizing high quality undergraduate and master's level education.

Types of Institutions

By the early 1960s, most of the state-controlled colleges in this group had become comprehensive, although a few were still somewhat specialized. Accordingly, they could be placed in various groups at that time, groups which have changed somewhat during the last 25 years as classification systems changed. Interestingly enough, the changing nature of these institutions caused some of the demand for reclassification.

In 1948–49, Ostheimer completed the *Statistical Analysis of the Organization of Higher Education in the United States*. The Carnegie Commission issued its *Classification of Institutions of Higher Education* in 1971 and revised it in 1976. In the period between these two reports, the "university" category had to be split into two groups, each with two subdivisions. Research Universities I and II comprised the first subdivision; the second Carnegie category was also dual with, Comprehensive Universities and Colleges I and II. The new category of "Research Universities" is in keeping with the previous discussion and would appear to be additional support for the thesis presented here. The new 1981 classification system of the National Center for Educa-

tion Statistics (NCES) also has different groupings for "comprehensive" and for "doctoral-granting" institutions.

The descriptions under the differing classifications are quite enlightening. Ostheimer, for example, developed for the Millett Commission the definition of a university involving three basic elements. The institution must offer an undergraduate liberal arts curriculum, graduate study, and professional education. Liberal arts was interpreted "broadly" by including sciences, and "graduate study" was taken to mean post-baccalaureate work in the humanities, social sciences, physical sciences, or biological sciences, preferably but not necessarily continuing through the level of the doctorate. "Professional education" was distinguished by two further factors: the kind of professional schools and whether or not they were accredited by their respective professional accrediting agencies. An institution satisfied the criteria of "professional education" if it had at least three professional schools, at least two of which must have been professionally accredited from the law, engineering, medicine, teacher education, and business group. The remaining school might be unaccredited from this group or accredited (where an accrediting agency existed) in some other field, such as social work, architecture, agriculture, dentistry, pharmacy, and so forth. The criteria might also be satisfied by four professional schools, at least one of which was accredited in the first group; the remaining three schools could be unaccredited in the first group or accredited from the second group (Ostheimer, 1951, pp. 6–7).

Interestingly enough, Ostheimer found that 15 of the 57 private universities failed to satisfy the minimal criteria; five of the 15 were members of the "invitational" Association of American Universities, the most selective of all the associations. Of the ten institutions which were not members of the AAU, all more nearly met the concept of a university than those which were members and had been admitted as special cases. Two of the state universities did not meet the criteria. Six of the state land-grant colleges did not meet the criteria, and one of the five municipal universities failed to meet the requirements. Ostheimer's classification system further provided for four types of institutions: universities, liberal arts colleges, professional schools, and junior colleges. The teachers colleges were considered specialized colleges in the professional school group, as were a number of the technological institutions which have become comprehensive institutions and are members of AASCU.

The Carnegie Classification of 1971 and 1976 included categories of research universities, doctoral universities, comprehensive univer-

sities and colleges, and liberal arts colleges, with each category subdivided into two groups. There was also a category for two-year colleges and institutes. Of course, each of these areas listed both publicly-supported and private institutions. Of particular interest in this review is the definition of comprehensive universities and colleges. They were considered institutions offering professional or occupational programs along with a liberal arts program, with many offering master's degrees but having no or very limited doctorate programs.

In order to be a Comprehensive University or College I, there had to be at least two professional programs and at least 2,000 students. A Comprehensive University or College II had to offer at least one professional program and, if public, have more than 1,000 students. In the Carnegie Classification revision of 1976, none of the current AASCU institutions was classified as a research university in either the first or second group.

The doctoral-granting universities included eight AASCU institutions in the Doctorate-granting Universities I group and ten in the Doctorate-granting Universities II group. Doctorate-granting universities in the first group had to award 40 or more Ph.D.s in at least five fields (plus M.D.s if on the same campus) or receive at least $3 million in total federal support in 1973–74 or 1974–75. In no case was an institution included unless it granted at least 20 Ph.D.s in at least five fields, regardless of the amount of federal support. Doctorate-granting Institutions II were those which awarded at least ten Ph.D.s in three fields. Also included in Doctorate-granting Universities II were a few institutions which the Carnegie Commission confidently expected would increase the number of Ph.D.s awarded within a few years.

The AASCU institutions included among Doctorate-granting Universities I were Georgia State University, Northern Illinois University, Southern Illinois University at Carbondale, the University of Southern Mississippi, Kent State University, the University of Toledo, North Texas State University, and Virginia Commonwealth University. Those AASCU institutions included in Doctorate-granting Universities II were the University of South Florida, Idaho State University, Illinois State University, Western Michigan University, Bowling Green State University, the University of Akron, Memphis State University, East Texas State University, Texas Woman's University, and the College of William and Mary.

Most of the remaining institutions which were members of AASCU in 1976 were included in the group described as Comprehensive Universities and Colleges, either group I or group II. A few were listed as liberal arts colleges, including such institutions as Mesa College in Colorado, the University of Maine at Machias, Mayville State College in North Dakota, the College of Charleston, the University of South Carolina campuses at Aiken and Conway, Texas Agricultural and Industrial University at Laredo, and the University of Houston—Victoria campus. Very few public institutions were listed among the specialized institutions of higher education: the Massachusetts College of Art, and three institutions considered teacher colleges—the District of Columbia Teachers College (now a component part of the University of the District of Columbia), the University of Maine at Fort Kent, and Harris-Stowe Teachers College in Missouri.

A catch-all area which the Carnegie group classified as "Other Specialized Institutions" contained a number of other AASCU colleges and universities: three maritime academies in California, Maine, and Massachusetts; the City University of New York's, John Jay College of Criminal Justice; the West Virginia College of Graduate Studies; the King of Prussia Graduate Center of Pennsylvania State University. One other institution with a relatively small enrollment was also included here, the University of Alaska's Juneau Senior College.

This rather lengthy description of the Carnegie Classification System and some of the institutions involved indicates the difficulty of providing a single total classification system of the varied institutions in the United States. It also suggests the marginal differences between the diverse institutions within the membership of the American Association of State Colleges and Universities.

The new classification system of the National Center for Education Statistics, put into use in 1981, provides three major classifications of general type institutions and ten designations of specialized and professional institutions with limited offerings in particular fields. As might be expected, the 406 institutions eligible for membership in AASCU and the 370 current members are spread throughout this grouping by arbitrary standards established for each of the groups.

The first category, Doctorate-granting Institutions, lists 16 institutions only. The criteria require the institution to grant a minimum of 30 doctoral degrees in three or more doctoral-level programs or in an interdisciplinary program at the doctorate level. Included as first professional doctorate degrees are the M.D. and other similar degrees. The second classification, Comprehensive Institutions, has a particularly significant definition in view of the history of the developing AASCU group. It states:

These institutions are characterized by strong, diverse postbacca-laureate programs including first-professional, but do not engage in *significant* doctoral-level education. Any institution which grants less than thirty or has less than three doctoral-level programs is included in the comprehensive institutional group.

The third group, General Baccalaureate Institutions, is defined as follows:

These institutions are characterized by their primary emphasis on general undergraduate baccalaureate education. They are not signifi-cantly engaged in postbaccalaureate education. Included are institu-tions not considered specialized institutions in which the number of postbaccalaureate degrees granted is less than thirty or in which fewer than three postbaccalaureate level programs are offered. Such institu-tions must also either (a) grant baccalaureate degrees in three or more baccalaureate programs or (b) offer a baccalaureate program in inter-disciplinary studies. In addition, over 75 percent of the degrees granted must be at the baccalaureate level or above.

This is particularly significant because several hundred members of the National Association of Land-Grant Colleges and State Universi-ties and of AASCU do continue to offer two-year and even less than two-year programs. Separate information about this particular activ-ity will be provided later in this chapter.

In summary, the current classification of the AASCU membership indicates two-thirds in the comprehensive institutions group (over 220). In the general baccalaureate group, there are 98 AASCU institutions. In the doctorate-group, 16 are listed as follows: the University of Northern Colorado, the University of South Florida, Georgia State University, Illinois State University, Northern Illinois University, Southern Illinois University at Carbondale, Ball State University, Western Michigan University, the University of Southern Mississippi, the University of North Carolina at Greensboro, Bowling Green State University, Kent State University, the University of Toledo, the University of Akron, Memphis State University, North Texas State University, and Texas Woman's University. It is interest-ing that institutions such as the College of William and Mary, which has been offering doctoral programs for decades, have not been included.

Finally, in the specialized grouping, the NCES classification in-cludes 18 of the AASCU institutions. Many are in this category because of a special characteristic. Three are experimental colleges, for example: Empire State College in New York, Thomas Edison College in New Jersey, and Metropolitan State University in Minnesota. Alaska-Juneau is listed as a specialized institution although it now has expanded programs in fisheries and is the Sea-Grant institution center of the University of Alaska System. A number of the institutions were probably included because they retain a small emphasis still on teacher education, but there is no way to determine for certain why they are considered specialized. This is an interesting and somewhat challenging problem derived from the classification of the various institutions. Of the AASCU institutions which are classified as specialized, however, the majority probably should be in the comprehensive category, emphasizing professional programs and, in most cases, with relatively strong general education requirements at the undergraduate level.

This coverage of classification and typologies of institutions will conclude by noting that current studies recognize the distinctiveness of state colleges and universities. For example, Bowen and Minter, in their recent series of annual reports of the financial condition and educational trends of public higher education, seemingly as a matter of course, include public state colleges and universities as one of the "major components". The other two components are community/junior colleges and public research universities (Bowen and Minter, 1980, p. iii). Birnbaum, whose eight-state study of diversity in higher education included 141 different types of institutions in 1960 and 138 in 1980, found that among the 18 most common were two public, large "comprehensive" types at the master's or doctoral level. A third type, public master's coeducational institutions, existed in 1960 but had vanished by 1980 (Birnbaum, 1983, pp. 135–136). Current literature of higher education is replete with similar references to these comprehensive institutions, clear recognition of the addition of this new category of public institution.

Establishment of New Public SCUs*

Hundreds of new colleges and universities were created by both private and public sources in the period between 1960 and 1985. Birnbaum reports that:

---

*For brevity, the abbreviation SCU will be used in the remaining text in lieu of public state colleges and universities.

Between 1969 and 1975, some 800 new colleges (many of them community colleges) were created, while roughly 300 were closed or consolidated, leaving a net gain of nearly 500 in just six years.

The historical development of private colleges has been discussed earlier with consideraton of their high degree of mortality in past years. Trow, in 1979, indicated that this is still true and that the extraordinary phenomenon of high fertility and high mortality rates among institutions of higher learning is still with us (quoted in Birnbaum, 1983, p. 35). Birnbaum has gone on to point out that "the maintenance of the total system [a diversified one] has required that institutions be allowed to fail so that new or more diversified institutional forms can develop and compete openly in the marketplace for resources and support" (Birnbaum, 1983, p. 36).

Under these circumstances, it is interesting to note that the public sector has created 83 new public comprehensive state-controlled institutions since 1960; all are fully operative. In 1960–69 alone, 65 new public institutions were created, and in 1970–79, 18. The decline in the 80s, however, resulted in the establishement of no new comprehensive, AASCU-type institutions during the decade through 1985. Seventy-three of these 83 institutions are currently members of AASCU. In 1986, however, Ohio created a new institution, Shawnee State University, making a total of 84. Three differentiated groups among them are worthy of note. First, many have been established as new campuses of state systems or as new campuses of multi-campus university systems within state systems. Second, a significant number were started since World War II as upper-division and graduate institutions only, with some reverting to type and becoming full four-year undergraduate institutions. Third, a few highly experimental and interesting nontraditional institutions have been established.

State organizations and statewide systems for the control, financing, and organization of public higher education institutions have had a very significant effect on the new comprehensive SCUs. In 1940, 33 of the 50 states had no coordinating mechanism; in 1975, all of the states had such a mechanism, and only Wyoming has disbanded it. Ten years later, statewide agencies were reported for every state (*Chronicle of Higher Education,* February 27, 1985, p. 16). Of course, in reporting the University of Wyoming as a statewide agency for its state, the report was in error. With that exception, however, it indicates that there are 21 governing boards and 30 coordinating agencies of various types in the states, Puerto Rico and the District of Columbia.

This is an exceedingly difficult area to categorize; the best organization has probably been developed by Millett. He separated the state government agencies for higher education as of 1982 (see Table 4) as first, statewide governing boards (22), second, state coordinating boards (18), third, statewide advisory boards (9), with a fourth grouping of 14 institutions called additional planning boards. A number of other attempts to categorize these different state government agencies have combined Millett's groups two and three and come up with 27 coordinating bodies. Millett, however, clearly differentiates between the coordinating boards in group two and the advisory boards in group three, based on particular kinds of authority. He indicates that the coordinating board has no authority for governance over public institutions but will have authority to prepare a master plan,

TABLE 4

State Government Agencies for Higher Education, 1982

Statewide Governing Boards (22)	Coordinating Boards (18)	Advisory Boards (9)	Additional Planning Boards (14)
Alaska	Alabama	California	Alaska
Arizona	Arkansas	Delaware	Arizona
Florida	Colorado	Michigan	Florida
Georgia	Connecticut	Minnesota	Georgia
Hawaii	Illinois	Nebraska	Iowa
Idaho	Indiana	New York	Maine
Iowa	Kentucky	Pennsylvania	Massachusetts
Kansas	Louisiana	Vermont	Mississippi
Maine	Maryland	Washington	Nevada
Massachusetts	Missouri		New Hampshire
Mississippi	New Jersey		North Dakota
Montana	New Mexico		Oregon
Nevada	Ohio		Rhode Island
New Hampshire			
North Carolina	Oklahoma		South Dakota
North Dakota	South Carolina		
Oregon	Tennessee		
Rhode Island	Texas		
South Dakota	Virginia		
Utah			
West Virginia			
Wisconsin			

Source: Millett, 1984, p. 24.

approve degree programs, and review and recommend the appropriation needs of institutions of higher education.

On the other hand, the advisory board may prepare a master plan and may review program offerings and budget requests, but it does not have the authority to approve degree programs or recommend operating and capital appropriations. Advisory boards, by Millett's classification, are boards which do not have at least two of the latter three types of authority. Governing boards, in contrast to either coordinating boards or advisory boards, are multi-campus boards with statewide authority, responsible for the governance of all public higher education within the state—at least for baccalaureate and graduate degree-granting institutions. In a number of states, a separate board governs the community colleges (Millett, 1984, pp. 99–102).

In a further refinement of the problem of defining multi-campus systems, a recent breakdown suggests the use of the designation "multi-campus systems" and includes four types: (1) private, (2) statewide, (3) heterogeneous public, and (4) homogeneous public multi-campus systems. In this categorization, beyond the statewide organization, there are multi-campus systems within various states which range from very small to very large and have significant effects upon the operation of the institutions which are a part of the system. In this plan, statewide multi-campus systems such as Hawaii, Georgia, Nevada, and Alaska have jurisdiction over the public institutions of the state and are very similar to Millett's classification of a statewide governing board. The heterogeneous public multi-campus system and the homogeneous multi-campus system, however, operate within a state which has a coordinating board or an advisory board with which the multi-campus governing board must work.

Heterogeneous systems include a variety of levels of institutions, while the homogeneous systems are in-state governing boards for a system of community colleges or a system or four-year and/or graduate institutions. Heterogeneous public systems would include examples such as Southern Arkansas University, Louisiana State University, the State University of New York, and the City University of New York. The multi-campus governing board, whether it is statewide or less-than-statewide and works with or through a coordinating board, has been a primary creation of the post-World War II period. In fact, many of the new institutions established since 1960, and particularly those which are AASCU members, have been established by and within these systems.

Texas is a particularly good example of this development. East

Texas State University at Texarkana, established in 1971, is a campus of East Texas State University. The University of Texas System established a number of additional campuses: at Dallas in 1969, of the Permian Basin in Odessa in 1969, at San Antonio in 1969, and at Tyler in 1971. The University of Houston's System established a campus at Clear Lake in 1971 and at Victoria in 1972. The University System of South Texas opened Corpus Christi State University in 1971 and Laredo State University in 1969. The University of South Carolina developed similarly, with Coastal Carolina College established in 1959, Aiken in 1961, and Spartanburg in 1967; these three campuses are members of AASCU. The Capitol Campus of Pennsylvania State University was established in 1966. In the City University of New York, the College at Staten Island was established in 1955, the John Jay College of Criminal Justice in 1964, Medgar Evers College in 1969, the State University College at Purchase in 1967, and Empire State College in 1971. Again, all of these institutions are members of AASCU.

Florida, Illinois and other states could be cited here as additional examples, but the key point has been well illustrated: the 1960 to 1985 development of additional public institutions in this professionally oriented new group has, in a high percentage of the cases, been as new campuses or colleges within existing multi-campus systems or as part of a state governing board operation.

Upper-division and graduate colleges and universities are primarily a phenomenon of the post-World War II period. They grew basically in states with significant numbers of existing or planned junior/community colleges which were designed to continue as two-year institutions. A few private institutions of this type have been described by Altman, including the College of the Pacific, Concordia Senior College of the Lutheran Church-Missouri Synod, and the New School Senior College in New York (Altman, 1970, pp. 159–160). The main effort has been through public institutions, however, and started in 1947.

The postwar boom in California led to the initial development of a number of upper-division and graduate colleges, primarily because of the existence of a strong statewide program of junior colleges. Some state colleges had been operating junior colleges on their campuses by contract with the local school districts, namely, San Jose', Fresno, and San Diego. Two other institutions, Humboldt State and Chico State, were operating junior colleges partially at local expense and partially at state expense. In the late 1940s and early 1950s, great demand emerged for a large number of new spaces in colleges and universities. The southern California legislators as a group became concerned about the state subsidy of junior colleges in the northern part of the state. In contrast, the full cost of junior college education was being borne by the county taxpayers in the southern part of the state, largely in the Los Angeles area.

As a consequence, the push for additional college operations in southern California led to early establishment of the Los Angeles State College of Applied Arts and Sciences, an upper-division and graduate institution housed on the same campus as the Vermont Street Campus of the City College of Los Angeles. The only common administrative employees were the president and the dean of students, Howard McDonald and Morton J. Renshaw. The state college rented space on the junior college campus and hired junior college teachers, as overload was available, to teach at Los Angeles State College. Shortly thereafter, Long Beach State College and Sacramento State College were started as upper-division and graduate institutions. A decade later, the state college for Alameda County and the state college for Orange County, now known as the California State University at Hayward and the California State University at Fullerton, were also established as upper-division and graduate institutions. The institutions at Long Beach, Los Angeles, and Sacramento became full four-year institutions within a short five- to six-year-period, and the same situation prevailed with the two later campuses at Hayward and Fullerton.

Thus, by the middle 1960s, the upper-division and graduate experiment in California had been terminated. The flood of students to be cared for required or allowed the institutions to become four-year undergraduate and graduate institutions without serious complaint by the junior college group. These two-year colleges were expanding so rapidly and their student bodies were so large that they had all they could take care of to provide spaces needed for students who wished to attend community colleges. Particularly in the Hayward area, where no community colleges had existed, new community college districts were developed—and still all the colleges were filled to overflowing.

Florida and Texas also started large numbers of upper-division colleges and universities. The Florida institutions—Florida Atlantic University, Florida International University, the University of Central Florida, and the University of West Florida—were upper-division and graduate institutions from the early 60s until they became four-year institutions in 1983–84. Texas, with a very strong community college system, still had ten upper-division-type colleges within the various systems in the State in 1986. These colleges were: Corpus Christi State

University, East Texas University Center at Texarkana, Laredo State University, Pan American University at Brownsville, University of Houston at Clear Lake, University of Houston at Victoria, University of Houston, Downtown, University of Texas at Dallas, University of Texas of the Permian Basin, Odessa, and the University of Texas at Tyler.

No other state in 1986 had more than two upper-division institutions. Those remaining were: West Oahu College in Hawaii, Governors State University and Sangamon State University in Illinois, the University of Baltimore in Maryland, Metropolitan State University in Minnesota, the SUNY College of Technology at Utica/Rome, and the Capitol Campus of the Pennsylvania State University. Missouri Southern State College and Missouri Western State College were added as upper-division institutions to existing two-year colleges. Operating with essentially the same boards, although they are separate jurisdictions, they have normally been regarded as four-year colleges rather than upper-division institutions.

Almost all institutions of this type are members of AASCU and as such participate as full colleges in the same way as any other institution. This very interesting experiment of the past 40 years still exists in these limited cases. With the slowdown in student enrollments, it appears that additional new institutions of this type will probably not be organized in the near future. On the other hand, as institutions search for students and as enrollments begin to fall in areas with serious losses in high school graduates, there may be continuing additional push for the existing upper-division colleges to move in the same direction as the California and Florida upper-division experiments.

Experimental Colleges. Student unrest and, in some places, student revolts of the 1960s led to very serious thinking about educational delivery systems. A number of states studied the need to provide persons at a distance with opportunities to continue through baccalaureate degree programs. Of course, there was some push for this development in all existing colleges; demands came for continuing education off-campus organized degree programs, and opportunities for students to take courses through talk-back TV and other methods. Simultaneously, a few states tried to develop special experimental colleges to provide organized statewide and, in some cases, nationwide programs designed to earn degrees through a variety of experimental delivery systems. Three of these institutions are in existence, fully accredited, and are full, organized members of AASCU.

These three institutions were established in 1971 and 1972: the

Empire State College in New York, a part of the State University of New York System; Thomas Edison College of New Jersey, part of the system operated by the Board of Higher Education in New Jersey; and in Minnesota, the Metropolitan State University located in Minneapolis/St. Paul, which works on a contract plan with individual students who have had previous college work and want a college degree. Over the years, each of these institutions has successfully developed programs leading to accreditation, programs which are considered some of the most innovative developments of the postwar period. A similar proposal for Lincoln University in Illinois actually did not get off the ground. The three institutions which do provide this special kind of service are especially noteworthy. During the same period, two entirely different but experimental institutions with non-traditional curricula were established: Evergreen State College in Washington and Grand Valley State College in Michigan. They are good examples of the true ingenuity of the American system to devise very different and diverse educational institutions to provide for professional education in this developing information/technology society.

Name Changes of Institutions

In the postwar period, a number of new institutions were named "university" or were part of a mass movement in a given state for the legislature to name all institutions "university" and get the problem out of the way. In a state where an institution contended strongly with the established state university to become a second state university, the solution to the problem was to make all the institutions universities. In this way, there was no single contender to the existing so-called flagship university; the newly-named universities were regarded as less competitive or less of a threat. This took place in many states, with most of the designations established in a given year. Over the three decades from 1950–1980, most of the AASCU institutions, with exceptions in a very few states, have been designated as university.

Oddly enough, a high percentage meet the original qualifications for university designation established by the Commission on the Financing of Higher Education of the Association of American Universities in 1948–49. The definition Ostheimer stated in his statistical analysis, as reported earlier in this volume, did not require the doctorate. Accordingly, a high percentage of existing AASCU members offering three or more professional degrees at the master's degree level and having significant numbers of graduates qualify easily. In the almost 40 years since that time, however, later definitions by the Carnegie Commission and the National Center for Educational Statistics have changed the designation of university, due particularly to the increase in the importance of the research function of the universities and the increased power and complexity of the doctoral programs they offer. Nevertheless, the term *university* has come to be almost generic for any institution which a state wishes to call by that name, and thus the designation as "research" university rather than as a "doctoral-granting" university has acquired considerable significance.

This process of change is still underway, and a number of states which had not seriously considered it in the past have recently made the statewide change for entire systems; Connecticut and Pennsylvania made the name change in 1983. North Dakota changed Minot State College to Dakota Northwestern University in 1985—then reversed the change in a state referendum and then, in 1986 reversed again, re-naming the four state colleges as the State University of North Dakota, at Dickinson, Mayville, Minot and Valley City respectively!

Southern Connecticut State University provides a good illustration of the process through which the institution progressed to this state. Founded as a two-year normal school in 1893, it was changed to a three-year normal school and converted to New Haven State Teachers College in 1937, with authority to grant the Bachelor of Science degree. In 1947, with a need for further growth, a new campus site was purchased and the institution initiated a cooperative Master of Arts program with Yale University. In 1954, the institution was authorized to grant the Master of Science degree for its own programs and five years later its name was changed to Southern Connecticut State College. With this came conversion to a multi-purpose institution and authorization to offer the Bachelor of Arts degree.

It is interesting to note that Southern Connecticut was able to offer the Master of Science degree in its particular professional field of teacher education five years before it was authorized to offer the general Bachelor of Arts degree. In 1965, it became a unit in the state system of public higher education and was soon authorized to grant the Master of Arts degree, a sixth-year certificate, and the baccalaureate degree in nursing. Authorization followed to offer the Master of Library Science degree and the Master of Social Work degree. In 1982, the academic divisions were reorganized, finally, into schools of arts and sciences, business/economics, education, library science, nursing, and social work, and a graduate school. The name was changed to Southern Connecticut State University in 1983. Clearly, this institution which had started as a two-year normal school in 1893 met the 1948–49 qualifications of the AAU study as a university. Currently, however, it is not a doctoral-granting institution but is basically a professional institution with strong liberal arts programs paralleling the undergraduate specialized degree programs. It is a modern university of this new type—contributed by the United States to the world as part of its postwar development in higher education.

A careful look at Appendix 4 will indicate how extensive these name changes have been for most of the institutions offering programs similar to Southern Connecticut State University's. Sixteen institutions are classified by the National Center for Educational Statistics as Class I or Type I doctoral institutions, but at least twice this many do offer doctorates—even though they may not offer the total number or the diversity required for that designation. Clearly, however, all these "universities" which are now members of AASCU offer the diversity of baccalaureate and master's level professional programs needed by modern society.

Curricular and Degree Programs

By 1960, the former state teachers colleges and technical institutions were ready for the curricular explosion of the next quarter-century. A 1964 analysis of higher education as a whole, published by the American Council on Education, revealed the beginnings of these institutions in professional fields (Cartter, 1964–65, pp. 75–141) and listed their accredited programs:

Art: Massachusetts College of Art.

Business Administration: Fresno State University, Los Angeles State University, Sacramento State University, San Diego State University, San Francisco State University, Georgia State University, Southern Illinois University at Carbondale, Bowling Green State University, Toledo State University, North Texas State University.

Engineering: Long Beach State University, San Jose' State University, the University of Wichita, the University of Southwestern Louisiana, the Montana School of Mines, the New Jersey Institute of Technology, the University of Akron, the University of Toledo, Youngstown University, The Citadel, South Dakota School of Mines and Technology, Lamar State University, the University of Houston.

Journalism: Fresno State University, San Jose' State University, Southern Illinois University at Carbondale.

Landscape Architecture: California Polytechnic State University at San Luis Obispo.

Law: Washburn University of Topeka, the University of Akron, the University of Toledo, the University of Puerto Rico, the College of William and Mary.

Music: Possibly because of long-time emphasis on the education of teachers, 55 institutions in 25 states were listed, far too many to name individually.

Nursing: Chico State University, Los Angeles State University, Sacramento State University, San Diego State University, San Francisco State University, San José State University, Northwestern State University, and the University of Southwestern Louisiana.

Pharmacy: Northeast Louisiana State University, Ferris State College, the University of Toledo, Southwestern State University.

Teacher Education: 178 institutions.

These data indicate very clearly the breadth of program which was already starting to develop in the SCU group, a development pointed up in the report of the California state universities and colleges between 1961 to 1981. In those two decades, the number of curricular programs accredited by national professional accrediting associations jumped over 1,000 percent, from 16 to 171. In 1981, the California State University and College System prepared three-fourths of the state's teachers and two-thirds of its nurses with baccalaureate degrees. The student body at this large system had grown from 95,000 students in 1961 to 314,000 students in 1981. The CSUC conferred more than half of all bachelor's degrees and one-third of all master's degrees conferred in California in 1981. Growth of this type, both in students and in proportion of degrees offered, coincides with the growth in the area of professional curricula, particularly the accredited professional programs which are so vital to the success of American society.

Between 1964 and 1975 four large studies were conducted to determine conditions in SCUs and to monitor ongoing changes. The studies were carried on by Smith in 1964 (with returns from 141 of 176 members), by Harcleroad and others in 1966 (231 returns of 260), in 1970 (191 returns of 303), and in 1974–75 (242 returns of 317). Of Smith's respondents, 90 indicated that they had historically been normal schools, here called normal colleges, and one was a normal university. In addition, there were six combinations of normal schools with either agricultural schools, three junior colleges, three state colleges, two seminaries, one commercial school, one polytechnical school, and one bible institute.

Smith's study indicated, for 141 institutions, that a number of fields other than teacher education had been widely developed by 1964. Business administration existed on 78 campuses—with graduate programs on 21; nursing, with baccalaureate programs on 22 campuses and graduate programs on two; agriculture, with major undergraduate programs on 20 campuses and graduate programs on three; social work, with major undergraduate programs on 19 campuses and a graduate program on one; engineering, an undergraduate program on ten campuses; baccalaureate degree programs in library science in 48 institutions; eight institutions with baccalaureate programs in medical technology; and 32 in journalism. Specialized programs reflected the regional service nature of the institutions in such fields as fisheries, forest management, park management, and American folk culture. These were offered, of course, in addition to the standard liberal arts majors characteristic of teacher education institutions. In 1964, these 141 institutions graduated 69,482 persons, with 58,018 at the baccalaureate degree level, 11,334 at the master's degree level, and 130 at the doctorate level. This study clearly demonstrated the beginnings of the SCU's "take-off" leading to their rapid expansion in the next two decades.

The three studies following Smith's reflect the postwar move to statewide or multi-campus systems—and its consequent effect on curricular developments. By the 1960s, American higher education had passed into the "era of the state educational system." The systemization of American higher education affected SCUs perhaps more than any other type of institution because of their close state control and their position between the community college and the federally encouraged research university. The SCUs had the greatest degree of overlap in functions and were most affected by the differentiation and coordination of roles.

Two types of *differentiation of educational function* took place: (1) level and kind and (2) emphasis. Historically, SCUs had been differentiated in the level and kind of programs they offered, first as noncollegiate or lower-division normal schools, then as single-purpose technological or teachers colleges, and most recently by the level of highest degree offered. In 1975, most SCUs were restricted by state statute and/or coordinating board decisions to less than doctoral-level degrees. Approximately one-fifth of these institutions were restricted to offering degrees only at the baccalaureate level.

Differentiation in emphasis has always been difficult to define and even more difficult to enforce in practice. Nevertheless, agencies responsible for statewide planning had to include differentiation in emphasis as a major concern. There have always been wide variations in educational programs with the same title. Some have been theoretically oriented, while others have been more practical. Some have been developed for high ability students, while others have been open to a wider range of students' abilities. The principal differentiation in emphasis is apparent most often between theoretically oriented versus applied-oriented curricula. This type of differentiation may include the assumption that theoretically oriented programs are more selective than those which are applied, although this often is not true.

As an illustration, both a state college and a major federal grant university might offer programs in business administration. The program at the university in some cases would be purely graduate or, if undergraduate, would likely emphasize economic and management theory in order to prepare the student for advanced graduate work. The program at the state college would also include some emphasis on theory but might focus on a more applied range of professional choices and prepare the student for middle-management positions in fields such as accounting or marketing. The emphasis of the two programs would be different, but it does not follow that a student must be more capable to succeed in one than the other.

The principle of differentiation has been most evident in SCUs at the graduate level. Master's degrees have traditionally been of an occupational nature. This is equally true at the doctoral level, where emphasis mostoften has been on applied professional work rather than theoretical research. SCUs generally have accepted a differentiated status initially in order to offer the new programs, and have modified them as necessary to meet the needs of their constituents.

Regionalism is another factor which clearly affected SCUs in their role as part of state systems. Since theoretically oriented, advanced graduate programs are normally expensive, these programs had usually been confined to a few established research universities. Applied professional programs, on the other hand, often had been dispersed on a regional basis. Recently, however, representatives of SCUs have asserted that economies of scale have reached a point of diminishing returns in research universities with national perspectives, and, therefore, advanced graduate education, some applied research activity, and regional public service activities should be allocated to regional state universities. Such reasoning often has been quite persuasive—and has extended even across state lines. As examples, Pennsylvania, Ohio, Minnesota, North Dakota, Tennessee, and

Kentucky have interstate agreements for cooperative attendance of students in degree programs. In some cases, however, regionalism worked against the development of more comprehensive regional universities. Several states decided to limit the size and functions of some regional SCUs and begin new institutions, rather than develop existing SCUs into comprehensive universities. The choice between differing conceptions of regionalism constitutes one of the key issues facing state systems of higher education and the SCUs which are members of the system.

The issues of differentiation and regionalism culminated in debates over actual university status for SCUs. The dispute over the name "university" as opposed to actual university status, in most states, has been resolved as described earlier. The more basic questions of university name and status revolve around which functions beyond the master's level SCUs should undertake and what level of resources should be provided. By 1975, it appeared that relatively few SCUs would become comprehensive federal grant universities within the next 15 years. By that year, however, many SCUs had a concentration of resources appropriate to *some* university-level research functions. Thus, the essential question exists: What functions are appropriate to a differentiated, highly professional, regional state university? Many critical social needs now receiving relatively little emphasis at fully developed research universities could be met to some degree through greater utilization of resources available to many SCUs.

Cooperative efforts with regional/business groups indicate great expansion in this area of response to social needs, and countless examples of these activities exist all over the United States. In the last three years, the Association has developed a full program of cooperation between AASCU institutions and neighboring industries. Chapter 5 will give more detail, but a few examples will highlight this development.

In 1985, Youngstown State University in Ohio established an Office of Technology Transfer Agent to provide technical assistance to area businesses lacking research and development capability. In the same year, George Mason University in Virginia established, in combination with the regional business community, what was listed as the nation's first school of information technology; a $3 million local contribution was combined with the $12.7 million appropriation from the state legislature. The school will include three major departments: systems engineering, computer and information sciences, and electronics engineering. Basically a new advanced school of engineering, it will be a key part of the regional "Center for Innovative

Technology" to be built close by the university and will promote corporate and university research in information technology, mathematical science, and computer-assisted design.

The University of Houston, through its Clear Lake campus, is working with the Lyndon B. Johnson Space Center to set up a Research and Development Management Center to study advanced technology management, human performance in space flight, and the use of computer science in these fields. In 1982, Morehead State University in Kentucky began collaboration with Martiki Coal Corporation in a joint agricultural research and development complex. This project was designed to develop the land from closed coal mines in order to provide for an improved agricultural base in the area. A year later, the Pocohantas Land Corporation, a subsidiary of Norfolk Southern Corporation, joined the partnership. The three organizations worked together on a 4,000 acre agricultural complex with an additional 10,000 acres devoted to upland pastures and forest land. In the process, the university provided a great deal of know-how, and the two companies provided the expertise in working with the land. As a result, the mining operation was expected to create more flat agricultural land than currently existed in the entire county.

These are only a few of dozens of similar cooperative projects combining professional degree programs and public service activities. Regional cooperative arrangements of this type indicate the importance of SCUs' expansion into diversified professional fields. Regional state universities which emphasize professional instruction, interpretive scholarship, applied research and development, and community-oriented public service make optimum use of scarce human and financial resources. In this way, they work directly toward solutions of immediate social problems and the long-term advancement of the regions.

Analysis of the four major studies of AASCU institutions shows that several examples of curricular diversification have been occurring simultaneously.

1. At the baccalaureate degree level, nearly all institutions offer majors in most of the arts and sciences fields and in most professional fields, while parallel general education programs are pervasive.
2. At the master's degree level, extensive growth is evident in professional fields and in a wide variety of subjects in the arts and sciences, especially those taught in secondary schools.
3. Over 15 percent of SCUs offered doctoral programs in 20 fields by 1975. Although over one-half of the doctoraldegrees were

awarded in education, there were several new doctoral degree programs in mathematics, business, physics, chemistry, engineering, psychology, fine arts, and English.
4. Significant numbers of less-than-baccalaureate technical and occupational programs were offered at approximately 40 percent of the SCUs.

At the baccalaureate and master's levels, the ability of the SCUs to adapt and change is particularly apparent. The period from 1968 through 1982 magnified the changes taking place, demonstrated most clearly in an analysis of undergraduate degrees and the fields in which they are offeredand completed. The National Commission on the Future of State Colleges and Universities, established in 1971, compiled data on all baccalaureate degrees granted by SCUs in 1969. These can be compared almost directly with the baccalaureate degrees granted by SCUs in 1981–82, as recorded by the U. S. Department of Education. The changes are dramatic in several selected areas, as shown in Table 5.

By 1969, the breadth of professional programs was already significant; the increases by 1981–82, a little over a decade later, are exceptional. Against an overall total increase of 37 percent, the growth is extremely large in agriculture, business, architecture, computer science, engineering, the health professions, and public affairs. The major decreases took place in education (− 37 percent), foreign languages (− 52 percent), social sciences (− 47 percent), and mathematics (− 65 percent). The drop in these four fields undoubtedly are directly connected with the shortage of teachers which the nation is experiencing at present, particularly in science and mathematics. These very significant modifications in just one decade give definite evidence of the shifts which American society has required in these institutions and underlines the magnitude of the changes they have accomplished. Comparable additions are also in place at the master's degree level.

A few examples of a professional nature will illustrate in a more graphic way the meaning of these numbers. A developing trend emerged at William Paterson College in New Jersey and Bowling Green State University in Ohio: professional majors are being subdivided in increasingly specialized areas.

At William Paterson College, the Bachelor of Music degree, with specialities in jazz studies and performance, and in classical performance, has added a new program of specialization, a baccalaureate degree in music management. Similar adaptation in the business field is illustrated by an additional new major program specialization in

TABLE 5

Baccalaureate Degrees Granted by AASCU Institutions in Selected Fields

Major Field	1968–69	1981–82	Percentage Changes
Agriculture and Natural Resources	2,003	4,236	plus 111%
Architecture	143	1,143	plus 707%
Business	25,920	75,352	plus 191%
Computer Science	231	11,114	plus 4711%
Education	73,468	49,808	minus 32%
Engineering	6,141	16,557	plus 170%
Health Professions	2,908	17,222	plus 492%
Home Economics	1,882	5,968	plus 217%
Public Affairs and Services	*	17,772	no basis for comparison
Psychology	6,686	12,220	plus 83%
Social Sciences	36,685	24,935	minus 47%
Physical Sciences	5,083	6,162	plus 21%
Biological Sciences	8,293	9,632	plus 16%
Fine and Applied Arts	7,857	11,253	plus 43%
Foreign Languages	4,787	2,011	minus 58%
Mathematics	9,440	3,339	minus 65%
Overall Totals of Degrees Awarded**	214,805	294,194	plus 37%

*In 1968–69 the only possible comparable field was city planning, with only 37 degrees awarded.

**Totals of the columns do not equal the grand totals since a few fields such as law, military sciences, and interdisciplinary studies are not included.

business administration at Bowling Green State University: hospitality management, an increasingly important part of the American scene. At Black Hills State College in South Dakota, a new major started several years ago in travel industry management includes work in four separate fields in order to provide graduates with competence in related fields and more opportunities for placement. The four areas are: the food service industry, the hotel industry, travel agency operations, and airline transportation. Students come to Black Hills State College from 26 different states because of the nature and well-known high standards of this baccalaureate degree program (Hause, 1984, pp. 1–2). At St. Cloud State University in Minnesota, a specialization in the field of biomedical sciences prepares physicians assistants (Mitau, 1974, p. 1).

Montclair State College in New Jersey again provides an excellent example of change in curricular emphasis from 1974–75 through 1984. At the undergraduate level, major changes have taken place in a number of professional fields, most strikingly in business administration and computer science. Bachelor's degrees in business administration rose from 262 in 1974–75 to 734 in 1983–84, an increase of 280 percent. The field of computer science saw astronomical increases. No students in the graduating classes of 1974–75 through 1977–78 majored in computer science, although during this period some math students took coursework in the field. In 1978–79, there were two graduates in this field; by 1983–84 there were 95, the fifth largest group of bachelor's degree majors in the college. In addition, Bachelor of Fine Arts degrees in specialized majors were started in 1979, 1980, and 1981. These grew from no graduates in 1978–79 to small but regularly increasing groups: Bachelor of Fine Arts in the arts, 14; Bachelor of Fine Arts in music, seven; Bachelor of Fine Arts in theatre, eight. Students in the music field began to go into music therapy during this decade, and in some years as many as ten to 12 students graduated in this field. The number of students taking degrees in philosophy/religion also increased. The first graduates completed the program in 1981–2 and, within three years, 11 students graduated in this field. A final new field developed in the recreation area starting in 1976–77; graduates varied from 39 through 57 in each of the years through 1984.

In addition to the undergraduate changes at Montclair, significant additional changes took place in the master's degrees awarded. In the decade from 1974–75 through 1983–84, 203 students graduated in business education and office systems administration. The first graduate in finance and quantitative methods received the MBA degree in 1983–84. The largest group of students, 1,182, earned a master's degree in student personnel services during this ten-year period. The second largest group was in communication sciences with 652 graduates during the decade, followed by psychology, including industrial psychology, with 422 graduates. Industrial education and technology had 153 master's degree completions, and home economics, with considerable emphasis in dietetics in many cases, had 154 persons complete the degree. In the area of mathematics and computer science, there were 276, of whom 40 took the degree in computer science after it became available in 1980–81.

Simultaneously, some fields were decreasing in the number of master's degrees awarded during this same decade. For example: the master's degree in history declined from 59 to five; Spanish and Italian went from six to 12 and then declined to one; biology (evidently for teachers, in the main) declined from 20 to 13; and physical education declined from 19 to 12 after increasing during the latter years of the 1970s. Degrees in the social science option in economics, on the other hand, averaged five per year during the end of this ten-year period. In the fine arts areas, an increase in speech and theatre actually coincided with an increase in speech and theatre at the undergraduate level of approximately 50 percent. It is clear from the data in 26 areas of master's degree and 36 areas in baccalaureate degree that a significant change in the direction of professional programs, outside of the teacher education profession, had developed at Montclair State College.

Montclair's cooperative programs were also expanding in the past decade. Thirty of the 40 major fields offered at the undergraduate level are now in the co-op program, with 384 companies in the region and 600 students participating. These include: Bell Laboratories, AT&T, Bendix Corporation, Exxon, Bankers National Life, Chase Manhattan Bank, Bristol Meyers, Brookhaven National Laboratory, and Dunn and Bradstreet Marketing Service.

The extensive sub-baccalaureate level degree programs offered by SCUs are yet another instance of the flexibility and change which have been built into these institutions. John Rowlett of Eastern Kentucky State University conducted studies in 1967, 1971, and 1976 to determine the status of these programs in both AASCU and NASULGC institutions and found large increases in both land-grant and AASCU institutions. In AASCU institutions alone, 1,462 less-than-baccalaureate-level degree or certificate programs were available in 1975. This was a large increase from 1971, which in turn had been a significant increase from 1967. In actuality, AASCU institutions accounted for over two-thirds of the total of 2,123 programs available in reporting institutions. In 1975, over 44,000 students were attending AASCU institutions and taking two-year or less-than-baccalaureate-degree programs. The technical and occupational programs available could be clustered in eight broad areas: environment and sciences, business, education, agronomy and animal husbandry, public service, mechanical and engineering technology, computer and electronics technology, and health.

Within these eight general areas, students could pursue highly specialized courses: petroleum technology, water quality, pollution control, hotel management, day care and nursery management, dairy herd management, fire service and safety, building construction technology, nuclear medicine technician, cytotechnology, air frame and power plant technology, and computer technology. In programs of this kind on four-year and graduate campuses, students were receiving a technical education and the beginning of a general/liberal education to achieve the associate degree. Having the less-than-baccalaureate program on a campus with the baccalaureate, master's, and doctoral programs (as was true in such cases at some of the AASCU institutions) provided students with an absolute optimum opportunity to start in a program of their choice and pursue it as far as they wished in the area of professional specialization. Although there has been no recent follow-up of these three studies, a random survey of institutional catalogs indicates that the two-year programs described in these less-than-baccalaureate-degree studies have not been changed. If anything, there have probably been further addition in the past ten years.

Degree program planning became a way of life for SCUs beginning in the early 1950s and continues today. Master planning is a major responsibility of coordinating boards and an important part of the work of multi-campus system central offices. If all of the needs of a rapidly changing society could be forecast accurately, demands for professional personnel could be met. One finding from the last two studies by Harcleroad, however, is most instructive in this area. It appears that degree program planning has not been very effective. Of the 434 degree programs planned in 1970 for implementation in 1972, only 192 or 44 percent were actually implemented. Problems with planning are also suggested by the fact that no 1970 plans had been made for 158 of the 350 new degree programs implemented in 1972.

In the future, flexibility will be a necessity within major fields and even in courses. The trend of the 1980s is not expansionist; adjusting to new needs will require internal changes. To illustrate, the Texas Coordinating Board at its April 1985 meeting considered only two new degree proposals for the entire massive system, the fewest in two decades. In the October 1984 report of the Oklahoma Regents for Higher Education, 24 programs were discontinued and no new programs were requested. The legislature, in fact, planned a thorough review of the existing 1,717 degree programs in all Oklahoma institutions "to identify weak and inefficient programs for possible consolidation or discontinuance" (Oklahoma Regents for Higher Education, October 12, 1984, p. 2). Under such conditions, internal planning, modifying existing majors, or updating and revising courses within majors may be the best and most desirable means of meeting changing economic and social conditions.

The summary for this period can be succinct and brief. It is clear that the SCUs represent a new and vigorous type of institution developed during the past 40 years, especially during the dynamic growth period from 1960–1985.

CHAPTER 5

AASCU: Twenty-five Years as Prologue

Introduction

Establishment of the American Association of State Colleges and Universities (AASCU) on February 12, 1961, formalized the emergence in the United States of a new type of public institution of higher learning.

AASCU had its origins in the Association of Teacher Education Institutions (ATEI), founded in 1951. Nearly all the original members of AASCU began as single purpose institutions, many as normal schools. By 1950, all the normal schools had become teachers colleges, and many were called state colleges or universities.

Prior to 1950, the activities and concerns of the teachers colleges had been confined largely to their respective states or, for a large number of them, to limited regions within their states. But with the rapid expansion of higher education enrollments following World War II, the teachers colleges became the fastest growing degree-granting institutions in the nation. As a result, their programs and services expanded and their horizons were greatly extended.

After ten years of coping with problems endemic to institutional expansion—the need for increased financial support, the impact on academic traditions of new curricula and a generation of ex-GIs, and the constant struggle for professional identity—ATEI members realized the urgency of creating a more broadly-based national organization. What was required, they decided, was an association that recognized the development of comprehensive, multi-purpose state colleges and universities as a growing, responsive, permanent presence on the nation's postsecondary, educational landscape. Time, the

American economy, and social change had made the "single-purpose" public institutions virtually obsolete. In fact, the close working relationship that had been established by the Association of State Universities and Land-Grant Colleges and the State Universities Association a few years prior to AASCU's birth had heralded a new order of things in the organization of American higher education.

So AASCU entered the scene as the "third force" in public higher education, a companion set of institutions with regional or statewide missions taking their seat at the national/policy table alongside the National Association of State Universities and Land-Grant Colleges (NASULGC, which resulted from a merger of the two associations mentioned above) and the American Association of Community and Junior Colleges (AACJC)—the triad that has formed the base of America's public postsecondary system for over a quarter century.

AASCU was established with its membership open to any regionally accredited institution of higher education offering programs leading to the degree of bachelor, master, or doctor, which was wholly or partially state-supported and, more specifically, state controlled. Coming as it did just three years following passage of the National Defense Education Act, the organization of AASCU and its growth over the past 25 years coincided with the impact of the federal government on higher education, particularly with respect to research grants and student financial assistance programs. In AASCU, member institutions have through the years had a strong, respected voice representing their interests at Congressional hearings dealing with legislation designed to expand educational opportunities in colleges and universities.

By 1962, 160 state colleges and universities had joined AASCU, including 22 which had not previously been members of the ATEI. They were attracted to the idea of the separate association representing a different, unique type of institution, not specialized in curriculum but comprehensive in outlook.

Dr. Walter Hager, AASCU's first executive officer, in his history, *AASCU's First Ten Years*, listed the four major purposes of the new association:

—To enable the members to make their influences felt in connection with national affairs . . . to be heard in national activities affecting higher education—as a voice, and not merely an echo.

—To present the strengths and services of state colleges and universities effectively to the public and to agencies and individuals from which grants of funds might be available.

—To represent the members of the Association in the National Commission on Accrediting (now the Council of Postsecondary Accreditation).

—To conduct studies of educational problems of common interest to the members.

By 1965—the high water mark of the banner Great Society legislation that earned President Lyndon B. Johnson (an alumnus of an AASCU institution, Southwest Texas State University in San Marcos) the acclaim of the academic world for being an "education president"—AASCU had grown to 170 members, and it was apparent that this new organization filled a pressing need in the higher education community. Older AASCU institutions had expanded, while in several states many new comprehensive public colleges and universities had been established. Determined to strengthen AASCU's services to its membership, the officers of the Association appointed Allan W. Ostar, formerly director of the Joint Office of Institutional Research of the National Association of State Universities and Land-Grant Colleges (NASULGC) to be AASCU's first full-time Executive Director. He assumed office in the fall of 1965, and has served AASCU continuously in this capacity, and now as President, to this date. Over the past 20 years membership in the Association has grown to 370 institutions and AASCU's voice is among the most respected in American higher education.

AASCU's first quarter century as an organization can best be presented in a three-period breakdown. The initial beginnings lasted from February, 1961, until November, 1965. The second period of early expansion lasted from 1966 until 1974, and the third period of early maturity of the Association covers the years from 1975 through 1986.

Early Beginnings, 1961–1965

From its voluntary origins, AASCU has been a membership-driven association. During its first years the officers served all functions of the organization on a voluntary, professional service basis. The founders and early officers of the Association often paid all or part of their expenses personally in order to get it started. The first presidents, Lloyd P. Young, John R. (Jack) Emens, and Eugene B. Elliott, gave freely of their time to lead the new organization. The first secretary, Charles R. Sattgast, president of Bemidji State College in Minnesota, served as the Association's focal point, acting as treasurer and taking care of all operational details as part of his professional responsibility to serve the greater educational community.

Much of the effort and cost involved in AASCU's beginning were absorbed in the budgets of the member institutions, and many of its early and continuing activities were conducted by college and university presidents, along with their staff members, in pursuing some of the important Association projects. Several examples of this characteristic of AASCU's early leaders illustrate the point graphically. President Jack Emens of Ball State University in Indiana, originated and carried out a number of the original studies which were completed and reported at the 1962 meetings of the Association. His Research Report #1 provides the basic summary data about member colleges, their enrollments, degrees granted, sources of income, and structure.

Concerned about the participation of member institutions in federal programs, Emens organized a study of this problem which was conducted by Ball State's director of research in 1962–63. In addition, Emens developed the consulting service for AASCU and organized and managed it for the Association for a number of years. As a former member of the Board of the American Council on Education and a colleague of many officials of NASULGC, he took a great deal of initiative in working with those organizations and was able to provide considerable help to AASCU in its cooperative relationships with other associations during its early years.

Several other examples include Glenn Kendall, president of Chico State College in California, who provided the time and encouragement for the dean of his college of education, Joe Smith, to take half-time for most of a year to conduct the first large study of AASCU institutions, described earlier, and prophetically titled "Challenge to Change" (1964). Fred Harcleroad, president of the California State College at Hayward, initiated the AASCU drive in the area of international education, and working with his administrative assistant, Fred Kilmartin, made the first study of international education in the state colleges and universities. Warren Lovinger, president of Southwest Missouri State College, conducted salary studies. Harold Hyde, president of Plymouth State College in New Hampshire, conducted the study of centralized controls and autonomy. President Earl Hawkins of Towson State College in Maryland, organized a conference on innovation which was an important AASCU project in its "beginnings" period. Finally, Harcleroad conducted, with considerable help, three baseline studies of the state colleges and universities referred to previously. This characteristic of AASCU's early years was carried into the following periods, with chairs and key members of the Association's committees constantly conducting special studies and organizing special projects in their fields of interest and expertise. Roland Dille, president of Morehead State University in Minnesota, and AASCU's board chair in 1980–81, took special note of this characteristic and emphasized it in his report to the Annual Meeting in 1981:

> "More than any other large organization that I know of (AASCU) involved its members in its work, in committees that do things and in meetings that are about something. To the sense of responsibility for our own institution and for higher education, a burden—if that is what it is—that none of us can escape is added a sense of responsibility both for one another and for the organization."

The Association meetings during its early period spent a great deal of time on federal programs which might be of benefit to the member institutions—for example, the National Defense Loan Program, the National Science Foundation, agencies providing federal aid in construction, and the International Cooperation Administration. AASCU representatives participated in continuing discussions concerning the National Commission on Accrediting, and in analyzing the implications of proposed federal legislation for public higher education. In its early years, however, AASCU determined that it would not take positions as an association relating to federal legislation. While this shortly gave way to an opposite decision, in the beginning period the members took no positions on pending bills in Congress. The variety of studies being conducted, previously listed under member activities, constituted the most active part of AASCU's early programs.

As a matter of policy, the Association executive boards early adopted a pattern of cooperation with other national higher education associations, particularly NASULGC. Russell Thackrey, NASULGC's first executive officer, was very cooperative and assisted greatly in the development of the new Association. While AASCU's budget was quite modest in its early years, the officers determined that a significant part of it—$8,000—would pay for sending members of the Association copies of the famous "green sheet" distributed privately by NASULGC to its members. This gesture was a special professional courtesy from NASULGC officials and provided AASCU members with very current and up-to-date information on the federal scene. In addition, AASCU was able to cooperate with NASULGC at a nominal cost to be part of the Joint Office of

Institutional Research. That office conducted many studies and provided AASCU members with a number of important publications. Cooperation in the research and information areas was a harbinger of the continuing cooperation between AASCU and NASULGC which exists today.

It soon became evident that the duties of executive secretary and treasurer were more than any one member of AASCU could be asked to carry out. Accordingly, the board of directors moved rapidly and in February, 1962, Walter E. Hager, retired president of the D.C. Teachers College, agreed to serve in a half-time capacity as the executive secretary and treasurer of the organization.

It was also possible at this time to arrange for an office in the same building with the American Council of Education (ACE) and NASULGC and its Joint Office of Institutional Research. Hager moved into this office on July 1, 1962, with a staff which consisted of himself on a half-time basis and one full-time secretarial assistant. In writing his brief history of the first ten years of AASCU, he noted that this was "a fortunate arrangement. It enabled the Association to be in close contact with other organizations serving higher education, including ACE itself. The Association became a constituent member of ACE at once."

One other change of considerable importance also was made during the early period. In 1963, AASCU's constitution was changed to provide for associate memberships. This made it possible for state educational agencies with a regulatory or administrative relationship with one or more institutional members of AASCU to be eligible for associate membership. Relatively few of the state educational agencies and commissions joined early, but there has been a significant increase over the years in this type of membership (see Appendix 5).

Clearly, by 1964–65, the new association had made significant strides in development. Nevertheless, it still had considerable distance to go in order to be recognized for its current and future value and importance. The AASCU leadership was ready to take the next step, which came immediately following the years of early beginnings.

AASCU's Period of Early Expansion 1966–74

The second period of AASCU's history—early expansion—begins with 1966 as a beginning because this was the first complete year in which a full-time executive director was employed to give total effort to the Association's operation and service. The 1974 closing date is arbitrarily chosen because it marked the end of the functioning of the

National Commission on the Future of State Colleges and Universities.

The executive board had made the important decision to move toward higher fees for AASCU members and the full-time service of an executive director and staff in the Washington office. The officers of the Association, with the agreement of Russell Thackrey of NASULGC, approached Allan Ostar, director of the Joint Office of Institutional Research; he agreed to accept the new position of executive director.

In November 1965, the executive board and newly-appointed executive director of the Association held a three-day retreat in a remote area on Captiva Island off the Florida coast. The nine proposals resulting from that meeting were presented to Association members for their consideration at the Annual Meeting in February 1966. The proposals were:

1. Establish an AASCU press, on a cooperative basis, for those members who wish to participate.
2. Set up a cooperative artist bureau in the area of the arts and humanities, which would serve the needs of institutions within particular regions seeking to obtain services of recognized artists and speakers.
3. Establish a special office in Washington to identify sources of federal support and to assist institutions in proposing projects which might be funded or contracts which might be secured with federal agencies.
4. Develop a program to help institutions in the area of fund-raising.
5. Establish programs at AASCU institutions in the health professions, particularly to prepare urgently needed allied health personnel.
6. Increase AASCU member involvement in international activities.
7. Develop research centers at AASCU institutions to conduct studies of administrative issues of special interest to AASCU presidents.
8. Establish an organized consulting service to assist AASCU members in obtaining specialists both from within and from outside the Association to deal with a variety of curricular and administrative problems.
9. Initiate a major national project to identify the role of state colleges and universities in American society.

These nine recommendations served as a springboard for a number of AASCU activities 1966–74 and in subsequent years.

One of the special AASCU committees which has been of particular importance to the Association as its services to institutional members expanded over the years has been the Committee on Policies and Purposes. This type of committee had been a part of the operation of the American Council of Education under the leadership of President Arthur Adams in the 1950s. AASCU members who had worked with Dr. Adams and knew his admiration for this kind of association operation encouraged the appointment of such a committee early in AASCU's development. This form of committee, rather than being administrative in nature, provides a different thrust for a professional association.

Shortly, after the Captiva retreat, the Committee on Policies and Purposes was given seven charges as a responsibility. Number six and seven were the outgrowth of Captiva recommendation number nine, calling for a study of the future role of AASCU institutions. However, the first five responsibilities of the committee are of even more long-term significance. With its on-going responsibility to observe the cutting edge of American society and the way in which higher education institutions should react to its challenges, the Policies and Purposes Committee continually keeps the Association alert to developing needs. As a consequence, it has been a major thrust of the Association in the past 20 years and continues to be extremely important.

Following are the seven responsibilities handed to the AASCU Committee on Policies and Purposes in 1966:

1. To review the purposes of AASCU and suggest to the Board of Directors actions or procedures which will advance these purposes.
2. To review suggestions originated by the Board and, if feasible, to develop procedures for implementing them.
3. To be alert to changing currents in the fields of higher education and to bring to the Board's attention developments which should engage AASCU's attention.
4. To conduct, at regular intervals, surveys of the Association's member institutions, through questionnaires designed to give up-to-date information regarding the growth and development of the institutions and make the results of such surveys available to AASCU members.
5. To review the information gained from periodic surveys and

recommend to the Board studies and projects which might be referred to the Committee on Studies.

6. To develop detailed plans for a comprehensive national study of the contributions that may be made by the member institutions of AASCU as they continue to evolve in programs and services.
7. To seek support from one of the national foundations to carry out the above study.

In the half-decade following the 1966 Annual Meeting, AASCU's membership grew significantly. It was a time of sweeping change not only in U.S. higher education, but in American society generally. The civil rights movement was at its peak. The nation was mired in the Vietnam war, rupturing the Great Society concept which had sparked so much progressive legislation. Student unrest swept campuses from coast to coast, climaxed by the shooting and deaths at two AASCU member institutions, Kent State University in Ohio and Jackson State University in Mississippi, in May 1970.

Many new AASCU-type institutions were created during this period, just as existing state colleges and universities expanded. New dormitories, new classroom buildings sprang up in urban centers and rural areas alike. So rapid was the growth of postsecondary education that, at the community college level at one point in the early 1970s, the country was building new campuses at the rate of one a week. "Computerese" was fast becoming the "in" language at many campuses. The federal role in higher education, particularly in the areas of student financial aid, institutional development grants, and research, expanded exponentially.

All of these developments served to spur AASCU's growth as an organization. Fledgling though it was on the national scene when compared with some of the older, better known associations, AASCU began to build a program of professional activities and services designed to meet the rapidly-shifting needs of its members. The Association's annual meetings, with member presidents involved in a wide range of committees, were well attended and soon regarded as among the most productive and best managed on the higher education scene. A series of summer "Council of Presidents" meetings was established, both to acclimate new chief executives to their responsibilities, but also to serve as a sounding board for new ideas.

Memo-to-the-President, AASCU's bi-weekly publication, became its principal channel of communication between the national office and all member presidents and their staffs. In addition, AASCU began regularly issuing a series of policy statements and position papers which had an important impact not just on AASCU campuses, but also throughout the higher education community. From testimony by AASCU presidents on federal legislation affecting postsecondary educational opportunities, to the need for internationalizing college curricula, to analyzing tensions between statewide higher education regulatory agencies and public colleges and universities, to setting forth principles of campus governance, AASCU learned during its period of early expansion how to make its presence known and felt.

For example, in 1972–73, working closely with the American Association of Community and Junior Colleges, AASCU initiated the Servicemembers Opportunity Colleges (SOC) project, which has since become one of the most innovative and successful programs in higher education. SOC is a partnership between the civilian and military educational communities sponsored by a consortium of 13 higher education associations, the five military services, and the Department of Defense; AASCU serves as the SOC fiscal and administering agent.

Currently, a total of 440 accredited postsecondary institutions comprise the SOC network, now in its fourteenth year. Of these, 320 are public, 120 are private, 193 are two-year, and 247 are four-year institutions. To be SOC designate, a college must: first, design its transfer practices for servicemembers to minimize loss of credit and avoid duplication of course work; second, limit residency requirements for servicemembers to no more than 25 percent of the undergraduate degree program, with courses taken at any time; third, award credit for specialized military training and occupational experience; and, fourth, award appropriate undergraduate-level credit for learning in extrainstitutional and nonacademic settings.

All told, some 500,000 servicemembers annually enroll during off-duty hours in courses offered for credit by SOC institutions on military installations or on nearby campuses in the United States and overseas. Thanks to the AASCU/AACJC initiative in the early 1970s, the SOC network now serves the world's largest student body.

AASCU'S early influence in the area of public policy initiatives captured widespread national attention in the fall of 1973, with the issuance of a statement entitled *Financing Postsecondary Education—the Case for Low-Tuition Public Higher Education*. As an AASCU staff paper prepared for the National Commission on the Financing of Postsecondary Education, the statement was intended to counter a number of reports issued in the early 1970s favoring higher tuition levels at public colleges and universities. AASCU regarded as particularly serious threats to the principle of low tuition two reports prepared by economists on behalf of the Carnegie Commission on Higher Education and the Committee for Economic Development.

In taking the case for low tuition to the American people, AASCU made these points:

1. The percentage of high school graduates going to college is generally lower in states with high tuition.
2. Among veterans receiving benefits under the G.I. Bill, the percentage who go to any college has generally been low in states with high tuition.
3. Research data show that parents of a great many students at public colleges can provide little or no financial assistance; these students earn a substantial part of their college expenses, and are very dependent on low tuition.
4. The great majority of working-class and minority students are dependent on low-tuition public colleges for an education.
5. A study found that lowering tuition significantly increases the number of students going on to college.
6. A Stanford Research Institute study showed that students from low income families would be more likely to go to college if tuitions were reduced.
7. Bureau of Labor Statistics calculations of family budget levels indicate that very few families have adequate funds to meet college costs.
8. Federal and state student aid programs are generally inadequate in meeting the needs of students from either lower-income or middle-income families, as inflation erodes the family ability to pay for college.

AASCU's leadership role in the legislative debates that swirled around the "tuition issue" in the early 1970s further earned it the respect, not only of the educational community, but also of public leaders in all parts of the country who periodically "feel the pressure" to increase tuition levels from groups opposed to the low tuition concept that undergirds public higher education.

Both the Captiva meeting in late 1965 and the Policies and Purposes Committee meeting early in 1966 had recommended a national study of the future of state colleges and universities, in order that AASCU members might develop a surer sense of direction. By January 1971, with support from the Ford Foundation, a National Commission on the Future of State Colleges and Universities had been formed under the chairmanship of the late Wayne L. Morse, former U.S. Senator from Oregon. The "Morse Commission" met regularly from early 1971 through mid–1973, taking as its primary responsibility "the encouragement of change for improvement in AASCU member institutions." It identified areas of growing concern in the present and the future of higher education and initiated what the Commission hoped would be a promising procedure to come to terms with these areas of concern "at the level that counts—back home," through the development of Campus Action Teams.

As noted earlier, the work of the Morse Commission marked an important, perhaps historic, point in AASCU's evolution as a major higher education association. Establishment of the Campus Action Teams induced a period of institutional self-analysis, criticism, and introspection which resulted in scores of campus-by-campus reviews of program priorities, goals, and mission statements. The state colleges and universities which, just a decade or so earlier, were seeking to find "unity in diversity" suddenly began to acquire institutional identities that differentiated them from the land grant/state universities, on the one hand, and the community/junior colleges, on the other. They were called, at one time or another, "the people's colleges" and "the colleges of the forgotten Americans." As AASCU enrollments grew and plants expanded, it became clear that public higher education in the United States had come of age.

In a series of publications, the Commission devoted its attention to the question of how the Campus Action Teams could help AASCU members improve themselves across a broad series of "issues categories." *Purposes, Goals, and Scope* was first, in which AASCU campuses were asked to develop a fuller understanding of their own particular missions and life-styles. Then came *Curriculum, Instructional Patterns, Governance and Organization, Student Access*—a "very contemporary and complicated area—*Finance, Student Life, Quality and Effectiveness* (thus presaging by at least a decade the preoccupation with "quality" and "excellence" that characterized higher education studies in the mind–1980's,) and *Planning and Improvement*, in which each member institution was urged to develop comprehensive long-range plans designed to take advantage of unique campus strengths.

Perhaps the best single word to describe what the work of the Morse Commission meant to AASCU, both in institutional and in association terms, is the word "maturity." By 1973–74, an organization that had its birth pangs at the outset of the "turbulent sixties" had begun to mature; it knew from whence it came and had started to carve out an identity that marked it as viable, productive, and distinctive. The work of the Morse Commission set the stage for AASCU's 1975–85 period, the era of "Early Maturity."

AASCU's Period of Early Maturity, 1975–1985

By the mid–1970s an AASCU organizational pattern—or perhaps "style" would be a better word—had started to emerge, in which the Association demonstrated remarkable skill in dealing successfully with a wide range of issues, projects, and programs in higher education. That success was (and is) attributable, it can now be seen in retrospect, primarily to the fact that, from the beginning, AASCU has been a *membership-driven* organization. Its founders sensed that an association of institutions could be resilient locally, regionally, nationally, and internationally only if it were governed from the bottom up, not from the top down; that it could be capable of continuous self-renewal only if its members were involved across the board in its many professional endeavors. The Association's charter members wanted the chief executive officers to "call the shots" with respect to Association policies and activities. AASCU began that way, in February 1961, and continued to function that way in the decade leading up to its Silver Jubilee—Year—November 1985 to November 1986.

The basic commitment led to three "hallmarks" which, by the mid–1970s, had brought about AASCU's organizational success. The Association in its formative years had learned how to fulfill these three functions essential to progress in a professional association:

First, the *partnership* function of working cooperatively and constructively with other organizations and agencies to achieve shared policy objectives;

Second, the *stewardship* function of guardian for the programs, values, and ideas that are central to the goals of public higher education; and

Third, the *leadership* function of breaking new ground in public policy formulation, pioneering in program innovation, and serving as an advance guard for identifying and resolving issues of national and state concern.

All three of these functions are, obviously, interdependent and inter-related. Given the complexities of organizational management, no single function can be completely separated from the other two. Nonetheless, during its decade of "early maturity" (1975–85) AASCU succeeded as partner, as steward, and as leader in many ways that advanced the mission of public higher education.

*AASCU as Partner.

AASCU leaders had learned the "partnership" concept early-on in the Association's history. First, in working closely with the American College Testing Program, the National Association of State Universities and Land-Grant Colleges, and the American Association of Community and Junior Colleges, and the AFL-CIO on policy questions relating to federal student financial assistance and the low tuition principle, and then in shaping the Higher Education Amendments in 1972, which strengthened and extended the provisions of the original Higher Education Act of 1965.

The Servicemembers Opportunity Colleges (SOC) project, described above, also symbolized the essence of a constructive, productive partnership, bringing together as it did the Department of Defense, the five military services, and 13 higher education associations in a consortium designed to expand postsecondary opportunities for men and women in the armed forces.

AASCU's role as partner in public policy development stemmed, in part, from the fact that the lifespan of the Association paralleled the growth of a massive program of federal assistance to colleges and universities, emanating not only from the U.S. Department of Education, but also from a wide array of other executive branch agencies, such as the Departments of Defense, State, Commerce, Labor, Agriculture, and Interior, and the National Endowments for the Arts and Humanities. AASCU's founders were correct in their assumption that the federal government would play an increasingly important role in higher education, and that state colleges and universities should have a national voice in defining and delineating that role.

AASCU "as partner" guided the preparation and publication in 1984 of *Early Planning for College Costs: A Guide for Parents,* a publication co-sponsored by the Association and the international accounting firm of Coopers and Lybrand. Designed to assist parents who fear they might not be able to afford to send their children to college, the "Guide" has proved to be especially helpful for those who do not have ready access to professional legal or tax advice. It is also a handy checklist for families seeking financial planning alternatives.

In 1980, AASCU expanded its partnership role in the international arena. Reflecting the need for a cooperative effort in higher education to increase students' awareness of global events and to participate more actively in international development, AASCU took part in the founding of the Consortium for International Cooperation in Higher Education (CICHE). The creation of CICHE was a collaborative effort of the National Association of State Universities and Land-Grant Colleges, the American Association of Community and Junior Colleges, the American Association of Colleges for Teacher Education, and the International Council on Education for Teaching, and AASCU. The American Council of Education joined in 1985. Through the consortium mechanism, AASCU continues to provide a point of contact for those outside the United States desiring access to U.S. Higher Education, a means for developing a global consciousness in American Colleges and Universities, and a source of professional and academic resources for development activities abroad.

*AASCU as Steward.

AASCU's role as "partner" in carrying forward new projects and programs is complemented by its functions as "steward" of concepts and policies essential to the integrity of the academic enterprise. The Association's leaders have from its inception believed that they had a continuing responsibility to keep public attention centered on ideas that sustain public colleges and universities and assure their unique contribution to the success of the American experiment.

The panoply of AASCU's enduring concern for staying close to the central educational issues of our time is reflected in the following sampler of policy statements approved by the Association membership:

—Quality and Effectiveness in Undergraduate Education (1971)
—Academic Freedom and Responsibility, and Academic Tenure (1971)
—The International Responsibility of Higher Education (1975)
—Career Education at the Four-Year College and University Level (1976)
—Value-Centered Education and Moral Commitment (1976)
—Academic Change and Improvement: Response for the 1980s (1978)
—Public Higher Education and the States (1980)
—AASCU and the Nation's Schools: An Action Program for Excellence and Opportunity in Education (1983)
—AASCU's Showcase for Excellence: Developing Models to Enhance the Teaching Profession (1984)
—Governance of State Colleges and Universities: Achieving Institutional Mission (1984)

In June, 1985, AASCU reprinted the Report on the Committee on Government and Higher Education, *The Efficiency of Freedom,* first issued in 1959. A virtual declaration of independence for trustees, administrators, and faculty members of state colleges and universities that seemed to be continually beleaguered by expanding state governmental bureaucracies, the findings of the Committee are as germane to the late 1980s as they were a quarter century ago: "must reading" in the future offices of every AASCU president and chancellor anxious about growing state intrusions on the management of institutional resources.

In 1974, with support from the Fund for Improvement of Postsecondary Education and the W. K. Kellogg Foundation, AASCU developed the Resource Center for Planned Change (now the AASCU Academic Affairs Resource Center) to institutionalize a systematic approach to future planning by AASCU members. The Center's services now encompass a summer institute for senior academic officers of Association members, two regional meetings and one national meeting each year for academic vice presidents, and workshops dealing with such topics as "Academic Personnel Administration" and "Changing Aspects of the Academic Mission." In addition, the Center publishes a newsletter for senior academic officers, *The Center Associate,* which provides a special forum for exchanging ideas about new dimensions in academic policy making and innovation.

During the past decade, AASCU has been particularly effective in functioning as steward for the idea that public postsecondary institutions bear a special responsibility for broadening opportunities for minorities in higher education. Early in its history, AASCU directed public and professional attention to the fact that minorities were seriously underrepresented in public four-year institutions. By means of conferences, workshops, and publications, the Association urged that "equity" and "opportunity" be co-equal in institutional priorities with "excellence" and "quality," so that catch phrases like "program quality" not be permitted to become code words for inequality of opportunity. "Excellence" and "equity," said an AASCU policy statement in 1984, are two sides of the same coin.

A 1985 AASCU study of *Minorities and Higher Education* was widely quoted in the media and quickly became the baseline analysis for critical questions that national and state administrations will be facing in 1986 and beyond. The study provided the general public and the press with valuable insights into the problem of coping with declining enrollment of minority populations in four-year institutions and future societal and educational implications resulting from such a drop-off.

A final illustration of significant AASCU service as a "steward" is in international education, where the Association's commitment has made a significant difference in the education of literally millions of students.

Since its inception, AASCU has stressed the field of international education. The post World-War II years had introduced a period of decolonization in Africa, Asia, and Latin America, and an attendant expansion of educational provisions (opportunities) for millions of young people and adults. Technological advances and communications breakthroughs began to shrink the world in terms of time and distance between neighbors and to increase the human interactions and relationships among nations. Future leaders in higher education joined the Peace Corps, participated in technical assistance projects in lesser developed countries, and began to understand the challenges and opportunities of international cooperation and completion. American society at large began to feel the effects of global interdepedence as it demonstrated against the conflict in Southeast Asia, waited impatiently in gasoline lines, and watched world events on its living room television sets. It had become obvious that higher education had an important role to play to prepare future generations for the complex world of tomorrow.

As early as 1966, the AASCU Board of Directors had formally proposed at the annual meeting to "increase AASCU member involvement in international activities." This set the course for 20 years of solid achievement in this field. An AASCU Committee on International Programs was established and through the years developed a series of three major goals to guide the work of the association and its members. They are: internationalizing the curriculum and the campus; involving the AASCU institutional resource base in international development; and influencing policies and priorities of federal, state, private and international agencies.

The activities of the committee have been directed by ongoing assessment of the needs of member institutions. The first study of its kind was conducted by Fred Harcleroad and Alfred Kilmartin in 1966. In subsequent years, AASCU undertook and published a series of surveys that recorded the accomplishments of member institutions in international education. These included a 1977 volume on *International and Intercultural Education in Selected State Colleges and Universities.*

A 1981/83 edition of *Internationalizing the Curriculum and the Campus* and a 1983 analysis of cost effective strategies for campus reform titled, *Without a Nickel.*

In reviewing these studies, one is struck by the variety of strategies used by colleges and universities to express their commitment to international education. The Washington-based Office of International Programs is designed to serve the institutional members of AASCU and does so by an equally diverse set of activities based on such policy statements as the "International Responsibility of Higher Education," first adopted by the membership in 1975 and most recently expressed in the 1984 document, *Guidelines: Incorporating an International Dimension in Colleges and Universities.* Campus-based and campus-directed activities, however, lie at the core of the association's projects.

Among the most influential of its projects are the overseas professional missions of presidents and chancellors to explore potential linkages with institutions of higher learning in other countries, leading to opportunities for the internationalization of the respective campuses. Since 1975, these missions have taken hundreds of presidents of AASCU institutions to the People's Republic of China (1975, 1981, 1984); Taiwan (1976, 1978, 1980, 1981, 1982, 1983, 1984); Argentina (1977, 1981); Egypt/Greece (1978); Cuba (1978, 1980); Mexico (1979); Israel (1980); Poland (1980, 1982); India (1980); Quebec (1981); Colombia (1982); France (1982); the Philippines (1983); Brazil (1983); Nigeria (1984); Korea (1984); Thailand (1984); Indonesia (1985); Japan (1985); Malaysia (1986); and Italy (1986).

As a result of these missions, AASCU has signed cooperation agreements with a large number of higher education agencies in Europe, Latin America, Asia and Africa. The importance of the missions lies, however, in the development of international contacts, exchanges, and experience that accrue to the individual institutions participating in the mission program.

TABLE 3
AASCU Missions 1975–1986

Mexico	November, 1970
Mexico	February 1972
India	May 1972
Malaysia	August 1974
People's Republic of China	April 1975
Taiwan	September 1976

Argentina	December 1977
Egypt/Greece	April 1978
Taiwan	June 1978
Cuba	December 1978
Mexico	November 1979
Israel	February 1980
Poland	April 1980
Taiwan	April 1980
Cuba	October 1980
Taiwan	October 1980
Argentina	December 1980
People's Republic of China	May 1981
Quebec	October 1981
Taiwan	January 1982
Colombia	April 1982
Taiwan	July 1982
France	September 1982
Poland	October 1982
Philippines	March 1983 (postponed)
Taiwan	April 1983
Brazil	April 1983
Nigeria	February 1984 (postponed)
Korea	June 1984
Thailand	June 1984
People's Republic of China	June 1984
Indonesia	October 1984
Japan	March 1985
Malaysia	October 1985
Italy	April 1986 (postponed)

AASCU institutions have also hosted reciprocal delegations from other nations which come to the United States to explore linkage with member institutions. The AASCU Office of International Programs serves, in these instances, as a liaison mechanism to appropriate AASCU institutions.

The professional development of administrators, faculty and directors of campus international programs has been a continuing effort of AASCU. The Association has sponsored conferences, workshops, and seminars on international education exploring such topics as funding international programs, corporate collegiate cooperation in international education, innovations in curriculum development, and interinstitutional linkages and exchange.

Useful publications have often resulted from these conferences, including *The International Funding Guide: Resources for International Activities at Colleges and Universities* (1985) and *International Education in the Global Marketplace* (1986). These publications are part of an association practice alerting AASCU member institutions to new developments in international education. The Office of International Programs also publishes an *International Memo* as an insert to the AASCU *Memo to the President* which gives member institutions information regarding grants and fellowship opportunities, innovative international programs on AASCU campuses, recent publications, international meetings, and pending federal and state legislation bearing on international education, funding and policies.

The Association also provides opportunities for students at AASCU institutions. In the 1970s, AASCU exerted national leadership in the development of regional international centers within its membership to encourage student exchanges with Europe, Canada, and Latin America. In recent years, AASCU has administered a scholarship program sponsored by the Taiwanese Ministry of Education for AASCU students to study Chinese language and culture at the Mandarin Training Center at National Taiwan University.

Throughout AASCU's history, institutions and faculty members have been involved in international development activities. To support these initiatives on the campus, AASCU has undertaken development projects which utilize the vast institutional resource base within its membership. Through the Consortium for International Cooperation in Higher Education (CICHE), of which AASCU is a founding member, a number of international projects have involved administrators, faculty and institutions. These development projects include: English professorships in the People's Republic of China; interinstitutional linkages in Asia, Africa, the Middle East and Latin America; international graduate student placement from Botswana, Pakistan, and Nigeria; a junior faculty development program supported by the Agency for International Development; and a development education program which involves some 30 member institutions.

The cooperative programs with CICHE illustrate the close working relationships that the Association has developed within the higher education community at home and abroad.

Future priorities for AASCU's involvement in international education will continue to be directed by membership needs as reflected by the work of the 25–member Committee on International Programs. Their activities will also reflect the changing educational needs of a world becoming increasingly interdependent, interactive and competitive.

*AASCU as Leader.

As was indicated earlier, there are no clear lines of demarcation between partnership, stewardship, and leadership; assignment of AASCU endeavors and activities to any of those three categories is, at best, an arbitrary method of contemplating the "early maturity" period of the Association's development. Thus, "leadership" in one era of a project may shift to "stewardship" in another, with "partnership" characterizing both. Nonetheless, AASCU's function "as leader" has highlighted the Association's record over the past decade.

In 1970, for example, AASCU took the lead in challenging certain aspects of the American Association of University Professors' traditional position with respect to policies governing academic freedom and academic tenure. At its Annual Meeting in San Antonio that year, AASCU decided—after an extended debate within its own membership, and with representatives of the AAUP—that policy statements dealing with academic freedom and academic tenure, to be truly valid, had to include references to the *responsibilities* faculty members must assume toward their students, toward one another, and toward their institutions. This debate marked the first time in over three decades that an institution-based association had successfully challenged the traditional AAUP position. Academic *responsibility* brought a constructive new dimension to the concepts of academic freedom and academic tenure at AASCU institutions.

Several years before the 1984–85 spate of national critiques centering on "issues of quality" in U.S. higher education, AASCU sponsored the Academic Planning and Evaluation Project (APEP), bringing together representatives of a dozen member institutions to develop curricular revisions and improvements in general education programs. The APEP experience led to an "involvement in learning", in which students and faculty members in participating institutions anticipated the "value-added" approach to the assessment of undergraduate education publicized by the National Institute of Education Higher Education Study Group in its landmark 1984 report.

AASCU was the first major association to establish networks of urban-based and rural-based state colleges and universities. The Association pioneered in the field of international education, education for the allied health professions, and the study of state systems of higher education. It developed strong relationships between the academic and business communities and led the way among public sector associations in holding fund-raising workshops for AASCU members and in the sponsoring conferences focused on resource development activities.

In the field of teacher education, AASCU was quick to respond to the challenges posed by *A Nation at Risk,* the U.S. Department of Education's 1983 study of America's schools. With AASCU institutions responsible for the undergraduate education of over 50 percent of the teachers certified annually in the United States, the Association's Board of Directors authorized the establishment of a Task Force on Excellence in Education; its charge was to develop an action program for AASCU members as they moved to strengthen teacher preparation and to improve teacher competence. In November 1983, the Task Force recommended to the Annual Meeting, and the membership approved, a policy statement and companion action program calling on the governing boards, administrative officers, and faculties of AASCU institutions to re-evaluate and revitalize programs for the preparation of teachers by giving top priority to the recruitment of talented students into the teaching profession.

In 1984, again on the recommendation of the Task Force, AASCU instituted its "Showcase for Excellence" Awards, designed to develop program models to enhance the teaching profession. At the 1985 annual meeting of the Education Commission of the States in Philadelphia, 17 program winners in the Association's institutional "Showcase for Excellence" were announced. The Awards project drew 83 nominees in its first year and was the subject of a special AASCU booklet published in 1986. In addition, the project will be continued for AASCU members during ensuing years. A new feature of the AASCU 1986 "Showcase Awards" included citations by the Association to the chief executives of three states which, in the 1983–86 period, did the most to strengthen education at all levels, with particular attention to the development and support of policies and programs designed to strengthen teacher preparation and enhance teacher performance. ECS and other organizations concerned with the need for improvements in the nation's educational system have widely praised AASCU for its leadership in the development of the "Showcase Awards" competition among its member institutions.

AASCU presidents and chancellors, responding to survey questions on proposed AASCU goals and objectives for the last half of the 1980s, placed two at the top of the list: to "reinforce the value of public higher education" and to "establish the national identity of state colleges and universities."

Accordingly, under the aegis of it's Committee on External Relations, the Association embarked on a three-year public-information program designed to sharpen the identity of AASCU institutions in order to strengthen support from a wide range of constituencies. The "identity issue" has consistently ranked high in recent years as AASCU members have grown more comprehensive in scope and more diverse in the publics they serve.

In another effort to strengthen its leadership role in public higher education, AASCU commemorated its Silver Jubilee Year with a successor to the Morse Commission of 15 years ago—the National Commission on the Role and Future of State Colleges and Universities, headed by the Hon. Terrel H. Bell, former U. S. Secretary of Education. The Silver Jubilee Commission was concerned with the question of how higher education and AASCU institutions in particular will respond over the next decade to emerging dramatic changes in American society: the growth in minority populations, accelerated obsolescence of job skills, increase in older part-time students, utilization of technology to enhance the teacher/learning process, and the need to add a greater international dimension to the undergraduate curriculum. The Commission report in November, 1986, identified the special functions AASCU institutions fulfill in American society and helped chart their course for the years immediately ahead.

Since AASCU's founding, its Board of Directors has asked itself every three years, "If this Association did not exist, would we invent it?" The Association's growth from 1961 to 1986, both in numbers and in stature, attests to the fact that all along the "prologue years" the membership has answered in a ringing affirmative.

CHAPTER 6*

Finance: A Special AASCU Concern

The member institutions of AASCU have always been low in cost to their students—and to their state constituents. Low or no tuition has made it possible, as a result, for millions of AASCU students to profit from higher education. The problems of financing public state colleges and universities have a special importance in any assessment of their future, thus, this chapter considers the entire background and problems of finance in higher education as well as those aspects critical to AASCU students and their institutions.

The investment made by state governments in higher education— an investment that has continued to grow throughout this century—is predicated on the notion that higher education benefits not only the individual, but the whole fabric of society.

These words of Thomas Jefferson are among the first in a long history of governmental encouragement, development, and enhancement of educational opportunities in the United States: "If a Nation expects to be ignorant and free in a state of civilization, it expects what never was and never will be . . . If we are to guard against ignorance and remain free, it is the responsibility of every American to be informed." Simply, stated, it is government's responsibility to provide citizens with the opportunity to expand their knowledge—to open the doors to advanced learning of all people.

In more recent years, Howard Bowen, a noted scholar on the philosophy and costs of American Education helped to explain the reasoning behind this public policy by defining more clearly the benefits that higher education provides for the nation and society. These benefits include:

---

*This chapter is based on a report prepared for AASCU by Scott Miller, Consultant on Economics of Higher Education.

- The advancement of knowledge, including the preservation of cultural heritage, the discovery of new knowledge, and the satisfactions of living in a world of advancing knowledge.
- The discovery and encouragement of talent.
- The advancement of social welfare, including economic efficiency and growth, enhancement of national prestige and power, progress toward solving social problems, positive improvement in social values and behavior, and progress toward social equality.
- The avoidance of negative outcomes for society (Bowen, 55–58).

The mission of providing access of higher education is more than just another of society's many responsibilities to its citizenry; it is an *investment* in that society's future, an *investment* in the talent and promise of the next generation. By investing in its own future, society, government, and all of the Nation's people can rest assured that the returns they receive will be many times greater than their initial outlays. Some of these returns can be judged in tangible ways—and this chapter will explore those ways—but others cannot be assigned a convenient price tag and weighed according to cost/benefit ratios or prevailing theories of economic returns.

As America stood on the threshold of the information age, President John Fitzgerald Kennedy alerted the nation that its very future rested in the hands of the young and, in turn, on the ability of these young people to gain access to higher education. JFK spoke of an "aristocracy of achievement arising out of a democracy of opportunity."

But whose responsibility is it to provide this access and to preserve the nation's future? The argument can be made that is a uniquely federal duty because, after all, it is our national government that is the defender of our society and of its democratic goals and constitution. Or, is it the states' responsibility? After all, aren't the states already responsible for elementary and secondary education, and haven't the states been responsible for creating and maintaining the bulk of higher education in this nation?

In 1947, President Truman's Commission on Higher Education was charged with defining the proper federal role in promoting access to higher education. According to the Commission's final report:

> The role . . . proposed for the federal government is that of a partner—a partner jointly responsible with states and localities for attaining the goals for higher education in a democracy (President's Commission, p. 63)

Today, we see this partnership in all aspsects of higher education finance. In examining the ways in which colleges support themselves, we find an intermingling of federal, state, student, parent, and philanthropic dollars. While federal student assistance programs have been designed to support the many, state policies are more attuned to the needs of each individual constituency—programs designed for laid-off auto or steel workers, programs to serve single parents, and programs to assist non-traditional students.

More than one-fourth of all college students today attend AASCU-type state-supported colleges and universities. Many of these students attend these schools because they represent an affordable alternative to high-cost private colleges and universities. Others choose these or other public colleges because of the excellent education they provide and the wide-range of facilities and course offerings that can be found on public college campuses. While numbers are difficult to come by, it is evident that public colleges serve more low-income and minority students than do their private counterparts; for untold number of students, public colleges provide the only avenue enabling them to take advantage of higher education opportunities.

Low tuition has been a cornerstone of public higher education since its inception. Today, public college tuitions are, on average, nearly $5,000 less than those at private colleges. Projections are that college costs will continue to rise throughout the remainder of this decade and that the gap between public and private college costs will widen.

The need to continue and strengthen this investment in people through low tuition has never been greater. As federal assistance to students lags behind inflation, the financial pressures of attending college will continue to mount. More and more students will be forced to forego college opportunities because they or their parents simply cannot afford its costs. By resisting the pressures for short-term gain through increased state college revenues and maintaining their commitments to low tuition, state governments will ensure that their long-term commitments to educational opportunity are investments that will pay off handsomely for many years to come.

Today, families face a greater challenge in meeting college costs than ever before. Despite their relatively modest tuition and fee charges, four years of education at a public college can total more than $20,000—about half the cost of four years of private college education. The vast majority of American families cannot meet these costs through their current discretionary income; once families have paid for life's necessities—food, clothing, shelter, transportation—and have put a little something aside for their retirement, they simply do not have enough of their current income left to pay for college. This applies to parents trying to give their children the opportunities that college offers as well as to "nontraditional" students trying to work their own financial way through college.

Given past performance and expected economic trends, it is almost certain that college costs will continue to climb and, consequently, families will be challenged to an even greater degree to meet the cost. It is difficult over time to control general economic inflation and its effects on the indirect costs of college attendance, but there is room now to put the brakes on rapid rises in tuition and fees—the direct costs of education.

Public colleges have succeeded to some degree in holding the line on cost increases. Over the past ten years, average charges for tuition and fees, room, and board at public colleges and universities have increased at a slower rate than the Consumer Price Index (CPI)—a measure of national economic inflation. During this time frame, the increases in the costs of private college education have outpaced the CPI.

Different Approaches

As budgetary pressures have mounted in Washington, D.C., and the federal government has begun to reduce its support for many domestic spending programs, states are facing increasing pressures to balance their own budgets without raising taxes. This, in turn, has resulted in calls for increased "user fees"—charges for the use of various public services, including parks, museums, recreational facilities, and educational services. Higher education, in the thick of this budget battle, has been expected to finance a growing portion of its operations with increased user fees—in this case higher college tuition and fees.

Pressure resulting from reduced federal support has been compounded by the desire of many states to upgrade the quality of the education they offer. Upgrading would include raising faculty salaries in an effort to recruit and retain highly qualified teachers and administrators, and beginning new initiatives to purchase or update equipment and facilities in order to keep pace with the demand for "high-tech" training and research.

States have a number of choices in determining just how to establish the tuition level at public colleges and universities. Perhaps the most frequently employed basis for tuition-setting is a formula-based

approach, such as defining a certain percentage of the cost of instruction that must be covered by tuition revenues. Under such a formula,
tuition costs rise in proportion to increases in the total "institutional"
or "educational" costs. In other words, if a college's operating costs
rise by ten percent in a given fiscal year, then tuition as well as state
appropriations would be raised by ten percent in order to cover the
next year's shortfall. The use of such a formula virtually guarantees
that tuition levels will grow at a steady rate. As faculty salaries rise, as
energy costs increase, and as new programs are begun to enhance
educational quality, tuition will have to be increased in order to
maintain a constant share of educational costs.

Another common method used for setting tuition rates is to peg the
amount students pay in tuition to their academic level. In other
words, juniors and seniors may pay higher tuition than freshmen and
sophomores, and graduate students are asked to pay even higher
costs. This is a widespread method for determining tuition levels; for
example, most community college students pay less than their four-
year counterparts in the same state. It may also be used in conjunction
with other formulas whereby lower-classmen pay a smaller proportion of the costs of instruction than upper-classmen or whereby
graduate students pay a higher proportion of the cost of instruction
than do undergraduates.

The final common method for determining tuition levels is to treat
tuition as a "user fee" for services rendered. When this logic is
employed in setting tuition, it is usually in conjunction with rhetoric
tying tuition revenues to a plan to close a gap in the state's fiscal
budget. When the state's budget deficit needs pruning, tuition may be
looked upon as a readily available source of income. It is, in some
quarters, a more palatable method for reducing the deficit than a tax
increase because it is a specific charge levied on those using a particular service rather than a levy imposed on all citizens (i.e., voters) in the
state.

States in recent years seemed to find a great many reasons to justify
tuition increases and to couch these in terms that make them seem a
necessary cost of doing business. In today's climate of budget restric-
tions, a tendency toward smaller governments, and resistence to
higher taxes, it takes vision, courage, and determination to buck the
trend and state the case for low-tuition. Those who founded public
colleges and conceived the idea of free public education were responding to the need for as many citizens as possible to avail themselves of higher education opportunities. Without economic assist-

ance in the form of low-tuition, America would be in danger of becoming a two-tiered society, a vision which our founding fathers had rejected.

Investing in Low Tuition

Why have AASCU-member institutions selected a path of low-tuition? Why continue to subsidize educational costs? There are many becauses: higher education is a good investment; states have historically been assigned the responsibility for educating their citizens; low-tuition is the key to overcoming the economic barriers that stand in the way of the educational aspirations of many American families; and because, as will be seen in this chapter, America may once again be heading down a path that leads to a severe division between the educated and the outcast. Let us begin by tracing the origins and development of one public investment in higher education, built originally upon a foundation of low tuition.

The City University of New York

In the 1830s, only about 250 of New York City's half million residents were enrolled in college (Rothbard, p. 31). Social reformers of the time saw a great inequity in that situation and came together to propose that the city establish a free college system that could serve all the people of the city.

Debate raged for ten years over the wisdom of establishing a "free academy" within the city's confines. Finally, in 1847, the New York State legislature adopted a measure that would put the question of the free academy before the voters of New York City. Thirty days later the voters approved the academy's creation and its policy of free tuition.

Those who argued against the free academy had claimed that such an institution would place a great burden on the city's finance, that it would provide education to those who were not worthy, and that it would cause great harm to the already established private colleges. In response to this charge, the *Evening Mirror* newspaper editorialized:

> We do not see how any intelligent man can oppose a plan like that of the Free Academy. Some are afraid it will injure Columbia College and the University . . . but if those institutions rest upon as ticklish a foundation as to be upset by such a rival, the sooner they are got rid of the better (Rothbard, p. 31).

Seventeen years later, the academy changed its name to the College of the City of New York. Over the century, the college grew into the City University of New York (CUNY, including two-year and four-year colleges, graduate centers, and medical school.)

By 1975, however, the CUNY Board of Higher Education succumbed to budgetary pressures from both the State and City of New York and voted to impose tuition for the first time. Although this tuition increase was accompanied by promises that students would be spared financial hardship through the existing state and federal financial aid programs, enrollment at CUNY dropped by 70,000 students in the three years following the imposition of tuition—no mere coincidence.

By imposing tuition, CUNY had taken a major step towards undoing its reputation for open access and opportunity. Where once all New Yorkers were assured that they could take advantage of the higher education opportunities offered by CUNY, now they had to be concerned with their ability to pay for the chance to better themselves. This was especially true among the thousands of students who attended school on a part-time basis. Many of these students were shut out of traditional sources of financial assistance, which are generally intended for full-time students, and thus were faced with insurmountable financial barriers to pursuing higher education. Several graduates of CUNY have been awarded Nobel prizes and have stated that they could not have attended without "free tuition."

Declining Participation

There is no way around it, families are finding it more and more difficult these days to pay for college. All of the available information points to the fact that low-income and minority students are not attending college at the rate that many had hoped and, it has been noted, their rate of attendance has been declining in recent years.

Why, when there are more dollars of student aid—federal, state, and private—available to students than ever before, when colleges are taking aggressive measures to recruit students and to fill their classrooms, and when there has been an increasing classroom emphasis on preparing students for college-level work, does it appear that a significant portion of the American public is opting not to pursue a college degree? The answer may be found in simple economics: going to college is just too expensive for many American families.

Throughout the 1980s, the rate at which black students attend college has been steadily declining. Overall, the proportion of "college-age" blacks who attended college dropped 18 percent from 1979 to 1984. As dramatic as these numbers are, they pale in comparison to the statistics on the participation rate of blacks whose families earn less than $10,000 per year. The participation rate for these low income blacks fell from approximately 33 percent in 1979 to nearly 23 percent in 1984—a decline of 29 percent in their rate of participation. At four-year public colleges, the participation rate of black students fell by more than 18 percent over this same period—a rate slightly lower than the overall decline, but still very disturbing. For comparison's sake, it should be noted that the participation rate for whites actually increased by nearly eight percent between 1979 and 1984. The participation rate for the lowest income whites, however, remained unchanged. (Applied Systems Institute, p. 55).

This evidence is reinforced by the findings from an AASCU-sponsored survey of student aid recipients in the 1983–84 school year. Data showed a considerable decline in the number and proportion of black students receiving financial aid at public colleges. In the report, *Student Aid and Public Higher Education: Recent Changes*, Dr. Jacob Stampen of the University of Wisconsin reported that in the 1983–84 academic year over 60,000 fewer minority students received financial aid at public colleges than in the 1981–82 academic year. In 1981–82, 32 percent of all need-based student aid recipients at public colleges were minority students; by 1983–84, that proportion had dropped to under 29 percent. Over this period, the total number of aid recipients remained stable (approximately 1.9 million students. Stampen, 1985).

Because these figures cover only students who received need-based financial aid, one can safely assume that most are from low or modest income families. In the years between 1981–82 and 1983–84, in fact, the rules for receiving financial aid were altered so that aid was more targeted on lower income students and their families. Certainly there is no evidence to suggest that minority families, as a group, became more affluent during this period and were no longer eligible for assistance. The only logical explanation for this phenomenon is a drop in the number of minority students applying for aid. It is apparent that the availability of federal, state, and private financial assistance was not enough to encourage increasing numbers of minority students to enter college and to apply for financial aid.

Family Purchasing Power

For most American families, each year represents a continuing battle against inflation and a struggle to maintain their present standard of living. Most economic statistics indicate that during the late 70s and on into the 80s, most families have been losing these battles and seeing their purchasing power decline.

While family income has risen modestly during this period, it has not risen fast enough to outdo the negative effects of general economic inflation.

The following chart illustrates the effect that inflation, as measured by the Consumer Price Index (CPI), has had on the median family income of American families:

Median Family Income in 1983
Constant Dollars for Selected Years, by Race

Year	All Families	White	Black	Spanish Oriented
1974	$26,062	$27,084	$16,172	$19,271
1976	26,177	27,190	16,174	17,953
1978	26,989	28,103	16,645	19,226
1980	25,438	26,504	15,336	17,806
1982	24,136	25,341	14,006	16,715
1983	24,580	25,757	14,506	16,956
1974–1983	−5.7%	−4.9%	−10.3%	−12.0%

Source: 1984 Statistical Abstract of the United States; U.S. Census Bureau

These data show that overall, the median family income of all Americans declined by 5.7 percent between 1974 and 1983 (when adjusted for inflation.) But the data also indicate that the effect of inflation has been even more acute among minority families; the median income for Black families fell by more than ten percent and the median income of families of Spanish origin dipped by 12 percent, while the median income of whites fell by less than five percent. In other words, minority families have lost more than ten percent of the purchasing power of their income; their earnings are ten percent less today than in 1974.

Families are not alone in losing the battle with inflation. Federal student aid programs also failed to keep pace with rising costs and, as a result, their value has shrunk. Between 1978 and 1983, the average Pell Grant increased by 13 percent; however, over this same time frame, the CPI rose by 57 percent. The value of Pell Grants was being steadily eroded by inflation; in 1983 the average Pell Grant could purchase only about two-thirds of the education that it could purchase in 1978.

The lowest income families, those who qualify for Pell Grants, are faced with locating alternative sources in order to fill in this gap in purchasing power. As will be discussed below, the implications for the newly emerging patterns of family financing raise a great deal of concern about the ability of low-income individuals to continue to have access to college.

Increasing Costs

Amidst these declines in the value of personal income, the costs of college have climbed at a steady rate over the past ten years. The American Council on Education recently predicted that the total costs of attending a public college will have doubled between the 1977–78 and 1987–89 academic years—a somewhat faster rate than the CPI's growth (Henderson, pp. 4–5).

There are two basic elements to the total cost of attending college: tuition and fees, and room, board and other personal expenses. Of these two elements, tuition and fees have been—and are projected to continue—rising at a faster rate. Although inflation has taken its toll on the ability of families to pay for college by pushing up the costs of food, shelter, transportation, and other basic necessities, tuition costs have caused the greatest strain on family budgets. At the start of the 1985–86 academic year, public colleges tuition and fees averaged $1,044 at public colleges as compared to $6,105 at private colleges. (Henderson, p. 4). While public colleges costs will have increaed by 100 percent between 1977–78 and 1987–88, costs at private colleges will rise by 128 percent over this same period (Henderson, p. 5). Nonetheless, neither collegiate sector provides any substantial relief for American families.

Average Undergraduate Tuition and Fee Charges by Sector

Academic Year	Public Colleges	Private Colleges
1977–78	$ 515	$2,604
1978–79	548	2,843
1979–80	586	3,089
1980–81	636	3,466
1981–82	713	3,935
1982–83	805	4,428
1983–84	895	4,897
1984–85	967	5,293
1985–86	1,044	5,706

Source: American Council on Education

This combination of rising college costs and the decreasing value of student aid, especially grant aid, is leaving low-income and minority students behind. In order to avoid the prospect of future indebtedness, more and more low-income and minority high school graduates are foregoing their college plans.

The secret to encouraging these young people to attend college is to reduce the need to borrow—to lower the gap between total college expenses and proportion of costs met through grant assistance. This can be accomplished by two complementary means: increase the amount of grant aid available to these students and lower or hold the line on tuition costs. Even if tuition costs remain constant, low-income and minority students will still be losing the battle to pay for college because of inflationary increases in such nontuition expenses as food, shelter, and transportation. Thus, it is essential that federal and state grant assistance be increased at a rate that is at least equal to increases in general economic inflation.

In effect, state governments are faced with trade-offs: if they raise tuition levels, then they must raise grant support in order to maintain the same degree of access; if they lower tuition levels, on the other hand, they can keep aid programs funded at the same level and still keep pace with inflation. In either case, there clearly must be two sides to any policy that is designed to promote or maintain access to higher education.

Borrowing to Pay for College

As college costs have continued to rise, American families have had to alter their ways of paying for college. In the middle and late 1970s, low-income families could count on government-sponsored grant assistance to pay a substantial portion of college costs. But, as noted earlier, the value of these grant dollars has fallen sharply over the past decade. In 1977–78, the maximum Pell Grant of $1,600 could meet about one-half of the average costs of a year in college. In 1985–86, despite an increase in the maximum grant to $2,100, a full Pell Grant meets only about one-third of the average cost of attendance.

A dramatic shift in how families meet college costs has already taken place. In 1975–76, more than 80 percent of the financial aid received by undergraduates was in the form of grants; only 17 percent of this aid was made up of loans; the remaining percentage was in Work-Study aid. By 1984–85, loans had become the dominant form of student assistance; 52 percent of all student aid was in the form of student borrowing, while grants made up about 45 percent of the aid received by college students (Gillespie, 1985).

Borrowing by college students has been rising steadily. The dollar value of the Guaranteed Student Loans secured by college students is soaring, despite changes that have made it more difficult to qualify for GSLs. In 1977–78, students secured approximately $1.7 billion in Guaranteed Student Loans; for 1985–86 that total is expected to reach $8.3 billion, five times the 1977–78 amount. College costs have not risen that much in the same period, but the gap between families' resources and the grant aid they may receive has! GSLs, of course, are only one of many federally sponsored student loan programs. An additional $1.5 billion in loans is secured by undergraduate and graduate students and their families through the National Direct Student Loan, and Health Education Assistance Loan programs. Today, 60 cents of every federal dollar spent on student aid goes toward the support of student loan programs (mostly in the form of subsidy payments to students and lenders.)

Even the lowest income collge students must borrow in order to meet the costs of college. A recent examination of the AASCU-sponsored survey of students who received financial aid in the 1983–84 academic year revealed that students who received aid at public colleges met at least half of their college costs through a combination of contributions from family resources, student earnings, and borrowing. Grant assistance generally covered no more than half of the college expenses for students whose families earned less than $15,000; there is no "free ride" for these students! (Miller et al., 1985).

Among independent students whose family incomes were under $7,500 per year, about 17 percent secured Guaranteed Student Loans. These loans averaged nearly $2,000 per year for students at this income level who attended public colleges. As income rises, a higher proportion of students use loans, especially GSLs, to help meet the costs of college. Grants only meet about one-third to one-quarter of a middle-income student's college costs; their family incomes are too high to make them eligible for most grant programs. As would be expected, a higher proportion of middle-income families borrow in order to pay for college. More than half of the dependent student aid recipients at public colleges whose family incomes were between $25,000 and $35,000 per year secured Guaranteed Student Loans in 1983–84.

Additional evidence of the link between borrowing and educational cost is found in the Department of Education's *High School and Beyond* study. This survey, which looked at the financial aid records of students who entered college immediately after high school graduation showed that students who attended low-cost schools—where tuition was less then $1,000—were the least likely to borrow, regardless of their family income level. Conversely, those who attended schools where tuitions were set at more than $3,000 per year were the most likely to borrow—more than half of these students took out loans regardless of their family's income (USDE, 1985, p. 32). The following chart summarizes this information:

Proportion of 1980 High School Graduates Entering Postsecondary Schools Immediately Following Graduation Who Received a Loan: Spring 1982

	Proposed Securing Loans		
Family Income	<$12,000	$12,000–$24,999	$25,000+
Tuition			
Less than $1,000	18.3%	20.8%	15.4%
$1,000–2,999	41.5%	47.2%	39.4%
$3,000 or more	59.3%	68.8%	51.3%

Source: U.S. Department of Education, National Center for Education Statistics, *High School and Beyond*

This chart clearly illustrates that those students fortunate enough to attend low-cost institutions are much less likely to borrow than their counterparts at high-cost schools. Students from the lowest income families, those with annual incomes below $12,000 per year, are more than three times as likely to borrow if they attend a high-cost school than if they choose a low-cost college. This three-to-one ratio holds up for students for all income levels. In all cases, if a student attends a high-cost college he or she is more likely to borrow than not, i.e., a majority of students at all income levels who attend high-cost schools use loans to help meet college costs.

A great deal of evidence supports the notion that low-tuition encourages college attendance and helps afford postsecondary opportunities to those who otherwise might not attend college. A review of some of the statistics regarding college students reveals the crucial role that low-cost, public colleges play in providing education opportunities.

In 1984, about 53 percent of all full-time college students were enrolled in four-year public colleges and universities. An additional 20 percent were attending two-year colleges, for a total of nearly 75 percent. A similar percentage of black college students were enrolled in public colleges in 1984, as were approximately 77 percent of all Hispanic students. For most Americans, and especially for members of minority groups, public colleges are more often than not the place where they can have access to higher education (Applied Systems Institute).

An analysis of data describing those students who received Pell Grants at public colleges also sheds light on the types of students served by this sector. In 1983–84, for example, approximately 75 percent of all students in the traditional collegiate sector who received Pell Grants attended public colleges (both two- and four-year). Among self-supporting students—who generally have minimal incomes and who are in many cases older, nontraditional students— over 80 percent of those receiving Pell Grants in collegiate settings were attending public colleges. In 1983–84, about 84 percent of all self-supporting student receiving Pell Grants had annual incomes of less than $9,000 (USDE Report, 1985).

Pell Grant recipients are usually the neediest of all college students. The average family income for all Pell Grant recipients attending public colleges in 1983–84 was about $9,300, approximately $1,000 less than the comparable figure for private college Pell recipients. The rules governing the Pell program generally restrict the number of recipients at low-cost schools by establishing a maximum percentage of educational costs that can be covered by the Pell Grant (currently 60 percent; in 1983–84 the figure was set at 50 percent of costs). Thus, in order to qualify for such a large portion of Pell Grant aid, students at public colleges would have to be considerably needier than their counterparts at higher cost institutions.

Low Tuition Assists Today's New College Students

The nature of the college student body has changed markedly over the past decade. More and more older students are attending the nation's colleges and universities—especially AASCU's institutions, and at an ever-increasing rate—supplementing "traditional" 18–24 year old college students. As the following table illustrates, a much greater proportion of the population over 25 years of age attended college in 1981 than in 1970:

Percentage Change in College Enrollment of Persons 14–34 Years of Age: 1981 and 1970

| | Percent Change: 1970–1981 | |
Age	Population	College Students
Total	30.9%	44.8%
14–17 years	−2.9%	−10.8%
18–19	16.6%	17.3%
20–21	36.7%	37.0%
22–24	31.8%	46.7%
25–29	47.4%	82.9%
30–34	63.3%	195.4%

Source: U.S. Census Bureau, Current Population Surveys

Obviously, there has been a dramatic shift in the college-going habits of persons 25 years of age and older. According to these Census Bureau data, persons between the ages of 30 and 34 are enrolling in college at three times their rate of growth as a proportion of the overall U.S. population. Persons between the ages of 25 and 29 have grown as a proportion of the college student body at twice the rate that would be expected given their growth in the overall population.

In 1981, students between the ages of 25 and 34 made up 29.9 percent of the college population as compared to 18.2 percent in 1970. This increase has been even more dramatic for women than for men students. In 1970, only 13.6 percent of the women enrolled in college were over the age of 25, while in 1981 that figure had more than doubled to 27.8 percent (U.S. Bureau of the Census, 1985).

These older students are not taking a traditional route through college, but are attending on a part-time basis. Nearly two-thirds of all those between the ages of 25 and 34 were part-time students in 1981. More than 82 percent of all students over 35 years of age attend college as part-timers. The majority of these older students are self-supporting, many are married, and a significant proportion have dependent children of their own.

Most of these students are not eligible for student financial assistance because they attend school part-time. Most federal aid is reserved for those who attend school half-time or more and only a handful of states have programs to assist part-time students. While recent proposals for expanding federal and state student aid programs to serve part-time students offer some rays of hope, the fact is that older, non-traditional students must rely on low tuition as their only readily available form of financial help in attending college. This is borne out by the fact that 42 percent of those 25–34 years old attend two-year colleges, which are generally less costly than four-year schools.

For many of these students tuition is just one of many costs in attending college. Transportation costs, reduced working hours, foregone income, and child care expenses can push the cost incurred by part-timers up to the levels normally associated with full-time enrollment. Without low tuition levels, many of these students would not be able to afford to attend school, to take advantage of retraining opportunities, or realize their hopes of completing a college degree—aspirations that could not be fulfilled immediately after graduating from high school.

Tuition and Access

This review of enrollment statistics presents compelling evidence of the role that low tuition plays in providing access to AASCU and other institutions. It is clear from these data that low-cost public colleges are not only educating the majority of those who attend college, but are serving an even higher proportion of those who may be considered to be economically disadvantaged.

A direct link between low tuition and educational access was established in the early 1970s in a study conducted at the University of Wisconsin (AASCU, 1985). The purpose of this study was to test the effects of lowering tuition on the enrollment behavior of students. It is one of the only studies in which an experimental design was used to test the role that tuition costs play in determining college attendances; in many ways the study was designed to be similar to a controlled laboratory experiment.

In 1973, the State of Wisconsin drastically reduced the tuition charges at two of its two-year colleges. At the same time, tuition remained constant at the state's other two- and four-year colleges. Tuition charges at the colleges in the study increased by 47 percent from $429 per year to $630 per year. After one year, enrollment at the two schools that had lowered their tuition charges increased by 47 percent and by 23 percent respectively. Based on these results, it was calculated that for every one percent decrease in tuition costs, enrollment rose by 1.3 percent—a very strong link between college costs and propensity to attend a given college. Further examinations of the students who enrolled because of the lower tuition charges revealed that it was indeed the low cost that spurred these students on to pursue postsecondary training and that, for the most part, they would not have attended college at all had it not been for the reduced costs. These students did not transfer from higher cost schools or from other University of Wisconsin institutions; rather, the low cost made higher education accessible to them for the first time.

Investing in Opportunities

There is no doubt that students who graduate from college absorb personal benefit from their educational experience. In a society that is rapidly changing from an industrial base to an information base, the need for better-educated, highly skilled workers is paramount. Those who do not have access to postsecondary opportunities simply fall behind in the race to better themselves and to raise their social and economic circumstance. In effect, low-tuition schools offer opportunities for self-improvement that otherwise would not be available. By investing in low tuition, state governments have, for the past 150 years, recognized the benefits of an educated citizenry and the need to unlock the doors of educational opportunity for all who can benefit from its services.

Despite their low-tuition policies, public colleges are not, by any means, monopolizing the market for college students. Private colleges serve a significant portion of college students and have held onto a constant share of college enrollment over the past ten years. For example, betwen 1977 and 1983, private four-year colleges increased their share of collegiate enrollments by approximately 1.5 percent; over the same period, enrollment at public colleges dipped by a very small count: 0.3 percent. In 1983, public four-year colleges enrolled 50.75 percent of students in the collegiate sector, while 22.91 percent of full-time undergraduates were enrolled at private four-year schools; the remainder were enrolled in two-year colleges.

The Return on the Investment

Judging the returns received on society's investment in higher education is no easy task. One cannot assume that every college graduate will contribute substantially to society as a result of his or her postsecondary experience. On the other hand, one cannot also assume that every person who does not enter college will become a drain on society, be unemployed, or become reliant on public assistance programs.

Additionally, one must resist the temptation to judge the returns on postsecondary investment solely in terms of dollars and cents. Investing in low-tuition and educational opportunity is not like investing in the stock market; the dividends received may come in nontangible ways—in the form of scientific advancement, artistic achievement, or self-improvement—and over many years. The very notion of trying to place a price tag on these items runs counter to the goals that society is trying to achieve by providing opportunities for higher learning. The value of the Nobel prizes received by graudates of CUNY, for example, is apparent by hard to quantify.

There is, of course, a great deal of evidence that a college education can bring with it some very substantial economic rewards—both to the individual and to society as a whole. Few economists would be willing to argue that college education does not produce monetary rewards. For example, Michael McPherson, a senior economic fellow, at the Brookings Institution has examined the returns on postsecondary education and concludes that there is enough economic evidence to justify continued government support of college opportunity. McPherson wonders, though, whether this is the yardstick by which the efficacy of government support for higher education should be measured:

> It is reassuring in a general way to know that much of our expenditure on education has an economic "payoff," and we would view teaching and research quite differently if we had reason to believe that no economic benefits flowed from them. Still an educational system geared single-mindedly to the maximization of economic benefits would be radically distorted from a social and educational point of view (McPherson, p. 35).

Dollars and Cents

In order to reassure those who are in need of tangible evidence that prove the economic return on investments in college opportunity, we present here the U.S. Census Bureau's estimates on the lifetime earnings of college graduates as compared to the estimates for those who terminate their educations at the high school level:

Lifetime Earnings and Level of Education

Sex	High School Graduates	Four-Year College Graduates
Male	$860,000–$1,870,000	$1,200,000–$2,750,000
Female	$380,000–$ 800,000	$ 520,000–$1,120,000

Source: U.S. Census Bureau

Obviously, both men and women can be expected to pay a great deal more in taxes as a result of their college educations. Male college graduates will return in the form of taxes nearly $8–10 for every dollar they received in tuition subsidies, while women, whose lifetime earnings are considerably lower than their male counterparts, still may return more than $3–5 in taxes for each dollar invested in low-tuition. From a cost/benefit viewpoint, maintaining low-tuition at AASCU and other public institutions makes a great deal of sense, and supports the "social-benefit" basic premises of the over four hundred low-tuition AASCU-type institutions over the past three hundred years.

This variety of facts and figures from numerous sources tell a rather simple tale: as a nation we are in grave danger of retreating from the policies of access to higher education that have been followed so successfully for the past century. In fact, this course was first charted by state-supported colleges nearly two-hundred years ago.

The warning signs are ominous. The rate at which minority and low-income students attend college is declining. The proportion of college costs must be met from out of the pockets of even the lowest income families is increasing. And, states and the federal government, under enormous financial pressures, are contemplating abandoning the low-tuition and student assistance policies that are the cornerstones of educational access in this nation.

As of 1986, we were faced with the prospect of creating an indentured class of college graduates—as well as those who do not complete their college educations but must still repay student loans. Combine this with an evergrowing proportion of the current generation of young people who are completely denied access to higher education and the prospects are that the United States will find it more and more difficult to produce the highly trained men and womanpower that will be necessary for this nation to maintain its competitive technological position in the world.

There is no doubt that free of low-tuition is a proven effective tool in promoting educational access. The University of Wisconsin's low-tuition study and the demographics of those who attend public colleges. The examination of the earnings power of college graduates as compared to those who end their educational careers at the high school level, and the extra revenue produced by taxing these earnings, testify to the efficiency of a low-tuition policy.

The terms "effective" and "efficient" are two of the reasons why states continue to invest in low tuition. After all, an effective, efficient investment should attract anyone who is wise with her or his money and is looking for the best return on the dollar.

But states are not alone in the struggle to promote educational access. Higher education in this nation is partnership—a compact between all of the beneficiaries of higher education. Parents and students are reaching deeper into their pockets than ever before to meet the rising costs of college. Students, themselves, are mortgaging their future earnings by going thousands and thousands of dollars into debt before they even reap the rewards of their educational experiences.

While states can hold the line on tuition increases, there is very little that they can do to stem the tide of general economic inflation which adds to the college bills of all students. The federal government has a responsibility to continue to expand its commitment to educational access that was enunciated so clearly in the Higher Education Act of 1965.

Most importantly, the foundation of student assistance, the Pell grant Program, should be expanded so that, at a minimum, a Pell Grant today covers the same proportion of educational costs that it did in 1973 (the first year of the program). It is only through this program that we can offer low-income students—those most in need of assistance—the opportunity to attend college without the dark cloud of debt hanging over their future.

These two goals—low-tuition and increased federal grant support—cannot be achieved without full cooperation between state and federal policymakers. If states hold the line on tuition, but federal grants lose the battle with inflation, then students and the cause of educational opportunity will be the ultimate loser.

Conversely, if Pell Grants rise and states increase their tuition in order to capture more of these federal dollars, then the states will be guilty of a breech of faith and will be in jeopardy of losing the aid that they currently receive—the political base for this grant support will have been shattered and the higher education community will have been outsmarted by its own greed.

A Struggle for the Future

Low tuition is an investment in the future. As Senator Kennedy so eloquently stated during the debate over reauthorizing the Higher Education Act of 1965, we are in a "struggle for the future."30 a struggle that can only be waged with armies of highly trained, highly able, and highly motivated troops who are adequately prepared to do battle in the information age.

In all quarters—scientific advancement, technological development, social and cultural enhancement, and our national security—there is, and will be, no substitute for a college-educated citizency. By opening the doors to educational access and by eliminating the economic barriers that prevent too many young people from pursuing higher educations, we are ensuring that the United States will be well-equipped to boldly step into the future. We cannot hope to win the coming battles if a large segment of our population is forced to sit on the sidelines.

The investment made today by state and federal governments is virtually risk-free—the returns will be great and will be counted for years to come. But, the losses sustained through short-sighted policies that close the doors on educational opportunity will be much greater and will have repercussions that can never be undone. In this case, the future of America is now!

CHAPTER 7

Prospects and Possibilities

Planning for the future is fraught with difficulty. Some serious errors in prediction in different areas illustrate this point, one from the distant past and two from more recent years. The first example, of science and technology, comes from the *New York Times*, which carried a story ridiculing the idea of human flight just one week before the Wright brothers made their first flight at Kitty Hawk. A second example, and one of many from the field of economics, occurred in 1978, when the major econometric models each forecast a major recession in 1979; none developed. A third, in the social sciences, shows even more graphically the problems inherent in social planning of all types, including higher education. In the late 1960s and early 1970s, the Commission on the Year 2000, led by Daniel Bell, attempted to anticipate developing social problems, design new social institutions, and devise options for choice in the next quarter-century. One of the participants has pointed out how wrong they were, basically because each major assumption on which their forecast was based turned out to be in error within a few years (Orlans, 1977, pp. 31–36).

With such total failures in mind, any predictions of the future development of over 400 different higher education institutions scattered through all the states must be approached gingerly.

Demography and Economics

Changing demographics have produced a significant change in the pool of potential college students, presaging a large—and probably needy—minority component. The birth rate among whites has dropped, while the rate among various minority groups has remained constant or risen. Poverty among this sector of the American population has not abated, but in fact continues to grow. The College Board has reported that one in five children in this country now lives below the poverty level. In 1973, the U.S. population below the poverty level stood at 11.1 percent. By 1983, it had grown to 15 percent. Minority groups have been hit especially hard, but the poverty level for whites also grew, from 6.6 to 9.6 percent during the decade. The need and desire for a college education is there for these young people of poor families, but the options are limited.

Because of the dropping birth rate and the economic changes that require job retraining, the average college student is becoming older. Although the number of 18–24 year-old college students dropped 2.6 percent in 1985, total college and university enrollment dipped just one percent—meaning that older students are taking up the slack.

The potential student pool is also becoming more and more urban. The rural student is almost an endangered species. Richard Richardson, Jr. and Louis Bender, in their 1985 report *Students in Urban Settings,* gathered a wide range of demographic information on the nation's present and future student population. "Twenty-eight percent of all white Americans (caucasians) are 18 or younger. For blacks, the comparable figure is 37 percent, for Hispanics, 42 percent," the report said. Most of these minority students live in highly urbanized districts, the researchers add. For example, 54.2 percent of all black children in the U.S. live in the city.

Yet, even as the nation's youth becomes increasingly disadvantaged, the federal government has been unable—or unwilling—to fill in the gaps. The nation's annual federal budget deficit has gone beyond the $200 billion mark. Should the deficit continue to grow, economists predict at best, a recession and, at worst, an economic collapse.

Although a consensus appears may have been reached, and Congress is attempting to balance government spending and the amount the nation collects in taxes, the poor and the minorities will be expected to carry a heavy load. Thus far, through 1986, Congress and the President have chosen to smooth out the deficit problem primarily through cuts in discretionary, non-Defense Department appropriations. Instead of increasing taxes, the elected representatives instead have concentrated their energies on tax reform legislation. Rather than solving or even easing the deficit, any changes in the tax laws are expected to be "revenue neutral," and will not bring new money into the nation's accounts.

Members of Congress who claim support of federal aid to education—and there are many—claim that Education Department expenditures have not dropped in recent years, despite the deficit. Federal student aid appropriations, not including Guaranteed Student Loans, were $3.74 billion in fiscal 1980 and reached $4.8 billion by fiscal 1986.

However, the Gramm-Rudman-Hollings balanced budget law cuts like a meat axe, at everything including student aid, and inflation has cut into the small gains that have been made. According to the American Council on Education, the vast majority of the financial resources that families use to pay for college continue to be in the form of self help.

"The most serious problem higher education faced [in the last decade] was inflation, not enrollment decline," Carol Frances wrote in a recent article in the *American Association of Higher Education Bulletin,* and it is difficult to discount her argument.

In fact, even as the American economy improved in the past three years, higher education has continued to become less affordable. Between 1980 and 1983, actual family income increased 10 percent, but college costs rose 40 percent. Moreover, the federal government has continued to tighten the eligiblity requirements for grants and subsidized student loans.

As we pointed out previously to fund the high cost of a college education, students increasingly turn to higher cost loan programs. Alternative, market rate programs are springing up at many profit and non-profit agencies and banks. In addition, the federal PLUS/ALAS program, initiated as a supplemental market rate loan program, has continued to grow.

Just how prevalent loans have become was revealed in a 1985 study by Carnegie Foundation researchers appearing in *Change* magazine. "In 1975, only 11 percent of all undergraduates borrowed to help pay college costs," the article said. "By 1984, the percentage had increased to 30 percent.

Thus, tuition debts are staggering, especially for students in professional fields. According to *Forbes* magazine, a typical medical student faces anywhere from $25,000 to $31,000 in unpaid bills upon graduation. Young attorneys owe an average of $16,300 to $16,900. Students completing their master's degree in business administration can expect to pile up loans totaling $11,200. "Those debts were rung up in a high inflation economy," according to *Forbes.*. "As inflation—and salary raises—moderate, it becomes more difficult to pay debts with harder dollars. The result is less money for future consumption."

The end product is what Frances calls an intergenerational shift of costs. The effect of inflationary college costs is being transferred to future generations. "This use of voluntary support for budget balancing instead of for investment in the future may have significant long-term effects on the vitality of the higher education enterprises," she writes.

Carnegie Foundation President Ernest Boyer agrees. The increasing cost of college, combined with the decreasing amount of scholarship money available, "suggest that . . . an education at a four-year institution would extend beyond the reach of many college students today," he said in 1985.

Minorities and Economics

As institutions committed to expanding educational opportunity, state colleges and universities continue to serve substantial numbers of first-generation college students—the first members of their families to seek postsecondary education. Yet, despite aggressive efforts to recruit black and Hispanic students, there has been a dramatic decline in the college participation rates of minority high school graduates in all of higher education. This key current problem will become even more critical in the future. According to the study prepared for AASCU in 1985, entitled *Student Aid and Minority Enrollments in Higher Education*, while the number of black high school graduates increased by 29 percent between 1975 and 1981, their college participation rate declined by 11 percent. During the same period the number of Hispanic high school graduates increased by 38 percent, while their college participation rate dropped by 16 percent. The number of white high school graduates increased by seven percent, and their college participation rate remained virtually unchanged. The study's author, John Lee, attributed the decline to economic factors. He concluded that minority students are less able now to afford to go to college than they were during the previous five-year period.

Federal student financial assistance programs have not kept up with the increasing cost of college attendance; median family income among minorities dropped by more than 12.5 percent between 1978 and 1982 (after adjustment for inflation)—and as a result, "an increasingly poorer population has faced steadily higher costs of education with shrinking amounts of aid." The study notes that a higher proportion of Hispanic and black families live below the poverty level (27.2 percent and 33 percent respectively, compared to 9.6 percent for white families.)

Not evident in the numbers on family income and proportion of population in poverty is the fact that black and Hispanic Americans represent a larger proportion of families with dependent children and thus, (in many cases) their income supports more people than that of white families.

The report notes that while the total American population grew by 50 percent between 1950 and 1980, the Hispanic population grew by 265 percent, and the number of black Americans increased by 150 percent. "In the years ahead," the report states, "the number of black and Hispanic individuals of college age will grow faster than the number of white individuals."

While the number of Hispanic college-age young people increased by 42 percent between 1975 and 1981, the number receiving bachelor's degrees increased by only 21 percent. The number of black college-age young people increased by 18 percent during that time, yet the number receiving bachelor's degrees increased by only 2 percent; the number receiving master's degrees actually dropped by 16 percent.

A subsequent AASCU report, *Student Aid and Public Higher Education,* published in May, 1985 found a sharp drop in minority students receiving student aid—down 12.4 percent in 1983–84 from 1981–82 levels. The total number of student aid recipients at public colleges during that period declined 2.3 percent, while overall enrollment remained stable. There was a seven percent drop in federal student aid dollars—from $7.2 billion to $6.7 billion, and a 5.5 percent drop in the number of need-based grants. The neediest students had to rely increasingly on loans to help pay for college, a deterrent to minority students.

Another deterrent to minority high school students was widespread publicity given to proposed cuts in federal student aid. The administration's budget proposals announced in 1985 would have caused over a quarter of a million students from families with incomes of less than $6,000 to lose an average of $1,160 in federal student assistance. An additional 96,000 students from families with incomes between $6,000 and $12,000 would have their aid reduced. More than 105,000 minority students from families with incomes below $25,000 would have received less assistance, with 80 percent of them coming from families with annual incomes of less than $12,000, and 60 percent from families with incomes of less than $6,000.

Faced with reductions of 25 percent in the value of federal student assistance since 1981, threats of more cuts to come, the shift from grants to loans, and the sharply rising costs of attending college, it was not surprising that low-income minority high school graduates decided not to pursue a college education.

A 1985 study prepared for the College Board by the Rand Corporation noted the importance of financial assistance for black students in reporting that in 1981, 48 percent of black college-bound seniors came from families with incomes under $12,000, as compared to only ten percent of their white counterparts.

According to the report, policy trends limiting black access and achievement in education include increasingly "tenuous" state, local, and federal funding for public elementary and secondary schools; cuts in student aid for higher education; new minimum competency tests and revised statewide graduation requirements for students; and a shortage of qualified teachers.

Increasing participation of blacks and Hispanics in postsecondary education is a responsibility shared by parents, the elementary and secondary schools, local, state, and federal policy makers, as well as the colleges themselves. The state colleges and universities, as the principal source of teachers, are in a strategic position to work with the public schools in encouraging minority junior high school students, for example, to go on to high school and take those courses which will give them the preparation necessary to succeed in college. Aggressive recruiting of high school seniors may increase the numbers enrolling in college, but of greater importance is the acquisition of academic skills in the public schools which will reduce the need for remedial courses in college and also increase the retention rate.

State colleges and universities are under pressure to reduce or eliminate remedial courses, tighten admission requirements, and increase tuition as limited state budgets are stretched to build more prisons, improve the quality of public schools, and assume a greater share of support for mass transit, welfare, and other programs being shifted from the federal to state government. The problems faced by state and local government are exacerbated by the phasing out of federal revenue sharing. These factors combine to increase the difficulty of reversing the downward trend of college participation of minority high school graduates, which making it all the more important for governing boards and presidents of state colleges and universities to take the leadership in expanding minority enrollments as a public policy issue of the highest priority in the years immediately ahead.

Among four-year institutions, the responsibility—and the opportunity—for serving minority students rests largely with AASCU colleges and universities. As reported by Alexander Astin, director of the Higher Education Research Institute at the University of California, Los Angeles, there is a severe under-representation of blacks, Hispanics, and American Indians in the nation's major public research universities. Of the 65 "flagship" state universities, 56 had significant under-enrollments of blacks, 48 of Hispanics and 46 of American Indians. Moreover, Astin noted, the degree of under-enrollment was greatest in those states with the largest minority populations. Astin concluded that "the major public universities in most states are not as accessible to low-income and minority students as are the public four-year colleges and, more particularly, the community colleges."

But it is not merely in the self-interest of state colleges and universities to increase minority enrollments; it is in the public interest. By the year 2000, blacks and Hispanics will constitute almost one-quarter of the U.S. workforce. The quality of their education and training will determine to a large extent the ability of the American economy to grow and compete successfully in world markets in terms of productivity, research, innovation, and quality of goods and services.

Denying opportunity may result in a lower standard of living for everyone, greater welfare costs. family destabilization, and social costs far greater than the cost of providing educational opportunity for all who can benefit.

Faculties of SCUs

A very high proportion of current faculties at SCUs took their doctoral degrees at research universities during the past three decades. This background seems to color their performance; they have allowed the ambience of the academic graduate school to determine their values.

In his early (1969) study of the developing SCUs, Alden Dunham of the Carnegie Commission saw this as a major problem for AASCU institutions.This attitude, he states:

> leads specifically to second-class status for applied programs. Teacher education, business administration, nursing, and other applied fields show a loss in respectability. The institution becomes increasingly national in outlook rather than regional, as exemplified in its programs as well as in its recruitment of faculty and students.

Dunham feels that the "graduate schools and the Ph.D are the culprits" in the case.

> A Ph.D. is a research degree and union card that means acceptance among one's colleagues within the guild, the academic discipline. So long as the only source of respectable faculty is the leading graduate

schools within major universities, state colleges will be automatically led toward these institutions as models. It is perfectly clear that research-oriented Ph.D.s from these graduate schools will do all they can to transform their employing institutions into what they have just left as students. This is bound to occur despite the evidence that 85 percent of those Ph.D.s never publish anything after their dissertation (Dunham, 1969, pp.156–157).

Ralph Tyler, one of the most distinguished analysts of higher education in history, also noted the same problem as he addressed the topic of academic excellence and equality of opportunity (Tyler 1970, p. 181).

Failure to provide essential conditions for learning is partly due to the fact that the typical college and university professor thinks of himself primarily as a scholar rather than a teacher. Hence, he has not given the problem the serious study that would be expected if he viewed the learning of his students as his chief purpose. When we are ready to give our major attention to providing essential conditions of learning for all our students, we can begin to realize the possibilities of increasing both academic excellence and equality of opportunity.

David Riesman, another of the leading analysts of postwar higher education in America, has pointed out further that:

It may also be true that some of them [faculty members in SCUs] unconsciously chose the state college as a place to settle down rather than the university because they did not want to be faced with the competitive pressures, and perhaps with the interdepartmental rivalries they found in their own graduate work at Berkeley or Columbia (Dunham, 1969, p. 171).

Dunham offered some solutions for this dilemma, recommending that the "strongest of AASCU member institutions should take the lead in the preparation of college teachers." He proposed, further, that a degree titled "Doctor of Arts" be developed, a degree to be given to people who will be primarily scholar-teachers rather than producers of new knowledge. Realistically, he pointed out that "one of the strongest objections to an alternative to the Ph.D. is second-class status." The answer to this objection, he said, is that only fully committed institutions should mount a Doctor of Arts program. Commitment, for Dunham, embraced providing sufficient resources, hiring graduates of the institution's program, promoting them, and giving them tenure as well. Said Dunham:

Wherever there are Ph.D. programs in existence, alternative doctoral programs are not likely to work. For this very reason, well-developed state colleges, . . . with strong master's programs are the most promising places to mount (new) Doctor of Arts programs" (Dunham, 1969, pp. 160–161).

The development of the Doctor of Arts degree, however, has been limited, paralleled by an occasional Ph.D. degree program emphasizing the preparation of the scholar-teacher for institutions not designed as research universities. Recently, a distinguished task force on professional growth of the American Association for Higher Education stated in its report that since the 1950s:

> Graduate schools of the post-Sputnik era embraced wholeheartedly and somewhat uncritically some variant of the model of professional training pioneered by Johns Hopkins University. Doctoral students were taught to do research in specialized branches of knowledge and with the passing of time academic specialties became ever more narrowly defined . . . During the 1960s, the pattern became common for all academic disciplines . . . In time, undergraduate colleges of arts and sciences, and even schools of education whose raison d'etre was the practical training of teachers, were advertising for faculty "with proven research ability and a record of substantial publications." . . . [This development] shaped the thinking of the generation of faculty who now occupy the tenured senior ranks at most four-year colleges and universities (Lovett, 1984, p. 3).

As institutions, some in the AASCU group, developed Doctor of Arts degree programs, they found that their graduates were in great demand for appointment. However, the large grants which started this program through the efforts of the Carnegie Foundation have dwindled; and currently around two dozen institutions offer such a degree program.

Dunham presented his findings early in the proceedings of the decade-long work of the Carnegie Commission. Twelve years later, Verne Stadtman, surveying the entire massive study, wrote:

> It is difficult to resist the speculation that the availability of faculty with Ph.D.s may be skewing the interests of faculty members at what were formerly teaching-oriented institutions somewhat away from teaching . . . Giving more emphasis to Doctor of Arts degree programs merits greater attention.

He also reported that 20 percent of all colleges had appointed persons with this degree since 1969–70, with none in Research

Universities I and Liberal Arts Colleges I, which is as it should be (Stadtman, 1980, pp. 56–57).

John Folger, thoughtful analyst of postsecondary education, has remarked that some of the AASCU members will probably continue to strive to be research universities, even though demographics and fiscal realities make this status an unobtainable objective for most. The nation does not need expanded production in very many doctoral or advanced professional fields, and the existing research universities can meet the needs for the rest of this country in a more efficient way than creating additional capacity. Following this warning to the few AASCU institutions which presently offer doctoral programs, Folger goes on to pose a great challenge:

> Could the comprehensive institutions accept a success model of student development, the value-added concept that Alexander Astin has been promoting (without much institutional response) for several years? . . . Most faculty want faculty prestige and autonomy more than they want student development; but could AASCU institutions provide rewards and prestige on the basis of student development rather than faculty research and scholarly output? . . . The AASCU has an opportunity to lead the way toward a student-centered model of academic quality which would put it in a better position to compete for public favor and public resources than trying to get into the lower rungs of the research university hierarchy (Folger, 1983, p. 1).

Hoke Smith, president of Towson State University in Maryland, has pointed out that during the 1990s, a high percentage of the existing faculty in AASCU institutions will be retiring and must be replaced. The persons who are appointed to replace them will set the tone of SCUs for another period of decades. Is it possible that between 1985 and 2000 some of the doctoral-granting institutions among the SCUs could establish and push such a creative program? This is one of the current genuine challenges to AASCU and its members.

Adult Students

The lifelong learner in large numbers is a new phenomenon in higher education. Longevity, retirement, and pure intellectual interest are bringing older adults to the campus. Many of them are not interested in a degree, though, which could change the focus of the instruction. Other adults, however, come to the campus from necessity: the need for professional retraining.

In looking toward the future, state colleges and universities increasingly will identify their appropriate role as major components of what has been called the learning society. Currently, most continuing education programs are viewed not as central to the mission of an institution, but as auxiliary enterprises often required to be self-supporting. But as institutions recognize that adults represent a primary group to be served, continuing education will move from the sideshow to the big top. Major changes in American society that will accelerate this process for adults were identified in a December 1984 conference sponsored by the W. K. Kellogg Foundation and the National University Continuing Education Association:

- The effect of rapidly changing technology on American industry and its competitive position.

- The increasing importance of the "knowledge industry" to the American economy.

- The accelerating need for rapid, effective knowledge transfer in developing and maintaining a labor force capable of "working smarter."

- Increasing national concern with human resource development.

- The impact of new technologies in creating and disseminating new knowledge and on facilitating the teaching-learning process.

- The dramatic growth in enrollments of older, mostly part-time students.

- The shrinking of the 18 to 24 year old population.

- New interest among institutions of higher education in entering into contractual relationships with business, industry, labor and public sector clients.

- Shifting patterns of federal and state funding for higher education.

A 1986 study prepared by AASCU staff members Meredith Ludwig and Gail Latouf noted that the population of the United States has been steadily aging; by the year 2000, 50 percent of students will be over age 25, and 20 percent of students will be over 35. The AASCU study of student aid in public higher education for 1983–84 showed that recipients were increasingly older, self-supporting, and attending college on a part-time basis.

More and more adults are either first-time students or are returning to school to finish degrees, and state colleges and universities are responding to that trend by placing greater emphasis on programs geared toward adults and by becoming more sensitive to the special needs of the adult population. Older women, especially single parents, see college as a way of broadening their education or preparing themselves for reentry or advancement in the job market.

State colleges, through adult reentry programs and continuing education offices, are making the campus less threatening by offering orientation and counseling programs tailored to the special needs of adults. Classes for degree programs and nondegree programs are being scheduled at more convenient times—during evenings and weekends so that adults with job and family responsibilities can attend.

An informal survey of AASCU institutions cited the following examples of how state colleges are responding to the growing interest in degree programs on the part of adults:

- A time-shortened program at the State University College at Brockport, New York, allows an individual to complete a degree with 96 credits. The college also has developed an interdisciplinary Bachelor of Science degree in Liberal Studies, specifically aimed at adults and offering courses off-campus in business, technical writing, and the humanities.

- A fee-waiver program at California State University, Sacramento, allows adults over the age of 60 to attend college free, just one of many similar programs.

- An orientation program for adults—called the Open Sesame Committee at Georgia State University in Atlanta—provides information, encouragement and role models to women who are considering college after a break in their education. It sponsors workshops that include panel discussions led by reentry students and faculty.

- The Adult Degree Program of the Herbert H. Lehman College of the City University of New York is expanding rapidly. Among its new programs is a bachelor's degree in nursing for licensed nurses 25 and older who have been out of school for at least five years. Nurses who qualify are exempted from some curriculum requirements, and credit is given for work experience.

- Establishing a career ladder for nurses, the College of Staten Island of the City University of New York allows working registered nurses with only associate or diploma school degrees to work toward the Baccalaureate in Nursing. The program includes off-campus instruction at hospital work sites and special schedules to accommodate working students with family responsibilities.

- At San Diego State University, the Educational Bridges to Options in High Technology Employment Project offers retraining and updating in biotechnology and analytical chemistry to about 100 mid-career adults who have a baccalaureate or higher degree in a scientific discipline and who completed their formal education over five years ago. This group includes some chemistry and biology high school teachers who are offering advanced placement courses at their institutions.

Several AASCU institutions were created in recent years specifically to serve adults through nontraditional programs. Three examples follow: Metropolitan State University in St. Paul, Minnesota offers only junior, senior, and graduate level courses for adults in different locations throughout Minneapolis and St. Paul. College credit is awarded for work experience by having a faculty member directly observe the working environment of the student and later test that student in the subject area related to the student's work. Two external degree colleges offer another alternative for adults—Empire State College in New York and Thomas A. Edison State College in New Jersey. These colleges assist students in identifying the available options that will allow them to gain credit for work experience. Among the methods that can be used to earn credits are the College Level Examination Program (CLEP) examinations, portfolio assessment, independent study, correspondence courses, and telecourses.

Armed Services and Veterans

Often overlooked in projections of part-time students in postsecondary education are men and women on active duty in the armed services, and those in the Reserves and National Guard. To maintain force requirements, the military will have to recruit an ever-growing share of a shrinking pool of 18 year-olds over the next decades. The competition between the military, higher education institutions, and business and industry will be especially keen for those in the age cohort group who are not only high school graduates but who have mathematics comprehension, and communications abilities.

Given the complexity of modern weaponry and equipment, the military is continually raising its educational requirements. Not only does it want recruits with a minimum of a high school education or its equivalent (GED), it wants noncommissioned officers to seek an associate degree, and commissioned officers to have bachelor's or master's degrees. And the military is prepared to pay the educational costs required to meet those standards.

As the costs of attending college continue to escalate, the military is spending millions of dollars on national advertising featuring educational benefits, including a G.I. Bill which can provide up to $25,200 to meet college costs upon completion of the enlistment period.

The tuition assistance program of the armed services involves an estimated 700,000 men and women who are, in effect, part-time students taking courses offered by colleges and universities on or near military installations in the United States and throughout the world. Through SOC (Servicemembers Opportunity Colleges), described in Chapter 5, the higher education community led by AASCU and the American Association of Community and Junior Colleges is responding to the unique postsecondary educational requirements of men and women in the armed services, many of whom will continue their college education after leaving the service. The challenge to the higher education community is to insure that the courses offered are comparable in quality to those taught on campus, and that obstacles to transfer of credit are reduced or eliminated so that the students can achieve their educational goals and earn the desired degrees.

AASCU's objective in organizing SOC was not only to find ways to respond to the particular educational needs of men and women in the armed service, but also to apply the lessons learned to help overcome similar barriers faced by older part-time civilian students. Part of AASCU's federal legislative agenda, for example, is extension of student financial aid benefits to less-than-half-time students.

Nontraditional Students

Among four-year public colleges and universities, AASCU institutions have a primary responsibility for serving the ever-growing pool of so-called nontraditional students. In *The Future of State Universities* published in 1985 by the Rutgers University Press, David Saxon, Chairman of the Corporation of the Massachusetts Institute of Technology and former president of the University of California, and Walter Milne, assistant to Dr. Saxon, expressed their conviction that in the years ahead there will be larger numbers of nontraditional students taught in a greater variety of nontraditional ways. "That doesn't necessarily mean," they write, "that they will be taught—not in great numbers at least—in our research universities. The reason is that these institutions are overwhelmingly geared to full-time students who are totally committed to full-time programs. The education of those students is the central obligation of these universities, and it must be discharged without dilution, just as other institutions already geared to part-time students must maintain their obligation to serve that population." AASCU institutions have a major future charge in this area.

Current Condition of SCU's

No one predicted the demise of the teachers college in 1948 or in 1961, but in 1985 there were no public colleges so named. And, out of the 406 SCUs (see Appendices 1 and 2), only 16 were classified by the National Center for Educational Statistics as "specialized." Of these only four were classified as teacher education institutions, and even these four are questionable. They were the University of Maine at Farmington, Harris-Stowe State College in Missouri, Western Montana College, and Western Oregon State College. Unpredicted and unplanned as the expiration was, it took place—and very rapidly. Its accomplishment was reflected in 1980 when the Carnegie Commission listed the nine major, consequential higher education decisions of the 1960–1980 period and included "the shift of teachers' colleges to comprehensive colleges and universities" (Carnegie, 1980, pp. 84–85). The use of this new nomenclature is now standard in the literature of higher education (including new classification systems of NCES), and the mission and responsibility of these institutions is well known by Congress and most state legislatures.

Because this change took place rapidly and somewhat unexpectedly the appearance of a third new type of higher education institution is still not recognized or well understood by many. In the late 1960s and particularly in the 1970s, it was quite common to read or hear that SCUs, caught in an amorphous position between the two types of institutions previously invented in America (land-grant colleges and community colleges), would be the institutions to suffer as enrollments dropped. Current enrollments clearly demonstrate that is not the case, and SCUs continue to attract huge numbers of students to their changing programs.

In 1984–85, early reports showed community colleges down 2.2 percent, four-year undergraduate enrollments up 2.8 percent, a difference of five percent (Fall 1984 Enrollment in Higher Education, 1985, p. 2). The high point of numbers of high school graduates was reached in 1977–78 at 3.2 million. The wavelike decline expected in high school graduates after that date (predicted by the Western Interstate Commission for Higher Education in 1984) was serious: to 2.9 million in 1980–81, to 2.6 million in 1983–84, to 2.5 million in 1986–87, back to 2.6 million in 1988, down again to 2.4 million by 1989–90, to 2.3 million in 1992–93, to 2.4 million in 1995–95, and to almost 2.7 million in 1999–2000.

Carol Frances has pointed out that although the drop from 1977–1982 was significant, the 1983–86 years alone would see 40 percent of the total decline in college-age population (Frances, 1984, p.4). Thus, it is quite significant that the enrollment in public SCUs rose to 2,873,467, in 1983–84, well over one percent of the total population in the U.S. Also, in 1984–85, with high school graduates declining six percent, SCU overall enrollments declined only one percent. An analysis of 362 AASCU member institutions indicated most of them were within one or two percent above or below 1983—with enrollment at 138 SCUs (38 percent) growing from one to 29 percent; one institution (Thomas Edison College) reported a 52 percent gain. The number of 18–year olds is expected to decline until about 1995. To the extent that colleges and universities depend on this pool of so-called "traditional" college-age people for their students, there is understandable anxiety on the part of higher education planners. Yet the decline in the size of this age group began in 1979 withouta corresponding decline in college enrollments. Older students, especially women, made up for part of the loss of 18–year olds, although the effect has been more pronounced on campuses located within driving distance of commuters.

AASCU institutions finally began to feel the effect of the decline in the 18–year old pool at the start of the 1985–86 school year, with a one percent decrease in enrollment from the previous year. Full-time student enrollments totaled about 1.7 million—a three percent decrease; at the same time, they enrolled 905,763 part-time students—a three percent increase. The number of full-time graduate students dropped by one percent, but the number of part-time graduate students increased by seven percent.

The Ludwig and Latouf study cited earlier analyzed population and societal trends as they relate to the mission and future enrollments in AASCU institutions. Their findings anticipate these emerging conditions:

the advancing age of the student body; the continued lack of minority student participation in higher education; the improving academic preparation of freshmen entering colleges; and the growing need for a college-educated workforce.

As the number of students between 18 and 24 declines, older students could well fill many of the vacant seats in college classrooms. Indeed, between 1970 and 1983, the enrollment rate for older students doubled—climbing from 2.4 million to 5 million.

Yet, Ludwig and Latouf emphasize, "no consensus has formed on precisely what effect this group will have on higher education." While the pool of potential students may be there, these adults will also have the options of other continuing education courses and "in-house" training programs.

The average full-time freshman coming into a public institution in 1984 was better prepared academically than the average incoming student the year before. Actions by local school districts and state governments to improve the quality of an elementary and secondary school education appear to be working. Ludwig and Latouf say that this academic improvement could eliminate the need for comprehensive remedial programs and increase the competition for able students.

Students continue to enter college with the incentive of a good job when they receive their diploma, and research indicates they may be right. Ludwig and Latouf caution, however, many of the jobs created by the growing economy are focused on a few categories. In addition, the projected growth rate (percent change) and actual growth (the number of jobs generated) are two distinctly different measures.

According to Ludwig and Latouf, public institutions "are doing well and maintaining their student population." AASCU presidents have closely monitored the factors that affect the needs and desires of the population they serve, and enrollment has not taken the major dive many had predicted. The outlook for public, four-year college and universities was "cautiously optimistic, if respect for the value of higher education is sustained within various student populations," Ludwig and Latouf concluded, pointing out that private, state and federal support in this endeavor is necessary.

Possible Near Future Contingencies

An intensified shortage of teachers may be the likeliest development that could affect public higher education in the near future.

The Rand Corporation and the National Center for Education Statistics reported that the nation's schools may need 100,000 new teachers this year.

Michael Kirst, professor of education and business at Stanford University, in his recent book *Who Controls the Schools?: American Values in Conflict,* noted several reasons for the decline in teachers and teacher quality, such as the relative dip in salaries compared to inflation, the erosion of public support for the profession, and the nature of the job itself. "Talented persons are not likely to choose a career that restricts them to an environment that is . . . unsuccessful and sometimes violent," Kirst wrote.

The Education Department's Assistant Secretary for Educational Research Chester Finn, then professor of education at Vanderbilt University, told *U.S News and World Report* in 1985 that "the lack of qualified teachers is a "national crisis," adding, "if trends" of the last few years continue, the average new teacher will be somebody most people won't want teaching their kids."

Some school districts are beginning to increase teacher pay scales, and the public may begin to appreciate its teachers, but colleges and universities should be conscious of the possibility that today's nagging troubles in teaching could become tommorow's crisis.

In addition to the major trends discussed so far a number of other areas of concern could affect higher education in the next few years— areas for which institutions might prepare. Here are ten to consider:

- The decline in the 18–20 year age group has also affected the armed services, and the federal government has the option of instituting a peacetime draft—a more formidable recruitment tool than any of the incentives a college or university could offer. Should a draft be instituted, and some sort of GI Bill remain, the higher education community may have to plan ahead in an attempt to assess exactly what the educational needs of these soldiers will be and what types of programs would be necessary to build on the specialties the draftees would gain while in the service.

- New educational services may be required for the nation's population. Many adults with strong professional backgrounds, lack general or liberal education and there may be a special need to develop such programs.

- The nation's immigration policy may be altered and, some suggest, liberalized. Under current law, the U.S. admits about

500,000 immigrants per year. Last year, *Forbes* magazine said the nation could absorb three times that number and suggested it do so. Should this occur, postsecondary education could well be flooded with yet another constituency and institutions would have to scurry to meet their needs.

- With computerized scientific research progressing at a rapid rate, some experts are predicting that a major scientific breakthrough could come at anytime in several different fields. A major discovery could spur an increased need for education in scientific areas and could dramatically increase enrollment in some science programs.

- Most college administrators might disagree, but the Labor Department says that only 20 percent of the jobs available in American society require a college degree. If 50 to 75 percent of our high schools' yearly graduates enter some form of higher education, a serious job shortage could develop.

- Even in fields where a college education has been an accepted requirement for job success, graduates may face trouble down the road. For example, the American Council on Education's Business-Higher Education Forum, in its report *America's Business Schools: Priorities for Change,* noted that business leaders are increasingly dissatisfied with the business education students are receiving. The *Harvard Business Review,* in a 1984 article, declared that MBA programs are churning out too many specialists and strategies and not enough graduates ready to tackle operational business problems. And, in an article published nearly two years ago, *Forbes* described many business schools as "MBA mills."

- Although it is not a problem per se, the number of state colleges and universities appears to have peaked. Few new state institutions have opened since the late 1970s, which means that states must adapt current institutions to meeting the changing needs of students.

- The nation's economy has turned a positive about-face in the early 1980s, but Wall Street analysts have been predicting the end of the bull market and the Federal Reserve Bank has been taking steps to head off a sluggish economy. Thus, the possibility of an economic depresion remains. Carol Frances, in the American Association of Higher Education *Bulletin,* reports college enrollments are counter-cyclical. "In most recessions, increased unemployment leads to higher enrollments because students without jobs go to college, either because they hope for higher incomes from better jobs later, or because their 'opportunity cost' of going to college—that is, the costs to them of foregone earnings from going to college instead of working—is zero because they don't have jobs anyway." Colleges should be aware of the potential enrollment windfall, and the problems that could arise from it.

• Some experts in the world of work are touting the need for sabbaticals in industry. Workers in a number of Scandinavian nations have been allowed periods off work for retraining purpose. With rapidly changing technology and increasing job complexity, some American corporations have conducted such retraining sessions for their own employees. However, there may be an opportunity for state colleges and universities to get involved. For this to happen, institutions might improve the lines of communication with industry and hammer out joint—and mutually beneficial—agreements.

• Government employment, especially federal government employment, continues to decline as the federal deficit remains high. The Reagan administration froze most federal hiring for two years and threatened to reduce the size of the federal workforce through layoff and early retirement programs. Because government jobs often are specialized and have little private sector applicability, a large number of federal workers could begin searching for retraining opportunitites in the next few years.

As Kenneth Mortimer, Mark Bagshaw, and Andrew Masland wrote in their recent book on academic staffing: "In the mid–1980s, the dominant feature of the institutional context is uncertainty in the face of scarce resources."

Prospects and Possibilities: Reprise

The prospects are that state colleges and universities will continue to meet the changes as they occur—responding as they have for over a dozen decades to the compelling demands of both the larger society and the individual student.

The possibilities are that these institutions will perform in the years to come as effectively as they have since their inception. Though the elements of future requirements are as yet unclear, the precedent for performance is absolute: the challenges, in whatever form they emerge, will be met.

A Coda

From its very beginning in 1961, AASCU has directed a major part of
its interest to new directions for state colleges and universities. It is
significant that one of AASCU's first publications was entitled *Challenge to Change.*

Of the many association committees, the Committee on Policies and
Purposes has been, and continues to be, both influential and preeminent. Its charge was to be the "pathfinder" committee for the association's membership—to look to the future, evaluate trends, and help
state colleges and universities respond to new challenges and opportunities.

This committee, in its role as AASCU's think tank, filled its responsibilties impeccably. Its efforts led to a 1971 Ford Foundation grant to
support the National Commission on the Future of State Colleges and
Universities, chaired by one of America's great educational statesmen,
the Honorable Wayne L. Morse, former U.S. Senator from Oregon.
The Commission, recognizing that effective change can occur only at
the campus level, resisted the temptation of similar national bodies to
prescribe solutions to problems. Instead, it identified issues and
alternatives for consideration by Campus Action Teams comprised
often of faculty, students, administrators, community leaders and
other citizens' groups. The work of these teams, over the next few
years, led to profound changes at state colleges and universities. New
curricula were introduced in fields such as allied health, human
services, engineering and technology, and business administration.
The relationship of general education to professional education was
given new emphasis. Campus planning was institutionalized. Enrollments increased rapidly as quality improved, making state colleges
and universities more attractive to both students and their prospective
employers, and eliciting financial support from from foundations,
business and industry, alumni, and other private donors.

A further committee achievement, the Kellogg Foundation major
grant in 1974, enabled AASCU to establish a Resource Center for
Planned Change. The Center's *Futures Planning Paradigm* soon be-

came a best-seller as both AASCU and non-AASCU institutions recognized the need for an instrument to identify trends more systematically and plan for the future. The Center became the focal point for chief academic officers of AASCU institutions to work on such issues as faculty development, academic leadership, assessment of outcomes of undergraduate education, and institutional management in times of crisis. The Center flourished as a catalyst for change at state colleges and universities, and continued as an on-going program for the association at the expiration of the grant from Kellogg.

Again, in 1985, as a result of the far-sighted work of the Committee, the Board of Directors of the Association established a new National Commission on the Role and Future of State Colleges and universities to help member institutions respond to new dramatic social changes: the growth in minority populations; accelerated obsolescence of job skills; increasing numbers of older part-time students; utilization of technology to enhance the teacher/learning process; and the need to add an international dimension to the undergraduate curriculum.

Chaired by former U.S. Secretary of Education Terrel H. Bell, and comprised of eminent higher education scholars and leaders from both the state colleges and universities and the broader community, the Commission focused its attention on the special roles of AASCU institutions in terms of changing missions, governance, curricula, students, faculty, and services for the remainder of this century and the beginning of the next.

The work of the Committee on Policies and Purposes during the past quarter century epitomizes the historical thrust of AASCU institutions: giving the process and substance of planned change the highest priority—yesterday, today and tomorrow.

Endnotes

Bowen, H. *Investment in Learning*. Jossey-Bass Publishers, San Francisco, CA: 1977. P. 58–59

President's Commission on Higher Education. *Higher Education for American Democracy, Volume V*. U.S. Government Printing Office, Washington, D.C.: 1947. P. 63

Rothbard, R. The Cost of Tuition: *A Study of the City University of New York*. Committee for Public Higher Education, New York, NY: 1982. P. 31

Applied Systems Institute. *Sectorial Balance of the Federal Student Aid Programs*. For the American Council on Education, ASI, Washington, D.C.: 1985. P. 55

Ibid. P. 55

Stampen, J. *Student Aid and Public Higher Education: Recent Change*. American Association of State Colleges and Universities, Washington, D.C.: 1985

Applied Systems Institute, Ibid. P. 9

Henderson, C. "Forecasting College Costs through 1988–89." American Council on Education, Washington, D.C.: 1986. PP. 4–5

Gillespie, G. and Carlson, N. *Trends in Student Aid 1982–83 and 1983–84*. The College Board, Washington, D.C.: 1984, 1985

Miller, S. and Hexter, H. *How Low-Income Families Pay for College*. American Council on Education, Washington, D.C.: 1985.

U.S. Department of Education. *The Condition of Education: 1985*. U.S. Government Printing Office, Washington, D.C.: 1985. P. 232

U.S. Department of Education. *Pell Grant End of Year Report: 1983–84*. U.S. Government Printing Office, Washington, D.C.: 1985

U.S. Bureau of the Census, Current Population Reports, Series P-20, No. 400, *Schools Enrollment—Social and Economic Characteristics of Students: October 1981 and 1980*. U.S. Government Printing Office, Washington, D.C.: 1985. Table D, P. 3.

American Association of State Colleges and Universities. *Low-Tuition Fact book*. AASCU, Washington, D.C.: 1983 P. 9

McPherson, M. "Higher Education: Investment or Expense," in Joy, J. and Bernstein, M. *Financing Higher Education*. Auburn House Publishing, Boston, MA: 1981. P. 35

Bibliography

A. GENERAL

A National Resource: Historically Public Black Colleges and Universities. Washington, D.C.: Office for Advancement of PUblic Negro Colleges, 1982.

Adams, Herbert Baxter. The College of William and Mary: A Contribution to the History of Higher Education with Suggestions for its National Promotion. Bureau of Education Circular of Information, no. 1–1887. Washington, D.C: Government Printing Office, 1887.

Agnew, Donald C. *Seventy-Five Years of Educational Leadership.* Atlanta, Georgia: Southern Association of Colleges and Schools, 1970.

Allen, Harry Kenneth, and Axt, Richard G. *Public Finance and State Institutions of Higher Education in the United States.* New York: Columbia University Press, 1952.

Altman, Robert A. *The Upper Division College.* San Francisco: Jossey-Bass, 1970.

American Association of Colleges for Teacher Education. *Directory/1967: Officers, Committees, and Members.* Washington, D.C.: American Association of Colleges for Teacher Education, 1967.

———. *Teacher Productivity—1966–.* Washington, D.C.: American Association of Colleges for Teacher Education, 1967.

American Association of State Colleges and Universities. "Educational Standards are Alive and Well in State Colleges and Universities." *Background,* July 1983.

American Association of Teachers Colleges. *Yearbook,* 1922.

Andersen, Charles J. *A Fact Book of Higher Education.* 1st issue. "Enrollment Data." Washington, D.C.: American Council on Education, 1968.

———. *A Fact Book on Higher Education.* 3rd issue. "Earned Degrees." Washington, D.C.: American Council on Education, 1967.

Ashby, Eric. *Any Person, Any Study: An Essay on Higher Education in the United States.* New York: McGraw-Hill, 1971.

Association of Colleges and Schools of the Southern States. *Proceedings of the Thirty-First Annual Meeting.* Birmingham, Alabama: Birmingham Publishing Company, 1926.

Association of State Colleges and Universities. *State Colleges and Universities*

Look to the Future: Proceedings of the Fifth Annual Meeting, Chicago, Illinois, 1966. Washington, D.C.: Association of State Colleges and Universities, 1966.

————. *New Opportunities for State Colleges and Universities in Federal Programs: Proceedings of the Sixth Annual Meeting, Washington, D.C., 1966.* Washington, D.C.: Association of State Colleges and Universities, 1967.

————. *Proceedings of the Seventh Annual Meeting, Columbus, Ohio, 1967.* Washington, D.C.: Association of State Colleges and Universities, 1968.

————. Research Report 1. Washington, D.C.: Association of State Colleges and Universities, 1962.

Barnard, Frederick A.P. *Letters on College Government, the Evils Inseparable from the American College System.* New York: D. Appleton. 1855.

Barnard, Henry. *Normal Schools and Other Institutions, Agencies, and Means Designed for the Professional Education of Teachers, Part I.* Hartford, Connecticut: Case, Tiffany and Company, 1951.

Beale, Lucrece. People to People: *The Role of State and Land-Grant Universities in Modern America.* Washington, D.C: Office of Research and Information of the National Association of State Universities and Land-Grant Colleges, 1973.

Berdahl, Robert O. *Statewide Coordination of Higher Education.* Washington, D.C.: American Council on Education, 1971.

Birnbaum, Robert. *Maintaining Diversity in Higher Education.* San Francisco: Jossey-Bass, 1983.

Blauch, Lloyd E., ed. *Education for the Professions.* Washington, D.C.: Government Printing Office, 1955. Reprint. Ann Arbor, Michigan: University Microfilms.

Boas, Louise Schutz. *Woman's Education Begins—The Rise of Women's Colleges.* New York: Arno Press and the New York Times, 1971.

Borrowman, Merle L. *Teacher Education in America—A Documentary.* New York: Teachers College Press, 1965.

Bowen, Howard and Minter, W. John. *Preserving America's Investment in Human Capital.* Washington, D.C.: American Association of State Colleges aand Universities, 1980.

Boyer, Ernest L. "Reflections on the Great Debate of 83." *Phi Delta Kappa,* April 1984, pp.525–530.

Branom, Mendel E. "One Hundred Years of Teacher Education in the St. Louis Public School System, Part 1: The St. Louis Normal School, 1857–1904." *Saint Louis Public School Journal,* Research and Survey Series no. 20, vol. 11, no. 1. St. Louis Public Schools, 1958.Brown, Jane A. *A Study of English as a Subject in the Curriculum of the College of William and Mary.* Ph.D. dissertation, College of William and Mary, 1982.

Brown, John Franklin. *The Training of Teachers for Secondary Schools in Germany and the United States.* New York: Macmillian Company, 1911.

Browning, Jane E. Smith, and William, John B. "History and Goals of Black Institutions of Higher Education." In *Black Colleges in America,* Willis, Charles V. and Edmonds, Ronald R., eds. New York: Teachers College Press, 1978.

Brubacher, John S., and Rudy, Willis. *Higher Education in Transition: A History of American Colleges and Universities—1636–1976*. New York: Harper and Row, 1976.

Brumbaugh, A. J. *State-wide Planning and Coordination of Higher Education*. Atlanta, Georgia: Southern Regional Education Board, 1963.

Brunner, Henry S. *Land-Grant Colleges and Universities 1862–1962*. Washington, D.C.: U.S. Department of Health, Education, and Welfare, 1962.

Bureau of Education. *Account of College-Commencements During 1873 in the Western and Southern States*. Washington, D.C.: Government Printing Office, 1873.

———. *Account of College-Commencements for the Summer of 1873 in Maine, New Hampshire, Vermont, Massachusetts, Rhode Island, Connecticut, New York, New Jersey and Pennsylvania*. Washington, D.C.: Government Printing Office, 1873.

Butts, R. Freeman. *The College Charts Its Course: Historical Conceptions and Current Proposals*. New York: McGraw-Hill, 1939.

Caffrey, John. "The Future Academic Community." *In The Future Academic Community: Continuity and Change*. Washington, D.C.: American Council on Education, 1968.

Carlton, Frank Tracy. *Economic Influences Upon Educational Progress in the United States, 1820–1850*. New York: Teachers College Press, 1908.

Carnegie Commission on Higher Education. *A Classification of Institutions of Higher Education*. Berkeley, California: Carnegie Commission on Higher Education, 1976.

———. The Capitol and the Campus: State Responsibility for Postsecondary Education. New York: McGraw-Hill, 1971.

Carnegie Council on Policy Studies in Higher Education. *Three Thousand Futures*. San Francisco. New York: McGraw-Hill, 1971.

Cartter, Allan M. "Accreditation and the Federal Government." In *The Role and Function of the National Commission on Accrediting*. Washington, D.C.: National Commissio on Accrediting, 1966.

———. *Scientific Manpower for 1970–1985*. Carnegie Commission on Higher Education, 1971.

Cartter, Allan M., ed. *Higher Education in the United States*. Washington, D.C.: American Council on Education, 1964–65.

Chambers, M. M. *Higher Education and State Governments, 1970–1975*. Danville, Illinois: Interstate, 1974.

Chandler, Marjorie O. *Earned Degrees Conferred: 1966–67. Part A—Summary Data*. Washington, D.C.: Government Printing Office, 1968.

Chronicle of Higher Education. Washington, D.C.: Chronicle of Higher Education, February 27, 1985, p. 16.

Clark, Willis G. History of Education in Alabama, 1702–1889. Bureau of Education Circular no. 3, 1889. Washington, D.C.: Government Printing Office, 1889.

Coulter, E. Merton. *College Life in the Old South*. New York: Macmillian Company, 1928.

Creswell, John W., Roskens, Ronald W., and Henry, Thomas C. "A Typology of Multicampus Systems." *Journal of Higher Education,* vol. 56, no. 1, January/February 1985, pp. 26–37.

de Tocqueville, Alexis. *Democracy in America.* Vol. II. (Translation by Henry Reeve, original publication in 1840). New York: Alfred A. Knopf, 1946.

Dunham, E. Alden. *Colleges of the Forgotten American—A Profile of State Colleges and Regional Universities.* New York: McGraw-Hill, 1969.

Eddy, Edward Danforth, Jr. *Colleges for our Land and Time, The Land-Grant Idea in American Education.* New York: Harper and Brothers, 1957.

Eells, Walter C., and Haswell, Harold A. *Academic Degrees.* Washington, D.C.: U.S. Government Printing Office, 1960.

El-Khawas, Elaine. *Campus-Trends.* Report No. 65. Washington, D.C.: American Council on Education, February 1985.

Emens, John. Personal correspondence files from 1950–1965 related to development of the Association of Teacher Education Institutions and the Association of State Colleges and Universities. Available in the AASCU Archives at Illinois State University, Normal, Illinois.

Fall 1984 Enrollment in Higher Education. Washington, D.C.: Association Council for Policy Analysis and Research, January 1985.

Fincher, Cameron. "Curricular Reform for the 1980s." *THE Newsletter.* Athens, Georgia: Institute of Higher Education, University of Georgia, 1978.

Finkin, Matthew W. *Federal Reliance on Educational Accreditation.* Washington, D.C.: Council on Postsecondary Accreditation, 1978. ED 172 591.

Flahive, Mark T. "The Origins of the American Law School." American Bar Association Journal, vol. 64, December 1978,pp. 1868–1871.

Frances, Carol. "1985: The Economic Outlook for Higher Education." *AAHE Bulletin,* December 1984, pp. 3–6.

Gambrell, Mary Latimor. Ministorial Training in Eighteenth Century New England. New York: AMS Press, 1967.

Gardner, J. W. *Excellence: Can We be Equal and Excellent Too?* New York: Harper and Brothers, 1961.

Geiger, Lewis G. *Voluntary Accreditation.* Chicago, Illinois: North Central Associatioin of Colleges and Secondary Schools, 1970.

Glenny, Lyman A. *Autonomy of Public Colleges: The Challenge of Coordination.* New York: McGraw-Hill, 1959.

Grant, W. Vance, and Simon, Kenneth A. *Digest of Educational Statistics.* Washington, D.C.: U.S. Office of Education, 1967.

Hager, Walter E. *AASCU: The First-Ten Years.* Washington, D.C.: AASCU, 1970.

Hall, Samuel Read. *Lectures to Female Teachers on School-Keeping.* 1832. Reprint. Ann Arbor, Michigan: University Microfilms.

Halstead, D. Kent. *Statewide Planning in Higher Education.* Washington, D.C.: Government Printing Office, 1974.

Handlin, Oscar, and Handlin, Mary F. *The American College and American Culture: Socialization as a Function of Higher Education.* New York: McGraw-Hill, 1970.

Harcleroad, Fred F. *Accreditation: History, Process, and Problems.* Washington, D.C.: American Association of Higher Education, 1980.

————. "Private Constituencies and Their Impact on Higher Education." In *Higher Education in American Society,* Altbach, Philip G. and Berdahl, Robert O., eds. Buffalo, New York: Prometheus Books, 1981.

————. *The Comprehensive Public State Colleges and Universities in America: A Pocket History.* Washington, D.C. American Association of State Colleges and Universities, 1983.

————. *Voluntary Organizations in America and the Development of Educational Accreditation.* Washington, D.C.: Council on Postsecondary Accreditation, 1980.

Harcleroad, Fred F., ed. *Institutional Efficiency in State Systetms of Public Higher Education.* Tucson, Arizona: University of Arizona, Center for the Study of Higher Education, 1975.

Harcleroad, Fred F., and Kilmartin, Alfred D. *International Education in the Developing State Colleges and Universities.* Washington, D.C.: Association of State Colleges and Universities, 1966.

Harcleroad, Fred. F., Molen, C. Theodore, Jr., and Van Ort, Suzanne. *The Regional State Colleges and Universities in the Middle 1970s.* Tucson, Arizona: University of Arizona, Center for the Study of Higher Education, 1976.

Harper, Charles Athiel. *A Century of Public Teacher Education: The Story of the State Teachers Colleges as They Evolved from the Normal Schools, Told by Charles A. Harper.* 1939. Reprint. Ann Arbor, Michigan: University Microfilms.

Hause, J. Gilbert. Personal correspondence regarding Black Hills State College, July 26, 1984.

Higher Education and National Affairs, February 1984, p. 3.

Hodgkinson, Harold L. *Institutions in Transition: A Profile of Change in Higher Education (Incorporating the 1970 Statistical Report).* New York: McGraw-Hill, 1971.

Hofstadter, Richard. *Academic Freedom in the Age of the College.* New York: Columbia University Press. 1961.

Hofstadter, Richard, and Hardy, C. DeWitt. *The Development and Scope of Higher Education in the United States.* New York: Columbia University, Press, 1952.

Hofstadter, Richard, and Metzger, Walter P. *The Development of Academic Freedom in the United States.* New York: Columbia University Press, 1955.

Irwin, Judith T., and Millett, John D. *The Campus Resources of Higher Education in the United States of America: A Taxonomy of Types and Geographical Distribution.* Washington, D.C.: Management Division, Academy for Educational Development, 1973.

Jenecks, Christopher, and Riesman, David. *The Academicm Revolution.* Garden City, New York: Doubleday and Company, 1968.

Jones, Thomas Jesse. *Negro Education—A Study of the Private and Higher Schools for Colored People in the United States.* New York: Arno Press and the New York Times, 1969.

Keiser, Albert. *College Names: Their Origin and Significance.* New York: Bookman Associates, 1952.

Kelley, Robert Lincoln. *Tendencies in College Administration.* New York: Robert Lincoln Kelly 1925.

Kendall, Glenn. Personal correspondence, February 15, 1980, including a copy of his speech on October 6, 1979 at the dedication of Glenn Kendall Hall at Chico State University

Kirst, Michael W. "Renewing the Teaching Profession." *The Standard Magazine,* Spring 1985, pp. 50–55.

Ladd, E. C., Jr. "The Work Experience of American College Professors: Some Data and Argument." *In Faculty Career Development.* Washington, D.C.: American Association for Higher Education, 1979.

Lahey, W. Charles. The Potsdam Tradition: *A History and a Challenge.* New York: Appleton-Century-Crofts, 1966.

Logan, Lawrence B. *AASCU Institutions and Industry: Partners in Progress.* AASCU Studeis 1984. Washington, D.C.: American Association of State Colleges and Universities, 1984.

Lovett, Clara M. *Vitality Without Mobility: The Faculty Opportunities Audit.* Washington, D.C.: American Association for Higher Education, 1984.

Low Tuition Fact Book. Washington, D.C.: American Association of State Colleges and Universities, 1983.

MacVittie, Robert W. Personal correspondence, July 14, 1975.

Makowski, David J., and Wulfsverg, Rolf M. *An Improved Taxonomy of Postsecondary Institutions.* Washington, D.C.: Department of Health, Education, and Welfare, 1980.

Mayhew, Lewis B. *Graduate and Professional Education, 1980: A Survey of Institutional Plans.* New York: McGraw-Hill, 1970.

Meriam, Dennis L. *Normal School Teaching and Efficiency in Teaching.* Privately published doctoral dissertation approved by the Faculty of Philosophy of Columbia University, New York, 1905.

Miller, Jerry W. *Organizational Structures of Non-Governmental Post-secondary Accreditation.* Washington, D.C.: National Commission on Accrediting, 1973. ED 082 591.

Millett, John D. *Conflict in Higher Education.* San Francisco: Jossey-Bass, 1984.

Minter, W. J., and Bowen, H. R.*Preserving America's Investment in Human Capital.* Washington, D.C.: American Association of State Colleges and Universities, 1980.

Mitau, G. Theodore. Personal correspondence regarding St. Cloud State College, January 16, 1974.

Morrison, Jack. *The Rise of the Arts on the American Campus.* New York: McGraw-Hill, 1973.

Newcomer, Mabel. *A Century of Higher Education for American Women.* New York: Harper and Brothers, 1959.

Norfleet, Morris. Personal correspondence regarding Morehead State University, November 28, 1984.

Oklahoma Regents for Higher Education. *Higher Education Report.* October 12, 1984.

Oliver, Kenneth D., Jr. and Miller, Kathryn J. *Organizational Patterns of Centain Colleges and Universities in the United States Enrolling 5,000–10,000 Students.* Springfield, Missouri: Southwest Missouri State College, 1966.

Orlans, Harold. *Private Accreditation and Public Eligibility.* Lexington, Massaschusetts: D.C. Heath and Company, 1975.

———. "Remembrances of Things Future." *Change,* April 1977, pp. 30–36.

Ostar, Allan W. "The Changing State College." *Manpower,* October 1971, pp. 25–28.

Ostheimer, Richard H. *A Statistical Analysis of the Organization of Higher Education in the United States, 1948–1949.* 1951. Reprint. Ann Arbor, Michigan: University Microfilms.

Pace, C. Robert. *Education and Evangelism—A Profile of Protestant Colleges.* New York: McGraw-Hill, 1972.

———. *The Demise of Diversity? A Comparative Profile of Eight Types of Institutions.* Carnegie Commission of Higher Education, 1974.

Pangburn, Jessie M. *The Evolution of the American Teachers College.* Teachers College, Columbia University Contributions to Education, no. 500. New York: Bureau of Publications, Teachers College, Columbia University, 1932.

Paradise, Michael E. Personal correspondence to Fred Harcleroad regarding the University of Alaska, Juneau, August 14, 1984.

Partridge, Arthur Ray. "The Rise of the University School of Education as a Professional Institution." Ed.D. dissertation, Stanford University, 1957. Ann Arbor, Michigan: University Microfilms.

Perkins, James A. *International Programs of U.S. Colleges and Universities: Priorities for the Seventies.* New York: International Council for Educational Development, Carnegie Commission on Higher Education, 1971.

Perkins, James A., ed. *Higher Education: From Autonomy to Systems.* New York: International Council for Educational Development, Carnegie Commission on Higher Education, 1971.

Peterson, Marvin W. "Decline, New Demands, and Qualitly: The Context for Renewal." *Review of Higher Education,* vol. 7, no. 3, Spring 1984, pp. 187–203.

Peterson, Paul E. "Did the Education Commisison Say Anything." *The Brookings Review,* Winter 1983, pp. 3–11.

Pilecki, Francis J. Personal correspondence to Allan Ostar regarding Westfield State College, March 13, 1984.

President's Commission on Higher Education. *Higher Education for American Democracy,* vols. 1 and 6. Washington, D.C.: Government Printing Office, 1948.

Proceedings of the Thirty-First Annual Meeting of the Association of Colleges and Secondary Schools of the Southern States, Jackson, Mississippi, December 3–4, 1926. Birmingham: Birmingham Publishing Company, 1926.

Puffer, Claude E. *Regional Association of Institutions of Higher Education: A Study.* Chicago, Illinois: Federation of Regional Accreditinig Commissions of Higher Education, 1970.

"Record." Maryland State Board of Education, vol. 10, no. 1, fall 1984.

Report of the Commission of Education for the Year 1885–'86. Washington, D.C.: Governement Printing Office, 1887.

Report of the Commission of Education for the Year Ended June 30, 1909, vol. I. Washington, D.C.: Government Printing Office, 1909.

Report of the Commission of Education for the Year Ended June 30, 1911, vol. II. Washington, D.C.: Government Printing Office, 1912.

Rice, David. "Participation in Selected Federal Programs by Institutions of the Associatio nof State Colleges and Universities Fiscal Year 1961," reported in *ASCU Studies No. 2*. Washington, D.C.: Association of State Colleges and Universities, 1963.

———. "Successful Participation in Selected Federal Programs by Institutions of the Association of State Colleges and Universities Fiscal Year 1963," reported in *ASCU Studies No. 3*. Washington, D.C.: Association of State Colleges and Universities, 1964.

Rincon, Frank L. *Factors Related to the Founding and Development of Special Purpose Private Institutions of Higher Education*. Ph.D. dissertation, University of Arizona, 1982.

Rivlin, Alice M. "Why and How to Cut the Deficit." *The Brookings Review*, Summer 1984, pp. 3–7.

Rowlett, John D. *Less-Than-Baccalaureate Level Technical Education Programs in Four-Year Public Colleges and Universities* (3 studies). Washington, D.C.: American Association of State Colleges and Universities, 1967, 1971, 1975.

Rudolph, Frederick. *The American College and University: A History*. New York: Random House, Vintage Books, 1962.

Selden, William K. *Accreditation: A Struggle Over Standards in Higher Education*. New York: Harper and Bros., 1960.

———. Official letter of March 8, 1961 to C. R. Stattgast, Executive Secretary, ASCU, Bemidji State College, Bemidji, Minnesota.

———. Smith, Hoke L. "Planning for the Coming Resurgence in Higher Education." *Change*, September 1984, pp. 37–41.

Smith, Joe. *Challenge to Change—The State Colleges and Universities in a Time of Expanding Responsibilities: A Position Statement*. Washington, D.C.: Association of State Colleges and Universities, 1965.

Stabler, Ernest, ed. *The Education of the Secondary School Teacher*. Middletown, Connecticut: Weselyan University Press, 1962.

Stadtman, Verne A. *Academic Adaptation*. San Francisco: Jossey-Bass, 1980.

Stetson, Fred L. *The History of the Northwest Association of Secondary and Higher Schools*, Newsletter vol. IV. no. 1. Seattle, Washington: University of Washington, 1971.

Strayer, George D., et al. *The Needs of California in Higher Education*. Sacramento, California: State Department of Education, 1948.

Swindler, William F. "William and Mary Marks Bicentennial of its First Chair of Law." *American Bar Association Journal*, vol. 64, December 1978, pp. 1872–1877.

Tewksbury, Donald G. *The Founding of American Colleges and Universities Before the Civil War*. New York: Archan Books, 1965.

Touraine, Alain. *The Academic System in American Society*. New York: McGraw-Hill, 1974.

Tyler, Ralph W. "Academic Excellence and Equal Opportunity," "Epilogue" in *Issues of the Seventies,* Harcleroad, Fred F., editor. San Francisco: Joseey-Bass, 1970.

Wahlquist, John T., and Thornton, James W., Jr. *State Colleges and Universities.* Washington, D.C.: Center for Applied Research in Education, Inc., 1964.

Wattenberg, Ben. "U.S. Still Believes Tommorrow Will Be Better Than Today." *U.S. News and World Report,* Decemberr 31, 1984, pp. 44–45.

Weathersby, George B. "Our Fading State Colleges." *Change,* January/February 1984, pp. 19–23, 49.

————. "State Colleges in Transition." In Froomkin, J., ed. *The Crisis in Higher Education.* New York: The Academy of Political Science, 1983.

Welte, Herbert D. Personal correspondence to Fred F. Harcleroad regarding (1) the National Commission on Accrediting and (2) Central Connecticut State University, March 12, 1984.

Williams, Robert L. *Legal Bases of Boards of Higher Education in Fifty States.* Chicago, Illinois: Council of State Governments, 1971.

————. Legal Bases of Coordinating Boards of Higher Education in Thirty-Nine States. Chicago, Illinois: Council of States Governments, 1967.

Woody, Thomas. *A History of Women's Education in the United States.* vols. 1 and 2. New York: Science Press, 1929.

Young, Lloyd. Official letter to John Caldwell, December 4, 1961.

B. State and International Histories

A Committee of the Alumni of the State Teachers College at Towson, Maryland. *Seventy-Five Years of Teaching Education.* Towson, Maryland: Alumni Association, 1941.

Adams, Herbert Baxter. *Thomas Jefferson and the University of Virginia.* U.S. Bureau of Education. Circular of Information no. 1, 1888. Washington, D.C.: Government Printing Office, 1888. Reprint. Ann Arbor, Michigan: University Microfilms.

Angell, James Burrill. From Vermont to Michigan: Correspondence of James Burrill Angell: 1869–1871. With a foreward by his son, James Rowland Angell. Edited by Wilfred B. Shaw. 1936. Reprint. Ann Arbor, Michigan: University Microfilms.

"Appalachian State Teachers College." Public Colleges of North Carolina, vol. 1, no. 1. Raleigh, North Carolina: North Carolina Board of Higher Education, 1964.

"A Presidential Report, 1955–1965: A Decade in Review." College Heights Bulletin, vol. 32, no. 4. Bowling Green, Kentucky: Western Kentucky State Colleges, 1965.

"A Short History of Western Washington State College." Bellingham, Washington: mimeographed. n.d.

A Study of the Need for Additional Centers of Public Higher Education in California. Prepared for the Liaison Committee of the California State Board of Education and the Regents of the University of California. Sacramento, California: California State Department of Education, 1957.

Bawden, William T. *A History of the Kansas State Teachers College of Pittsburgh, 1903–1941.* Pittsburgh, Kansas: Kansas State Teachers College, 1952.

Belsheim, Thomas Osbourne. *The Story of Dickinson State: A History of Dickinson State College 1918–1968.* Dickinson, North Dakota: Dickinson State College, 1968.

Boyden, Arthur Charles. *The History of Bridgewater Normal School.* Bridgewater, Massachusetts: Bridgewater State College, 1933. Reprint. Ann Arbor, Michigan: University Microfilms.

Brush, Carey W. *In Honor and Good Faith: A History of the State University College at Oneonta, New York.* Oneonta: State University Teachers College, 1965.

Burgess, John W. *Reminiscences of an American Scholar: The Beginnings of Columbia University.* 1934. Reprint. New York: AMS Press, 1966.

California Joint Committee on Higher Education. *The Academic State: A Progress Report to the Legislature on Tuition and Other Matters Pertaining to Higher Education in California.* 1968.

California State Department of Education. *A Restudy of the Needs of California in Higher Education.* Sacramento, California: State Department of Education, 1955.

Callahan, Helen, and Cashin, Edward J. *A History of Augusta College.* Augusta, Georgia: Augusta College Press, 1976.

Carnegie Foundation for the Advancement of Teaching. *A Study of Education in Vermont.* New York: Vermont Educational Commission, 1914.

Carter, Albert F. *Forty Years of Colorado State Teachers College, Formerly the State Normal School of Colorado, 1890–1930.* Colorado Teachers College Education Series, no. 11. Greeley: Colorado State Teachers College, 1930.

Cates, Edwin H. *A Centennial History of St. Cloud State College.* Minneapolis, Minnesota: Dillion Press, 1968.

Coffelt, John J. *The Status and Direction of Oklahoma Higher Education.* Oklahoma City: Oklahoma State Regents for Higher Education, 1968.

Coleman, Charles H. "Eastern Illinois State College; Fifty Years of Public Service." Eastern Illinois State College Bulletin, no. 189, 1950.

Cooper, Frank A. *The Plattsburgh Idea in Education, 1889–1964.* Plattsburgh, New York: Plattsburgh College Benevolent and Educational Association, State University of New York, College at Plattsburgh, 1964.

Cope, Quill E. "A Ten Year Report 1958–1968, Middle Tennessee State University." Mufreesboro, Tennessee: Middle Tennessee State University, mimeographed, 1968.

Cornette, James P. "A History of the Western Kentucky State Teachers College." Teachers College Heights, vol. XIX, no. 1, n.d.

Curti, Merle, and Christensen, Vernon. *University of Wisconsin: A History, 1848–1925.* 2 vols. Madison: University of Wisconsin Press, 1949.

Dansbury, B. Baldwin. *A Brief History of Jackson College: A Typical Story of the Survival of Education Among Negroes in the South.* Jackson, Mississippi: Jackson College, 1953.

Detroit Institute of Technology . . . Today, Tomorrow, and in the Generation Ahead: A Report to the President and the Board of Trustees of the Institute. New York: Academy for Educational Development, 1968.

Dew, Lee A. *The ASU Story: A History of Arkansas State University, 1909–1967.* Jonesboro: Arkansas State University Press, 1968.

Dingledine, Raymond C. *Madison College: The First Fifty Years, 1908–1958.* Harrisonburg, Virginia: Madison College, 1959.

"Draft of Academy History." Buzzards Bay, Massachusetts: Massachusetts Maritime Academy, duplicated, n.d.

Education in North Carolina Today and Tomorrow: The Report of the State Education Commission. Raliegh, North Carolina: United Forces for Education, 1948.

Elmendorf, Edward M. *Statewide Coordination and Planning of Postsecondary Education in the State of Vermont-Interim Report.* Raleigh, North Carolinnna: United Forces for Education, 1948.

"Faculty Publications, 1968–1969." *Appalachian State University Bulletin.* Boone, North Carolina: Appalachian State University.

Falk, Charles J. *The Development and Organization of Education in California.* New York: Harcourt, Brace and World, 1968.

Farmerie, Samuel A. *Clarion State College: A Centennial History.* Clairon Pennsylvania: Alumni Association, 1968.

Farrand, Elizabeth M. *History of the University of Michigan.* Ann Arbor: Register Publishing Houses, 1885.

Fay, Abbott. *Mountain Academia: A History of Western State College of Colorado.* Boulder, Colorado: Pruett Press, 1968.

"Five Decades of Progress; Eastern Kentucky State College, 1906–1957." *Eastern Kentucky Review,* vol. XLVII, no. 5. Richmond, Kentucky: Eastern Kentucky State College, 1957.

Fleming, Donald. *Science and Technology in Providence, 1760–1914: An Essay in the History of Brown University in the Metropolitan Community.* Providence, Rhode Island: Brown University, 1952.

Florida Atlantic University. *Bulletin, 1967–1968,* vol. 3, no. 1. Boca Raton: Florida Atlantic University, 1967.

Fowler, Herbert E. *A Centruy of Teacher Education in Connecticut: The Story of the New Britain State Normal School and the Teachers College of Connecticut, 1849–1949.* New Britain: Teachers College of Connecticut, 1949.

Gamble, Richard D. *From Academy to University, 1866–1966: A History of Wisconsin State University, Plattesville, Wisconsin.* Plattesville: Wisconsin State University, 1966.

Gannon, Robert I. *Up to the Present: The Story of Fordham.* New York Doubleday and Company, 1967.

Gilbert, Benjamin Franklin. *Pioneers for One Hundred Years: San Jose State College, 1857–1957.* San Jose: San Jose State College, 1957.

Graver, Lee. "Beacon on the Hill; A Centennial History of Kutztown State College." Kutztown, Pennsylvania: *The Kutztown Bulletin,* vol. 99, no. 1, 1966.

Hanawalt, Leslie A. *A Place of Light: The History of Wayne State University,* a Centennial Publication. Detroit, Michigan: Wayne State University Press, 1968.

Harris Teachers College. *General Catalog, 1968–1969.* St. Louis, Missouri: Harris Teachers College.

"Harris Teachers College, St. Louis Public Schools, 1857–1966." St. Louis: Harris Stowe College, mimeographed, n.d.

Hart, Irving H. *The First 75 Years: A History of Ideas Fundamental to the Development of the Iowa State Normal School (1876–1909) and the Iowa State Teachers College (1909–1951)*. Cedar Falls: Iowa State Teachers College (University of Northern Iowa), 1951.

Hartman, William Frederick. "The History of Colorado State College of Education—The Normal School Period—1890–1911; Field Study No. 1." Ed.D. dissertation, Colorado State College of Education, 1951.

Hawk, Grace E. *Pembroke College in Brown University: The First Seventy-Five Years, 1891–1966*. Providence, Rhode Island: Brown University Press, 1967.

Hickey, Philip J. "Highlights of One Hundred Years of Teacher Education in the St. Louis Public Schools, 1857–1957." An Address delivered at the January 24, 1957 Commencement Exercises of Harris Teachers College.

Hoeglund, Harold A. *History of Pueblo College, Pueblo, Colorado, 1953–1963*, n.d.

Hubley, John E. *Fountainhead of Good Teachers: A History of the First Ninety Years of Shippensburg State College*. Shippenburg, Pennsylvania: News-Chronicle Publishing Company, 1964.

Isbell, Egbert R. *A History of Eastern Michigan University, 1849–1965*. Ypsilanti, Michigan: Eastern Michigan University Press, 1971.

Johns Hopkins University. *Celebration of the Twenty-Fifth Anniversary*. Baltimore: John Hopkins University, 1902.

Kennedy, Gail, ed. *Education at Amherst: The New Program*. Amherst, Massachusetts: Amherst College, 1955. Reprint. Ann Arbor, Michigan: University Microfilms.

Learned, Williams S., Bagley, William C., McMurry, Charles A., Strayer, George D., Dearborn, Walter F., Kandel, Issac L., and Josselyn, Homer W. *The Professional Preparation of Teachers for American Public Schools: A Study Based Upon an Examination of Tax-Supported Normal Schools in the State of Missouri*. New York: Carnegie Foundation for the Advancement of Teaching, 1920.

Lentz, Harold H. *A History of Wittenberg College (1845–1945)*. Springfield, Ohio: Wittenberg Press, 1946.

Lynch, William O. *A History of Indiana State Teachers College (Indiana State Normal School, 1870–1929)*. Terre Haute: Indiana State Teachers College, 1946.

McAdow, Beryl. *From Crested Peaks: The Story of Adams State College of Colorado*. Denver: Big Mountain Press, 1961.

Mangun, Vernon Lamar. *The American Normal School, Its Rise and Development in Massachusetts*. 1928. Reprint. Ann Arbor, Michigan: University Microfilms.

Mann, Aubrey Eugene. "The History and Development of Eastern New Mexico University." Ed.D. dissertation, Colorado State College, 1959. Reprint. Ann Arbor, Michigan: University Microfilms.

Mansfield Alumni-College Pictorial Bulletin: Centennial Issue, 1857–1957. Mansfield, Pennsylvania: Mansfield State College, n.d.

Meader, James Laurence. *Normal School Education in Connecticut.* 1928. Reprint. Ann Arbor, Michigan: University Microfilms.

Meriwether, Coyler. *History of Higher Education in South Carolina With A Sketch of the Free School System.* Washington, D.C.: U.S. Bureau of Education, Circular of Information, no. 3, 1888. Reprint. Ann Arbor, Michigan: University Microfilms.

Mohler, Samuel R. *The First Seventy-Five Years; A History of Central Washington State College, 1891–1966.* Ellensberg: Central Washington State College, 1967.

Moore, D. E. *The History of Sacramento State College (1947–1967): 20 Years of Higher Education.* 2nd edition revised. Sacramento: Associated Students of Sacramento State College, 1967.

Morison, Samuel Eliot. *Three Centuries of Harvard, 1636–1936.* Cambridge: Harvard University Press, 1936.

Neyland, Leedell W., and Riley, John W. *The History of Florida Agricultural and Mechanical University.* Gainesville: University of Florida Press, 1963.

Overman, James Robert. *The History of Bowling Green State University.* Bowling Green, Ohió: Bowling Green University Press, 1967.

Peirson, Cyrus. *The First State Normal School in America; the Journals of Cyrus Peirce and Mary Swift.* Framingham, Massachusetts: Framingham State College, 1926. Reprint. Ann Arbor, Michigan: University Microfilms.

————. *Yale College: An Educational History, 1871–1921.* New Haven, Connecticut: Yale University Press, 1952.

Pittard, Homer. The First Fifty Years. Murfreesboro, Tennessee: Middle Tennessee State College, 1961.

Powers, Alfred, and Corning, Howard M., eds. *History of Education in Portland.* Corvallis, Oregon: WPA Adult Education Project under sponsorship of the General Extension Division, Oregon State System of Higher Education, 1937.

Report of the Master Plan Committee to the Illinois Board of Higher Education. *Governing Structure.* Springfield, Illinois: Illinois Board of Higher Education, 1966.

Report of the Board of Regents for the Biennium Ending June 30, 1968. Pensacola, Florida: University of West Florida.

Rogers, Dorothy. *Oswego: Fountainhead of Teacher Education; A Centruy in the Sheldon Tradition.* New York: Appleton-Century-Crofts, 1961.

Rose, Hary Eugene. "The Historical Development of a State College: Morehead Kentucky State College, 1887–1964." Ed.D. dissertation, University of Cincinnati, 1965. Reprint. Ann Arbor, Michigan: University Microfilms.

Shaw, Wilfred B. *A Short History of the University of Michigan.* Ann Arbor: Georgia Wahr, 1937.

Slonaker, Arthur Gordon. *A History of Sheperd College, Shperdstown, West Virginia.* Parsons, West Virginia: Sheperd College Foundation, 1958.

Smith, Morris Euguene. "A History of California State Polytechnic College;

The First Fifty Years, 1901–1951." Ed.D. dissertation, University of Oregon, 1958. Reprint. Ann Arbor, Michigan: University Microfilms.

Spechts, Ellen L. *History of the Wisconsin State University at Stevens Point*. Stevens Point, Wisconsin: Alumni Association, 1969.

Towson State College. *Centennial*. Baltimore: Towson State College, 1966.

University of California. Office of University Relations. *A Brief History of the University of California*. Berkeley: University of California, 1966.

University of Michigan 1837–1887. The Semi-Centennial Celebration of the Organization of the University of Michigan, June 26–30, 1887. Ann Arbor: University of Michigan, 1888.

University of West Florida. *Biennial Report*, 1964–66, pp. 141–146.

Vasche, J. Burton. "The California State Colleges: Their History, Organization, Purposes, and Programs." California Schools, vol. XXX. no. 1, 1959, pp. 1–23.

White, Glenn. *The Ball State Story: From Normal Institute to University*, Muncie, Indiana: Ball State University, 1967.

White, Kenneth B. *Paterson State College; A History, 1855–1966*. Wayne, New Jersey: Student Cooperative Association of Paterson State College, 1967.

Wooster, Lyman Dwight. *Fort Hays Kansas State College: An Historical Story*. Fort Hays: Fort Hays Kansas State College, 1961.

Wright, David Sands. *Fifty Years at the Teachers College: Historical And Personal Reminiscences*. Illustrated Souvenir edition, 1876–1926. Cedar Falls: Iowa State Teachers College, 1926.

Wyman, Walker, C., ed. *History of the Wisconsin State Universities*. River Falls, Wisconsin: River Falls State University Press, 1968.

C.
SPECIAL PUBLICATIONS OF THE AMERICAN ASSOCIATION OF STATE COLLEGES AND UNIVERSITIES

How to Order

To order AASCU publications, please use the form provided herein or Xerox copies of them. Indicate the quantity, total costs, and ordering codes. Return the form with your check, money order, or purchase order. Note: All orders must be prepaid or accompanied by a purchase order.

Postage

All publications are mailed Fourth Class—Book Rate. Please allow up to four weeks for delivery.

Discounts

Quantity discounts of 15 percent are available on orders of tweenty or more copies ofa single publication. A 25-percent discount is available for orders of 100 or more copies; 30 percent on 200 or more.

Bulk Orders of Free Publications

Please add a $3.00 postage and handling fee for orders of twenty or more copies of AASCU publications identified in the catalog with the notation "single copies free." For orders of fifty or more, add $4.50.

Mail Order Form To:

AASCU Publications
One Dupont Circle, Suite 700
Washington, DC 20036-1192

Order Form

_____
Name

_____
Institution

_____
Address

_____
City, State, Zip

Please send me the following publications:

_____
Title

| quantity | code no. | unit price | total price |

_____
Title

| quantity | code no. | unit price | total price |

_____
Title

| quantity | code no. | unit price | total price |

Subtotal

handling charges (if any)
$3.00 for bulk orders of
20 or more free publications + _____

quantity discount (15% on 20
or more copies of 1 publication) − _____

total enclosed

☐ Check or money order enclosed.
☐ Purchase order enclosed.

Mail to: AASCU Publications, One Dupont Circle, Suite 700, Washington, DC 200236-1192

Index of Publications by Order Code

127 Value-Centered Education
128 Academic Freedom and Responsibility
133 Institutional Efficiency
139 Views on System Governance
140 Can Man Transcend His Culture?
146 Intercultural Education
148 International Responsibility
149 Trends and Issues in Globalizing
150 Enrollment Trends and College Costs
159 Value of a College Education
161 Cooperative Arrangements
162 Businessperson-in-Residence
163 Faculty/Management Forum
164 Northwestern University Programmatic College
170 Public Higher Education and the States
202 Beyond 1984
204 Student Aid and Public Higher Education
205 Efficiency of Freedom
206 Facts about AASCU Institutions
207 Annual Report, 1985
208 Fulfilling the Urban Mission
209 Public Service at Public Colleges
210 Innovation and Change 1985
211 More Good Ideas 1985
212 When Colleges Lobby States
214 AASCU 1986
215 Publications Catalog 1986
216 Exemptions for Executives
217 Showcase for Excellence 1985 (winners)
218 Quality and Effectiveness
219 Urban State Colleges and Universities
220 Urgent Imperative
221 Annual Report 1986
222 The Higher Education-Economic Development Connection
223 Retrospect and Prospect
224 Partnership Model
225 Issues in Higher Education and Economic Development
226 To Serve the Blessing of Liberty
227 Office of International Programs
228 Innovation and Change 1986
229 More Good Ideas 1986
230 Guide For Grant Seekers in Higher Education
231 Student Charges at Public Institutions 1986–87

AASCU Member Institutions
June 30, 1986

Membership in the American Association of State Colleges and Universities is open to "any regionally accredited institution of higher education which offers programs leading to the degree of bachelor, master or doctor, and which is wholly or partially state supported and state controlled." The over four hundred eligible institutions make up most of the group designated in this book as the comprehensive public colleges and universities. Appendix 1 lists, by state, the names and dates of establishment of those 370 which have voluntarily chosen to be members. Appendix 2 similarly lists 40 institutions which probably are eligible. Many of these institutions are in governance systems, and Appendix 3 lists those 32 state systems which have chosen to be members of the AASCU.

State	Institution	Date Established
ALABAMA	Alabama A & M University	1875
	Alabama State University	1874
	Auburn University at Montgomery	1967
	Jacksonville State University	1883
	Livingston University	1835
	Troy State University	1887
	University of Alabama in Huntsville	1950
	University of Montevallo	1896
	University of North Alabama	1872
	University of South Alabama	1963

State	*Institution*	*Date Established*
ALASKA	University of Alaska, Anchorage	1970
	University of Alaska, Juneau	1972
ARIZONA	Northern Arizona University	1899
ARKANSAS	Arkansas State University	1909
	Arkansas Tech University	1909
	Henderson State University	1890
	Southern Arkansas University	1909
	University of Arkansas at Little Rock	1927
	University of Arkansas at Monticello	1909
	University of Central Arkansas	1907
CALIFORNIA	California Maritime Academy	1929
	California Polytechnic State University, San Luis Obispo	1901
	California State College, Bakersfield	1965
	California State University, San Bernardino	1960
	California State University, Stanislaus	1957
	California State Polytechnic University, Pomona	1938
	California State University, Chico	1887
	California State University, Dominguez Hills	1960
	California State University, Fresno	1911
	California State University, Fullerton	1957
	California State University, Hayward	1957
	California State University, Long Beach	1948
	California State University, Los Angeles	1947
	California State University, Northridge	1958

State	Institution	Date Established
	California State University, Sacramento	1947
	Humboldt State University	1913
	San Diego State University	1897
	San Francisco State University	1899
	Sonoma State University	1960
COLORADO	Adams State College	1921
	Fort Lewis College	1911
	Mesa College	1925
	Metropolitan State College	1963
	University of Colorado, Colorado Springs	1965
	University of Colorado at Denver	1912
	University of Northern Colorado	1889
	University of Southern Colorado	1933
	Western State College of Colorado	1911
CONNECTICUT	Central Connecticut State University	1849
	Eastern Connecticut State University	1889
	Southern Connecticut State University	1893
	Western Connecticut State University	1903
DISTRICT OF COLUMBIA	Gallaudet College	1857
	University of the District of Columbia	1975
FLORIDA	Florida A & M University	1887
	Florida Atlantic University	1961
	Florida International University	1965
	University of Central Florida	1963
	University of North Florida	1965
	Universith of South Florida	1956
	University of West Florida	1963

State	Institution	Date Established
GEORGIA	Albany State College	1903
	Armstrong State College	1935
	Augusta College	1925
	Columbus College	1958
	Georgia College	1889
	Georgia Southern College	1906
	Georgia Southwestern University	1906
	Georgia State University	1913
	Kennesaw College	1966
	North Georgia College	1872
	Savannah State College	1890
	Southern Technical Institute	1948
	Valdosta State College	1906
	West Georgia College	1933
GUAM	University of Guam	1952
HAWAII	University of Hawaii at Hilo	1947
	West Oahu College	1973
IDAHO	Boise State University	1932
	Idaho State University	1901
	Lewis-Clark State College	1893
ILLINOIS	Chicago State University	1867
	Eastern Illinois University	1895
	Governors State University	1969
	Illinois State University	1857
	Northeastern Illinois University	1961
	Northern Illinois University	1895
	Sangamon State University	1969
	Southern Illinois University at Carbondale	1869
	Southern Illinois University at Edwardsville	1965
	Western Illinois University	1899
INDIANA	Ball State University	1918
	Indiana State University	1865
	Indiana University-East	1946
	Indiana University-Southeast	1941

State	*Institution*	*Date Established*
	Indiana University at Kokomo	1945
	Purdue University, Calumet	1943
	University of Southern Indiana	1965
IOWA	University of Northern Iowa	1876
KANSAS	Emporia State University	1863
	Fort Hays State University	1902
	Pittsburg State University	1903
	Washburn University of Topeka	1865
	Wichita State University	1892
KENTUCKY	Eastern Kentucky University	1906
	Kentucky State University	1886
	Morehead State University	1923
	Murray State University	1922
	Northern Kentucky University	1968
	Western Kentucky University	1906
LOUISIANA	Grambling State University	1901
	Louisiana State University in Shreveport	1965
	Louisiana Tech University	1894
	McNeese State University	1938
	Nicholls State University	1948
	Northeast Louisiana University	1931
	Northwestern State University of Louisiana	1884
	Southeastern Louisiana University	1925
	University of Southwestern Louisiana	1898
MAINE	Maine Maritime Academy	1941
	University of Maine at Augusta	1965
	University of Maine at Farmington	1864
	University of Maine at Fort Kent	1878
	University of Maine at Machias	1909

State	Institution	Date Established
	University of Main at Presque Isle	1903
	University of Southern Maine	1878
MARYLAND	Bowie State College	1965
	Coppin State College	1900
	Frostburg State College	1898
	Morgan State University	1867
	Salisbury State College	1925
	Towson State University	1866
	University of Baltimore	1925
	University of Maryland, Baltimore County	1963
MASSACHUSETTS	Bridgewater State College	1840
	Fitchburg State College	1894
	Framingham State College	1838
	Massachusetts College of Art	1873
	Massachusetts Maritime Academy	1891
	North Adams State College	1894
	Salem State College	1854
	Southeastern Massachusetts University	1895
	University of Lowell	1894
	Westfield State College	1838
	Worchester State College	1874
MICHIGAN	Central Michigan University	1892
	Eastern Michigan University	1849
	Ferris State College	1884
	Grand Valley State College	1960
	Lake Superior State College	1960
	Northern Michigan University	1899
	Oakland University	1957
	Saginaw Valley State College	1963
	Western Michigan University	1903
MINNESOTA	Bemidji State University	1913
	Mankato State University	1866
	Metropolitan State University	1971
	Moorhead State University	1885

State	Institution	Date Established
	Southwest State University	1963
	St. Cloud State University	1869
	Winona State University	1858
MISSISSIPPI	Alcorn State University	1871
	Delta State University	1924
	Jackson State University	1877
	Mississippi University for Women	1884
	Mississippi Valley State University	1946
	University of Southern Mississippi	1910
MISSOURI	Central Missouri State University	1871
	Harris/Stowe State College	1857
	Missouri Southern State College	1965
	Missouri Western State College	1915
	Northeast Missouri State University	1867
	Northwest Missouri State University	1905
	Southwest Missouri State University	1873
	Southwest Missouri State University	1906
	University of Misouri at St. Louis	1963
MONTANA	Eastern Montana College	1927
	Montana College of Mineral Science and Technology	1893
	Northern Montana College	1929
	Western Montana College	1893
NEBRASKA	Chadron State College	1911
	Kearney State College	1903
	Peru State College	1867
	University of Nebraska at Omaha	1908

State	Institution	Date Established
	Wayne State College	1909
NEVADA	University of Nevada, Las Vegas	1955
NEW HAMPSHIRE	Keene State College	1909
	Plymouth State College	1871
NEW JERSEY	Glassboro State College	1923
	Jersey City State College	1927
	Kean College of New Jersey	1855
	Montclair State College	1908
	New Jersey Institute of Technology	1881
	Ramapo College of New Jersey	1969
	Stockton State College	1969
	Thomas A. Edison State College	1972
	Trenton State College	1855
	William Paterson College of New Jersey	1855
NEX MEXICO	Eastern New Mexico University	1927
	New Mexico Highlands University	1893
	Western New Mexico University	1893
NEW YORK	City University of New York—Brooklyn College	1930
	City University of New York—Graduate School and University Center	1961
	City University of New York—Herbert Lehman College	1931
	City University of New York—John Jay College of Criminal Justice	1964
	City University of New York—Medgar Evers College	1969

State	*Institution*	*Date Established*
	City University of New York—Queens College	1937
	City University of New York—College of Staten Island	1955
	Empire State College	1971
	Fashion Institute of Technology	1944
	State University College at Brockport	1867
	State University College at Buffalo	1867
	State University College at Cortland	1866
	State University College at Fredonia	1867
	State University College at Geneseo	1867
	State University College at New Paltz	1828
	State University College at Old Westbury	1967
	State University College at Oneonta	1887
	State University College at Plattsburgh	1889
	State University College at Potsdam	1816
	State University College at Purchase	1967
	State University College of Technology at Utica/Rome	1966
NORTH CAROLINA	Appalachian State University	1899
	East Carolina University	1907
	Elizabeth City State University	1891
	Fayettesville State University	1877
	North Carolina State University	1910
	Pembroke State University	1887

State	Institution	Date Established
	North Carolina Agricultural and Technical State University	1891
	University of North Carolina at Asheville	1927
	University of North Carolina at Charlotte	1965
	University of North Carolina at Greensboro	1891
	University of North Carolina School of the Arts	1963
	University of North Carolina at Wilmington	1947
	Western Carolina University	1889
	Winston-Salem State University	1892
NORTH DAKOTA	Dickinson State College	1918
	Mayville State College	1889
	Dakota Northwestern University	1913
	Valley City State College	1889
OHIO	Bowling Green State University	1910
	Cleveland State University	1887
	Kent State University	1964
	University of Akron	1910
	University of Toledo	1872
	Wright State University	1964
	Youngstown State University	1908
OKLAHOMA	Central State University	1890
	East Central University	1909
	Northeastern Oklahoma State University	1851
	Northwestern Oklahoma State University	1897
	Oklahoma Panhandle State University	1909
	Southeastern Oklahoma State University	1909

State	Institution	Date Established
	Southwestern Oklahoma State University	1901
	University of Science and Art of Oklahoma	1908
OREGON	Eastern Oregon State College	1929
	Oregon Institute of Technology	1946
	Portland State University	1946
	Southern Oregon State College	1926
	Western Oregon State College	1856
PENNSYLVANIA	Bloomsburg University of Pennsylvania	1839
	California University of Pennsylvania	1852
	Cheyney University of Pennsylvania	1837
	Clarion University of Pennsylvania	1867
	East Stroudsburg University of Pennsylvania	1893
	Edinboro University of Pennsylvania	1857
	Indiana University of Pennsylvania	1872
	Kutztown University of Pennsylvania	1866
	Lincoln University	1854
	Lock Haven University of Pennsylvania	1870
	Mansfield University of Pennsylvania	1854
	Millersville University of Pennsylvania	1852
	Pennsylvania State University, Behrend College	1926
	Pennsylvania State University at Harrisburg	1966
	Shippenburg University of Pennsylvania	1871

State	Institution	Date Established
	Slippery Rock University of Pennsylvania	1889
	University of Pittsburgh at Bradford	1963
	University of Pittsburgh at Johnstown	1927
	West Chester University of Pennsylvania	1871
PUERTO RICO	Rhode Island College	1854
SOUTH CAROLINA	Coastal Carolina College of the University of South Carolina	1959
	College of Charlestown	1770
	Francis Marion College	1970
	Lander College	1872
	The Citadel Military College of South Carolina	1842
	University of South Carolina at Aiken	1961
	University of South Carolina at Spartanburg	1967
	Winthrop College	1886
SOUTH DAKOTA	Black Hills State College	1883
	Dakota State College	1881
	Northern State College	1901
	South Dakota School of Mines and Technology	1885
TENNESSEE	Austin Peay State University	1927
	East Tennessee State University	1911
	Memphis State University	1912
	Middle Tennessee State University	1911
	Tennessee Technological University	1915
	University of Tennessee at Chattanooga	1886
	University of Tennessee at Martin	1927

State	Institution	Date Established
TEXAS	Angelo State University	1926
	Corpus Christi University	1971
	East Texas State University	1917
	Lamar University	1971
	Laredo State University	1923
	Midwestern State University	1969
	North Texas State University	1922
	Pan American University	1890
	Sam Houston State University	1927
	Southwest Texas State University	1899
	Stephen F. Austin State University	1921
	Sul Ross State University	1919
	Texas A & I University	1917
	Texas A & M University of Galveston	1962
	Texas Southern Woman's University	1917
	University of Houston-Clear Lake	1971
	University of Houston-Downtown	1974
	University of Texas-Victoria	1973
	University of Texas at Dallas	1969
	University of Texas at San Antonio	1969
	University of Texas at Tyler	1971
	University of Texas of the Permian Basin	1969
	West Texas State University	1909
UTAH	Southern Utah State College	1897
	Weber State College	1889
VERMONT	Castleton State College	1787
	Johnson State College	1828
	Lyndon State College	1911
VIRGIN ISLANDS	College of the Virgin Island	1962
VIRGINIA	Christopher Newport College	1960

State	Institution	Date Established
	Clinch Valley College	1954
	College of William and Mary	1693
	George Mason University	1957
	James Madison University	1908
	Longwood College	1839
	Mary Washington College	1908
	Norfolk State University	1935
	Old Dominion University	1930
	Radford University	1910
WASHINGTON	Central Washington University	1890
	Eastern Washington University	1890
	The Evergreen State College	1967
	Western Washington University	1899
WEST VIRGINIA	Bluefield State College	1895
	Concord College	1872
	Fairmont State College	1865
	Marshall University	1872
	Shepherd College	1871
	West Liberty State College	1837
	West Virginia College of Graduate Studies	1972
	West Virginia Institute of Technology	1895
	West Virginia State College	1891
WISCONSIN	University of Wisconsin-Eau Claire	1916
	University of Wisconsin-Green Bay	1965
	University of Wisconsin-La Crosse	1909
	University of Wisconsin-Oshkosh	1871
	University of Wisconsin-Parkside	1965
	University of Wisconsin-Plattesville	1866
	University of Wisconsin-River Falls	1874

State	Institution	Date Established
	University of Wisconsin-Stevens Point	1894
	University of Wisconsin-Stout	1893
	University of Wisconsin-Superior	1893
	University of Wisconsin-Whitewater	1868
	University of Wisconsin Centers	1972

AASCU Non-Members
June 30, 1986

State	Institution	Date Established
ALABAMA	Athens State College	1822
	Troy State University at Dothan-Fort Rucker	1965
	Troy State University at Montgomery	1966
CALIFORNIA	San Jose State University	1857
COLORADO	Colorado School of Mines	1869
INDIANA	Indiana University-Fort Wayne	1964
	Indiana University-Northwest	1921
	Indiana University-South Bend	1940
	Indiana University-Purdue University of Indianapolis	1969
MARYLAND	St. Mary's College of Maryland	1839
MASSACHUSETTS	University of Massachusetts, Boston	1965
MICHIGAN	Michigan Technological University	1885
	University of Michigan-Dearborn	1959
	University of Michigan-Flint	1956
MINNESOTA	University of Minnesota, Duluth	1947

State	Institution	Date Established
	University of Minnesota, Morris	1959
NEW JERSEY	Rutgers University-Camden Campus	1927
	Rutgers University-Newark Campus	1892
NEW MEXICO	New Mexico Institute of Mining and Technology	1889
NEW YORK	City University of New York, Bernard Baruch College	1919
	City University of New York, City College	1847
	City University of New York, Hunter College	1870
	City University of New York, York College	1966
	State University of New York, College of Arts and Science at Oswego	1861
	State University of New York, College of Environmental Science and Forestry	1911
	State University of New York, Maritime College	1874
OKLAHOMA	Cameron University	1909
PENNSYLVANIA	Pennsylvania State University-Radnor Center for Graduate Studies	1963
TENNESSEE	Tennessee State University	1912
TEXAS	Pan American University at Brownsville	1973
	Sul Ross State University, Uvalde Center	1973
	Tarleton State University	1899
	University of Texas at Arlington	1895
	University of Texas at El Paso	1913
VIRGINIA	Virginia Military Institute	1839

APPENDIX 3

System and Associate Members of AASCU

June 30, 1986

ALASKA
University of Alaska System

CALIFORNIA
California State University

COLORADO
Consortium of State Colleges in
    Colorado
Colorado State University

FLORIDA
State University System of Florida

GEORGIA
University System of Georgia

MARYLAND
Board of Trustees of the State
    University and Colleges

MASSACHUSETTS
Board of Regents of Higher
    Education

MICHIGAN
President Council, State Colleges
    and Universities

MINNESOTA
Minnesota State University System

NEBRASKA
Board of Trustees, Nebraska State
    college
University of Nebraska System

ILLINOIS
Board of Governors of State
    Colleges and Universities,
Board of Regents, Southern Illinois
    University System

MAINE
University of Maine System

NORTH DAKOTA
Board of Higher Education

OREGON
Oregon State System of Higher
    Education

PENNSYLVANIA
Commission for the Universities
Pennsylvania State University
Pennsylvania System of Higher
    Education

PUERTO RICO
University of Puerto Rico

NEW YORK
City University of New York
State University of New York

NORTH CAROLINA
University of North Carolina,
    Central Office

SOUTH DAKOTA
Regents of Education, State of
    South Dakota

TENNESSEE
Board of Regents, State University
    and Community College System
    of Tennessee

TEXAS
Coordinating Board, Texas College
    and University System
University System of South Texas

VERMONT
Vermont State Colleges

WISCONSIN
University of Wisconsin System

Institutional Name Changes— 1966 to 1985

AASCU MEMBERS (BY STATE)

Institutional Names of June 1986   *Institutional Names of 1966*

ALABAMA

Alabama A & M University	Same
Alabama State University	Alabama State College
Auburn University at Montgomery	New
Jacksonville State University	Same
Livingston University	Livingston College
Troy State University	Same
University of Alabama in Huntsville	Same
University of Montevallo	Alabama College
University of North Alabama	Florence State College
University of South Alabama	Spring Hill College

ALASKA

University of Alaska, Anchorage	New
University of Alaska, Juneau	Southeastern Senior College

ARIZONA

Northern Arizona University	Same

ARKANSAS

Arkansas State University	Same
Arkansas Tech University	Arkansas Polytechnic
Henderson State University	Henderson State College
Southern Arkansas University	Southern State College
University of Arkansas at Little Rock	Little Rock University
University of Arkansas at Monticello	Arkansas A & M College
University of Central Arkansas	Arkansas State Teachers College

Institutional Names of June 1986	*Institutional Names of 1966*
CALIFORNIA	
California Maritime Academy	Same
California Polytechnic State University, San Luis Obispo	California State Polytechnic College
California State College, Bakersfield	Same
California State University, San Bernardino	California State College, San Bernardino
California State University, Stanislaus	Stanislaus State College
California State Polytechnic University, Pomona	California State Polytechnic College
California State University, Chico	Chico State College
California State University, Dominguez Hills	California State College Dominguez Hills
California State University, Fresno	Fresno State College
California State University, Fullerton	California State College, Fullerton
California State University, Hayward	California State College, Hayward
California State University, Long Beach	California State College, Long Beach
California State University, Los Angeles	California State College, Los Angeles
California State University, Northridge	San Fernando Valley State College
California State University, Sacramento	Sacramento State College
Humboldt State University	Humboldt State College
San Diego State University	San Diego State College
San Francisco State University	San Francisco State College
Sonoma State University	Sonoma State College
COLORADO	
Adams State College	Same
Fort Lewis College	Same
Mesa College	Same
Metropolitan State College	Same
University of Colorado, Colorado Springs	Same
University of Colorado at Denver	Same
University of Northern Colorado	Colorado State College
University of Southern Colorado	Southern Colorado State College
Western State College of Colorado	Same
CONNECTICUT	
Central Connecticut State University	Central Connecticut State College
Eastern Connecticut State University	Eastern Connecticut State College

Institutional Names of June 1986	*Institutional Names of 1966*
Southern Connecticut State University	Southern Connecticut State College
Western Connecticut State University	Western Connecticut State College

DISTRICT OF COLUMBIA

Gallaudet College	Same
University of the District of Columbia (merger, 1975)	District of Columbia Teachers College, Federal City College (opened 1968)

FLORIDA

Florida A & M University	Same
Florida Atlantic University	Same
Florida International University	New
University of Central Florida	Florida Technological University
University of South Florida	Same
University of West Florida	New

GEORGIA

Albany State College	Same
Armstrong State College	Same
Augusta College	Same
Columbus College	Same
Georgia College	Georgia College at Milledgeville
Georgia Southern College	Same
Georgia Southwestern University	Georgia Southwestern College
Georgia State University	Georgia State College
Kennesaw College	Same
North Georgia College	Same
Savannah State College	Same
Southern Technical Institute	Same
Valdosta State College	Same
West Georgia College	Same

GUAM

University of Guam	College of Guam

HAWAII

University of Hawaii at Hilo	New
West Oahu College	New

IDAHO

Boise State University	Boise State College
Idaho State University	Same
Lewis-Clark State College	Lewis-Clark Normal School

ILLINOIS

Chicago State University	Chicago State College
Eastern Illinois University	Same

Institutional Names of June 1986	*Institutional Names of 1966*
Governors State University	New
Illinois State University	Same
Northeastern Illinois University	Northeastern Illinois State College
Northern Illinois University	Same
Sangamon State University	New
Southern Illinois University at Carbondale	Same
Southern Illinois University at Edwardsville	Same
Western Illinois University	Same

INDIANA

Ball State University	Same
Indiana State University	Same
Indiana University-East	Same
Indiana University at Kokomo	Same
Indiana University-Southeast	Same
Purdue University, Calumet	Same
University of Southern Illinois	Same

IOWA

University of Northern Iowa	Same

KANSAS

Emporia State University	Kansas State Teachers College
Fort Hays State University	Fort Hays State College
Pittsburg State University	Kansas State College of Pittsburg
Washburn University of Topeka	Same
Wichita State University	Same

KENTUCKY

Eastern Kentucky University	Same
Kentucky State University	Kentucky State College
Morehead State University	Same
Murray State College	Same
Northern Kentucky University	Northern Kentucky State College
Western Kentucky University	Same

LOUISIANA

Grambling State University	Grambling College
Louisiana State University in Shreveport	Same
Louisiana Tech University	Louisiana Polytechnic Institute
McNeese State University	McNeese State College
Nicholls State University	Francis T. Nicholls State College
Northeast Louisiana University	Northeast Louisiana State College
Northwestern State University of Louisiana	Northwestern State College of Louisiana
Southeastern Louisiana University	Southeastern Louisiana College

Institutional Names of June 1986	*Institutional Names of 1966*
University of Southwestern Louisiana	Southwestern Louisiana College

MAINE

Maine Maritime Academy	Same
University of Maine at Augusta	Same
University of Maine at Farmington	Farmington State College
University of Maine at Fort Kent	Fort Kent State College
University of Maine at Machias	Washington State College of the University of Maine
University of Maine at Presque Isle	Aroostook State College of the University of Maine
University of Southern Maine	University of Maine at Gorham and University of Maine at Portland

MARYLAND

Bowie State College	Same
Coppin State College	Same
Frostburg State College	Same
Morgan State University	Morgan State College
Salisbury State College	Same
Towson State University	Towson State College
University of Baltimore	Same
University of Maryland, Baltimore County	Same

MASSACHUSETTS

Bridgewater State College	Same
Fitchburg State College	Same
Framingham State College	Same
Massachusetts College of Art	Same
Massachusetts Maritime Academy	Same
North Adams State College	Same
Salem State College	Same
Southeastern Massachusetts University	Southeastern Massachusetts Technical Institute
University of Lowell	Lowell State College and Lowell Technological Institute
Westfield State College	Same
Worcester State College	Same

MICHIGAN

Central Michigan University	Same
Eastern Michigan University	Same
Ferris State College	Same
Grand Valley State College	Same
Lake Superior State College	Same
Northern Michigan University	Same

Institutional Names of June 1986	*Institutional Names of 1966*
Oakland University	Same
Saginaw Valley State College	Saginaw Valley College
Western Michigan University	Same

MINNESOTA

Bemidji State University	Bemidji State College
Mankato State University	Mankato State College
Metropolitan State University	Minnesota Metropolitan State College
Moorhead State University	Moorhead State College
Southwest State University	Southwest Minnesota State College
St. Cloud State University	St. Cloud State College
Winona State University	Winona State College

MISSISSIPPI

Alcorn State University	Alcorn Agricultural and Mechanical College
Delta State University	Delta State College
Jackson State University	Jackson State College
Mississippi University for Women	Mississippi State College for Women
University of Southern Mississippi	Same

MISSOURI

Central Missouri State University	Central Missouri State College
Harris/Stowe State College	Harris Teachers College
Missouri Southern State College	Missouri Southern College
Missouri Western State College	Missouri Western College
Northeast Missouri State University	Northeast Missouri State College
Northwest Missouri State University	Northwest Missouri State College
Southeast Missouri State University	Southeast Missouri State College
Southwest Missouri State University	Southwest Missouri State College
University of Missouri at St. Louis	Same

MONTANA

Eastern Montana College	Same
Montana College of Mineral Science and Technology	Same
Northern Montana College	Same
Western Montana College	Same

NEBRASKA

Chadron State College	Same
Kearney State College	Same
Peru State College	Same
University of Nebraska at Omaha	Municipal University of Omaha
Wayne State College	Same

NEVADA

University of Nevada, Las Vegas	Nevada Southern University

Institutional Names of June 1986	*Institutional Names of 1966*
NEW HAMPSHIRE	
Keene State College	Same
Plymouth State CollegeSame	
NEW JERSEY	
Glassboro State College	Same
Jersey City State College	Same
Kean College of New Jersey	Newark State College
Montclair State College	Same
New Jersey Institute of Technology	Newark State College of Engineering
Ramapo College of New Jersey	New
Stockton State College	New
Thomas A. Edison State College	New
Trenton State College	Same
William Paterson College of New Jersey	Paterson State College
NEW MEXICO	
Eastern New Mexico University	Same
New Mexico Highlands University	Same
Western New Mexico University	Same
NEW YORK	
City University of New York—Brooklyn College	Same
City University of New York—Graduate School and University Center	Same
City University of New York—Herbert Lehman College	Same
City University of New York—John Jay College of Criminal Justice	Same
City University of New York—Medgar Evers College	New (1969)
City University of New York—Queens College	Same
City University of New York—Staten Island	New (1971)
Empire State College	Same
Fashion Institute of Technology	New
State University College of New York at Brockport	Same
State University College of New York at Buffalo	Same
State University College of New York at Cortland	Same

Institutional Names of June 1986	*Institutional Names of 1966*
State University College of New York at Fredonia	Same
State University College of New York at Genesco	Same
State University College of New York at New Paltz	Same
State University College of New York at Old Westbury	Same
State University College of New York at Oneonta	Same
State University College of New York at Plattsburgh	Same
State University College of New York at Potsdam	Same
State University College of New York at Purchase	Same
State University College of Technology at Utica/Rome	State University at Utica/Rome

NORTH CAROLINA

Appalachian State University	Appalachian State Teachers College
East Carolina University	East Carolina College
Elizabeth City State University	Elizabeth City State College
Fayettesville State University	Fayettesville State College
North Carolina Central University	North Carolina College at Durham
Pembroke State University	Pembroke State College
North Carolina Agricultural and Technical State University	Same
University of North Carolina at Asheville	Same
University of North Carolina at Charlotte	Same
University of North Carolina School of the Arts	Same
University of North Carolina at Wilmington	Same
Western Carolina University	Western Carolina College
Winston-Salem State University	Winston-Salem State College

NORTH DAKOTA

Dickinson State College	Same
Mayville State College	Same
Dakota Northwestern University	Minot State College
Valley City State College	Same

OHIO

Bowling Green State University	Bowling Green Normal College
Central State University	Same

Institutional Names of June 1986	*Institutional Names of 1966*
Cleveland State University	Same
Kent State University	Same
University of Akron	Same
University of Toledo	Same
Wright State University	Same
Youngstown State University	Same

OKLAHOMA

Central State University	Central State College
East Central University	East Central State College
Northeastern Oklahoma State University	Northeastern State College
Northwestern Oklahoma State University	Northwestern State College
Oklahoma Panhandle State University	Oklahoma Panhandle State College
Southeastern Oklahoma State University	Southeastern State College
Southwestern Oklahoma State University	Southwestern State College
University of Science and Art of Oklahoma	Oklahoma College of Liberal Arts

OREGON

Eastern Oregon State College	Eastern Oregon College
Oregon Institute of Technology	Oregon Technical Institute
Portland State University	Portland State College
Southern Oregon State College	Southern Oregon College
Western Oregon State College	Oregon College of Education

PENNSYLVANIA

Bloomsburg University Pennsylvania	Bloomsburg State College
California University of Pennsylvania	California State College
Cheyney University of Pennsylvania	Cheyney State College
Clarion University of Pennsylvania	Clarion State College
East Stroudsburg University of Pennsylvania	East Stroudsburg State College
Edinboro University of Pennsylvania	Edinboro State College
Indiana University of Pennsylvania	Same
Kutztown University of Pennsylvania	Kutztown State College
Lincoln University	Same
Lock Haven University of Pennsylvania	Lock Haven State College
Mansfield University of Pennsylvania	Mansfield State College

Institutional Names of June 1986	*Institutional Names of 1966*
Millersville University of Pennsylvania	Millersville State College
Pennsylvania State University, Behrend College	Same
Pennsylvania State University at Harrisburg	Pennsylvania State University, Capitol Campus
Shippenburg University of Pennsylvania	Shippenburg State College
Slippery Rock University of Pennsylvania	Slippery Rock State College
University of Pittsburgh at Bradford	Same
University of Pittsburgh at Johnstown	Same
West Chester University of Pennsylvania	West Chester State College

PUERTO RICO

University of Puerto Rico	Same
University of Puerto Rico—Cayney University College	New
University of Puerto Rico—Humacao University College	Same

RHODE ISLAND

Rhode Island College	Same

SOUTH CAROLINA

Coastal Carolina College of the University of South Carolina	Same
College of Charleston	Same
Francis Marion College	New (1970)
Lander College	Same
The Citadel Military College of South Carolina	Same
University of South Carolina at Aiken	Same
University of South Carolina at Spartanburg	Same
Winthrop College	Same

TENNESSEE

Austin State University	Same
East Tennessee State University	Same
Memphis State University	Same
Middle Tennessee State University	Same
University of Tennessee at Chattanooga	Same
University of Tennessee at Martin	Same

Institutional Names of June 1986	*Institutional Names of 1966*
TEXAS	
Angelo State University	Angelo State College
Corpus Christi State University	New (1971)
East Texas State University	Same
East Texas State University at Texarkana	Same (1971)
Lamar University	Lamar State College of Technology
Laredo State University	New (1969)
Midwestern State University	Midwestern University
North Texas State University	Same
Pan American State University	Pam American College
Sam Houston State University	Sam Houston State College
Southwest Texas State University	Southwest Texas State College
Stephen F. Austin State University	Stephen F. Austin State College
Sul Ross State University	Sul Ross State College
Texas A & I University	Same
Texas A & M University of Galverston	Same
Texas Southern University	Same
Texas Woman's University	Same
University of Houston—Clear Lake	New (1971)
University of Houston—Downtown	New (1974)
University of Houston—Victoria	New (1973)
University of Houston—Dallas	Same
University of Texas at San Antonio	New (1969)
University of Texas at Tyler	New (1971)
University of Texas at Permian Basin	New (1969)
West Texas State University	Same
UTAH	
Southern Utah State College	College of Southern Utah
Weber State College	Same
VERMONT	
Castleton State College	Same
Johnson State College	Same
Lyndon State College	Same
VIRGIN ISLANDS	
College of the Virgin Islands	Same
VIRGINIA	
Christopher Newport College	Same
Clinch Valley College	Same (branch of Univ. of Va.)
College of William and Mary	Same
George Mason University	George Mason College (branch of Univ. of Va.)

Institutional Names of June 1986	*Institutional Names of 1966*
James Madison University	Madison College
Norfolk State University	Same
Old Dominion University	Norfolk State College
Radford University	Radford College

WASHINGTON

Central Washington University	Central Washington State College
Eastern Washington University	Eastern Washington State College
The Evergreen State College	New (1967)
Western Washington University	Western Washington State College

WEST VIRGINIA

Bluefield State College	Same
Concord College	Same
Fairmont State College	Same
Glenville State College	Same
Marshall University	Same
Shepherd College	Same
West Liberty State College	Same
West Virginia College of Graduate Studies	New (1972)
West Virginia Institute of Technology	Same
West Virginia State College	Same

WISCONSIN

University of Wisconsin—Eau Claire	Same
University of Wisconsin—Green Bay	Same
University of Wisconsin—La Crosse	Same
University of Wisconsin—Oshkosh	Same
University of Wisconsin—Parkside	Same
University of Wisconsin—Plattesville	Same
University of Wisconsin—River Falls	Same
University of Wisconsin—Stevens Point	Same
University of Wisconsin—Stout	Same
University of Wisconsin—Superior	Same
University of Wisconsin—Whitewater	Same
University of Wisconsin—Centers	New (1972)

AASCU Members That Are Units or Branches of University Systems

University of Alabama in Huntsville
Auburn University of Montgomery

University of Alaska, Anchorage
University of Alaska, Juneau

University of Arkansas at Little Rock
University of Arkansas at Monticello

California Polytechnic State University, San Luis Obispo
California State College, Bakersfield
California State University, San Bernardino
California State University, Stanislaus
California State Polytechnic University, Pomona
California State University, Chico
California State University, Dominguez Hills
California State University, Fresno
California State University, Fullerton
California State University, Hayward
California State University, Long Beach
California State University, Los Angeles
California State University, Northridge
California State University, Sacramento
Humboldt State University
San Diego State University
San Francisco State University
Sonoma State University

University of Colorado, Colorado Springs
University of Colorado at Denver

Southern Illinois University at Edwardsville
Southern Illinois University at Carbondale

Purdue University—Calumet
Indiana University—East
Indiana University at Kokomo
Indiana University—Southeast

Louisiana State University in Shreveport

University of Maine at Farmington
University of Maine at Fort Kent
University of Maine at Machias
University at Maine at Presque Isle
University of Southern Maine

University of Missouri at St. Louis

University of Nebraska at Omaha

University of Nevada, Las Vegas

City University College of New York—Brooklyn College
City University College of New York—Graduate School and
    University Center
City University College of New York—Herbert Lehman College
City University College of New York—John Jay College of Criminal
    Justice
City University College of New York—Medgar Evers College
City University College of New York—Queens College
City University College of New York—Staten Island
Empire State College
Fashion Institute of Technology
State University College of New York at Brockport
State University College of New York at Buffalo
State University College of New York at Cortland
State University College of New York at Fredonia
State University College of New York at Geneseo
State University College of New York at New Paltz

State University College of New York at Old Westbury
State University College of New York at Oneonta
State University College of New York at Plattsburgh
State University College of New York at Potsdam
State University College of New York at Purchase
State University College of New York at Utica/Rome

University of North Carolina at Asheville
University of North Carolina at Charlotte
University of North Carolina at Greensboro
University of North Carolina at Wilmington

Pennsylvania State University, Behrend College
Pennsylvania State University at Harrisburgh
University of Pittsburgh at Johnstown
University of Pittsburgh at Bradford

University of Puerto Rico, Cayey University College
University of Puerto Rico, Humacao University College

Coastal Carolina College of the University of South Carolina
University of South Carolina at Aiken
University of South Carolina at Spartanburg

Dakota State College

University of Tennessee at Chattanooga
University of Tennessee at Martin

Texas A & M University at Galveston
University of Houston—Clear Lake
University of Houston—Downtown
University of Houston—Victoria
University of Texas at Dallas
University of Texas of the Permian Basin
University of Texas at San Antonio
University of Texas at Tyler

University of Wisconsin—Eau Claire
University of Wisconsin—Green Bay
University of Wisconsin—La Crosse
University of Wisconsin—Oshkosh

University of Wisconsin—Parkside
University of Wisconsin—Plattesville
University of Wisconsin—River Falls
University of Wisconsin—Stevens Point
University of Wisconsin—Stout
University of Wisconsin—Superior
University of Wisconsin—Whitewater

Index